The Conceptual Approach to Genealogy

The Conceptual Approach to Genealogy

David C. Chamberlin

Heritage Quest®
Bountiful, Utah

Heritage Quest®, a division of AGLL, Inc., P.O. Box 329, Bountiful, UT 84011-0329

Copyright © 1998 by David C. Chamberlin
All rights reserved. Published 1998
Printed in the United States of America
02 01 00 99 98   5 4 3 2 1

No part of this book may be reproduced or utilized in any form or by any means, electronic or mechanical, including photocopying, recording, or by an information storage or retrieval system, without permission in writing from the Publisher.

International Genealogical Index (IGI) is a trademark of The Church of Jesus Christ of Latter-day Saints

LifeNumber™ (LN), Genealogical Coordinate System™ (GCS), and GenStor™ are trademarks of David C. Chamberlin.

Library of Congress Catalogue Card Number: 98-071082

Chamberlin, David.
    The Conceptual Approach to Genealogy: organization, processing and compilation of genealogical records

ISBN: 1-877677-87-6

To Bobbie, my beloved wife and best friend

Bobbie Noe Chamberlin (1930-1995)

This dedication was one of the very first things I thought about when I first began this book. Sadly, my dearest one did not live to see this work published. But, I cannot see this book printed without saying something about Bobbie. Her unconditional love and faith in me during the nearly 20 years of our life together and her belief in this book are what has made it possible. Bobbie was, and still is my good angel—my better half, and I can never see or hear her name without every chord in my heart vibrating at the touch. There are no words that can express my love, gratitude, and appreciation to have had this wonderful woman in my life all those years.

Contents

List of Illustrations	xv
List of Tables	xvii
Foreword	xix
Preface	xxi
Chapter 1 – Introduction	1
Computers and Genealogy	4
Getting Started	4
Evolution of a System	5
The Ideal Genealogical Process	7
Planning Your Genealogical Project – First Step	8
Research and Source Extraction – Second Step	8
Organizing and Filing Source Extractions – Third Step	9
Logging and Indexing Source Extractions – Fourth Step	9
Compilation of Genealogical Records – Fifth Step	11
Indexing and Filing Genealogical Records – Sixth Step	12
Genealogical Process Summary	12
Chapter 2 – Planning Your Genealogical Work	15
Types of Genealogies	15
Who is Your Audience?	16
Advantages of Organization and Planning	18
Using a Computer	19
Planning Guidelines	20
Planning Log	21

Chapter 3 – Source Extractions 25

    Primary Sources 26
    Secondary Sources 27
    Research Log 29
    Source Extraction Files 33
    Source Extraction Number 33
    Indexing Your Source Extractions 35
        Essential Elements for Genealogical Indexing 36
        Names 37
        Sex or Gender 37
        Race 39
        Era Correlation Key 40
    Source Extraction Example 41
    Source Extraction Summary 44

Chapter 4 – Unique Identification 47

    Name 48
    Spelling 49
    Birth Date 51
    Location 52
    Proving an Identification 56
    Linking Families 59
        Numbering Systems 61
        Absolute Numbers 62
        Example 64

Chapter 5 – Jurisdictional Tracking 67

    Events 68
        Elements of Jurisdictional Tracking 69
        Era Correlation Key 73

Contents

Jurisdictional Tracking Format	76
Jurisdictional Hierarchy	77
Name Changes	78
Incomplete Time Periods	78
Exercise	80

Chapter 6 – The Family Group Record — 81

Recommended Conventions and Guidelines	82
Incomplete, Missing, or Ambiguous Names	83
Marriage Anomalies	84
Recording Dates	85
Baptisms and Christenings	86
Abbreviations	87
Event Modifier	87
Date Modifiers	88
Jurisdictional Modifiers	89
Family Numbering	90
Generation Numbering	90
Birth-order Numbering	91
FGR Structure	91
Parent's Section	93
Number	94
Name	94
Key Events	94
Parentage	95
Parent Section Example	96
Children's Section	97
Biographical Section	99
Data Analysis & Evaluation Section	101
References Section	103
Summary	105

Chapter 7 – Genealogical Charts and Numbering 107

    Ancestral or Pedigree Charts 107
        Numbering Considerations 110
        Pedigree Chart Numbering 112
        Computing Pedigree Chart Numbers 113
        Pedigree Numbering Systems 115
            Standard Numbering System 116
            Ahnentafel System 116
    Pedigree Numbering Comparisons 118
    Descendancy Charts 118
        Descendancy Numbering Systems 121
            The Index and Henry Systems 122
            The New England or Register System 123
            The Modified Register System 124
            Descendancy Numbering Comparisons 125
        FGR Numbering Example 129

Chapter 8 – Using a Database 135

    Types of Databases 136
        Flat-file Databases 137
        Relational Databases 138
    Source Extraction Indexing 140
    Database Queries 143
    Indexing Family Group Records 147
    Jurisdictional Tracking 149
    Database Summary 152

Chapter 9 – Summary 153

    Important Concepts to Remember 154
    Preferences in Notation 155
    Clarity in Presentation 156
    Computer Programs for Genealogy 156

Contents

Appendix A – Planning Log Examples 159
Example 1 159
Example 2 160
Example 3 160
Example 4 161
Example 5 161
Example 6 161
Example 7 162

Appendix B – Source Extraction Examples and Exercises . 163
Source Extraction Examples 163
    Example 1 163
    Example 2 167
    Example 3 170
    Example 4 173
    Example 5 176
Source Extraction Exercises 180
    Exercise 1 180
    Exercise 2 181
    Exercise 3 181
    Exercise 4 182
    Exercise 5 183
    Exercise 6 183
    Exercise 7 184
    Exercise 8 185
    Exercise 9 186
    Exercise 10 187

Appendix C – Jurisdictional Tracking Exercises 189

Exercise 1 189
Exercise 2 190
Exercise 3 190
Exercise 4 191
Exercise 5 193
Exercise 6 195
Exercise 7 197

Appendix D – Family Group Record Examples 199

FGR Parents 199
FGR Children 201
FGR Biographical 202
Data Analysis & Evaluation 204
    Example 1 204
    Example 2 205
    Example 3 205
    Example 4 206
FGR References 208

Appendix E – Pedigree Chart Numbering 211

Numbering from the First Chart 211
Extended Chart Numbering 213
    Chart Numbers From Tables 213
    Chart Numbering Examples 219
Numbering Systems 220
    Positional Notation 221
    Radix 221
    Counting 222
    Multiplication and Division by Radix 223

Contents

Number Structure	224
Equivalent Numbers	224
Binary Numbers	225
Decimal-Binary Equivalents	226
Binary to Decimal Conversion	228
Decimal to Binary Conversion	228
Hexadecimal Numbers	230
Decimal-Hexadecimal Equivalents	230
Hexadecimal to Decimal Conversion	232
Decimal to Hexadecimal Conversion	233
Conversions Between Binary and Hexadecimal Numbers	234
Binary to Hexadecimal	235
Hexadecimal to Binary	235
Glossary	**237**
Bibliography	**253**
Index	**255**

Illustrations

1-1	Process Comparisons, Sources, and Compiled Records	13
3-1	Elements of a Source Extraction Number	34
3-2	Research Log Example	42
3-3	Source Extraction Example	43
3-4	Source Extraction Index Example	44
6-1	Family Group Record (FGR) Outline	92
6-2	FGR Typical Parent's Section	96
6-3	FGR Typical Children's Section	97
6-4	FGR Typical Biographical Section	101
6-5	FGR Typical Data Analysis & Evaluation Section	103
6-6	FGR Typical References Section	106
7-1	Four-generation Pedigree Chart	109
7-2	Pedigree Chart Linking	110
7-3	Typical Descendancy Chart Outline	120
7-4	Typical Descendancy Chart Detail	121
7-5	FGR Numbering Example 1	131
7-6	FGR Numbering Example 2	132
7-7	FGR Numbering Example 3	133
8-1	Simple Database Table	136
8-2	Relational Database Table 1	139
8-3	Relational Database Table 2	139
8-4	Linking Tables in a Relational Database	140
8-5	Relational Database Example	146
8-6	FGR Index Database	150
B-1	Research Log, Example 1	165
B-2	Source Extraction Example 1	166
B-3	Source Extraction Index, Example 1	167
B-4	Research Log, Example 2	168
B-5	Source Extraction Example 2	169
B-6	Source Extraction Index, Example 2	170
B-7	Research Log, Example 3	171

B-8	Source Extraction Example 3	172
B-9	Source Extraction Index, Example 3	173
B-10	Research Log, Example 4	174
B-11	Source Extraction Example 4	175
B-12	Source Extraction Index, Example 4	176
B-13	Research Log, Example 5	177
B-14	Source Extraction Example 5	178
B-15	Source Extraction Index, Example 5	179
D-1	Parent's Section Example 1	199
D-2	Parent's Section Example 2	200
D-3	Children's Section Example	201
D-4	Biographical Section Example 1	202
D-5	Biographical Section Example 2	203
D-6	FGR References Section Example	208
D-7	Linking FGR References to Key Events	209
E-1	Chart and Range Relationships	214

Tables

3-1.	Era Correlation Key Characters and Interpretation	40
5-1.	Era Correlation Key Characters and Interpretation	74
7-1.	Pedigree Numbering Comparisons	119
7-2.	Original Descendancy Numbering Assignments	126
7-3.	Revised Descendancy Numbering Assignments	128
E-1.	Powers of 2	211
E-2.	Extended Pedigree Chart Numbers (First Chart No. 0)	212
E-3.	Extended Pedigree Chart Numbers (First Chart No. 1)	212
E-4.	Chart Grouping by Ranges	213
E-5.	Pedigree Chart Numbers for Ranges C and D	215
E-6.	Decimal-binary Equivalents	227
E-7.	Powers of 2 and Equivalents	227
E-8.	Decimal to Binary Conversion	229
E-9.	Decimal-hexadecimal Equivalents	231
E-10.	Powers of 16 With Decimal and Hexadecimal Equivalents	232
E-11.	Decimal to Hexadecimal Conversion	234
E-12.	Decimal-binary-hexadecimal Equivalents	234

Foreword

Having spent more than forty years teaching genealogy seminars, I have learned that most family historians are primarily concerned with finding records or sources. However, what they really need first is "a system."

In other words, they need to have a system of notekeeping and organization. This is why there are so many "stone-wall" problems. Most researchers simply do not know how to conduct and keep track of historical research.

This is the single greatest need in the world of genealogy today. Until this important principle is addressed, we will continue to perpetuate the same mistakes. Researchers need to know how to keep proper research notes and how to evaluate record sources.

This book, more than any other, teaches these concepts. If you want to know the best course available on the subject, this is it! It teaches you how to think properly and evaluate your information.

While much has been written on this important subject, this is the best ever. It is indeed the greatest work a genealogist could ever read. It sets the industry standard.

I challenge every genealogist to not only read *The Conceptual Approach To Genealogy*, but to practice the concepts and techniques it expounds.

Ron Bremer
Professional Genealogist
Author and Lecturer

Preface

The idea for this book probably had its inception more than 15 years ago from a conversation with my very good friend, Ron Bremer, who liked the genealogical system I had developed. At his urging, a very brief outline for a book was made, but for many reasons too tedious to relate, nothing was done at this time. It wasn't until late 1994, more than a year after I had taken an early retirement from my position at the Intel Corporation in Hillsboro, Oregon, that I really got serious about trying to put something down on paper.

Had it not been for the constant encouragement from my dear wife, Bobbie, and the continuing support from my friend, Ron Bremer, I doubt that you would be reading this now. I had hoped to complete this book over a year ago, but the two years that have elapsed since my dearest one passed away have been the most difficult ones of my life. There have been many days and weeks when it was all I could do just to get out of bed, let alone write a book.

Most of the techniques and concepts presented in this book are the fruits of nearly 40 years of experience as a genealogist coupled with my technical knowledge and experience in the electronics and computer industries over a similar period of time. Virtually everything in this book came out of constant trial and error and the empirical results of many experiments. If there is a pervading theme in this book, it is precision, clarity and verification.

The focus of this book is not on genealogical research per se, but instead attempts to provide the reader with the underlying concepts and techniques to best implement the genealogical process. In mathematics it is always more useful to understand how a formula is derived rather than just memorizing it. Similarly, a better understanding of good genealogical principles is much more valuable than just outlining a series of specific steps.

Preface

Some advantages of using computer applications to better implement certain concepts in the genealogical process are described and illustrated. Though the use of a computer is not mandatory in genealogy, its benefits are overwhelming.

Special thanks are due my son, David C. Chamberlin Jr., for executing most of the technical illustrations used herein. In addition, he and my daughter, Mrs. Ginny Eggen, my cousin, Mrs. Betty Chamberlin, my friend and distant kinsman, Dr. Theodore Chamberlain, and my friend, Mrs. Debbie Wetzel, kindly reviewed my first draft. I wish to take this opportunity to gratefully acknowledge their helpful comments, suggestions and encouragement. I am further indebted to my friend, Steve Sonntag, for his very thorough review of the final draft and suggestions for further improvement.

I also wish to express my gratitude and appreciation to other members of my family and friends in addition to those already named for their love and enthusiastic support over the years; my sisters, Mrs. Laura Anne Levy, Mrs. Phyllis Barkofski, Miss Mary Joan Chamberlin, and Mrs. Alice Lynn; my daughters, Mrs. Diana Sall, and Miss Moira Chamberlin; my sister-in-law, Mrs. Beverly Marts; friends, Mrs. Linda Stribich, Mr. Leo Toscano-Martinez, Mrs. Yvonne Craig, and Ms. Skye Ciel.

In all human endeavors, there comes a time when every project must be brought to a close, in spite of the fact there will always be room for improvement. But this is good because if it were not so, nothing would ever be finished. I think the desire for perfection particularly applies to those individuals who are involved in the creative arts, such as writers, artists, composers, and musicians who are probably never entirely satisfied with their efforts. I wish I could have devoted more space to some of the issues addressed in this book, but time and circumstances have decreed that I must soon turn my attention to other matters.

Thus, the mistakes, errors, and omissions that are bound to emerge are my own, and I hope the reader will overlook them. Whether you are a novice or an experienced genealogist, it is hoped that this book will give you some new ideas and techniques that you heretofore have not considered.

Introduction 1

The dictionary defines genealogy as a record or table of the descent of a person, family, or group of people from an ancestor or ancestors; a family tree; a person's lineage or pedigree; the study or investigation of ancestry and family. While these definitions seem straight-forward, there are quite a few considerations to take into account that may not be obvious at first glance. At the very minimum, a genealogy involves the following phases:

- Research (gathering information)

- Organization (processing information)

- Compilation (integrating information)

There are many excellent books that deal with genealogical research, and there is no question that the very foundation of a genealogy depends upon good research. However, the main focus of this book is on organization and compilation rather than on research, though certain aspects of research are discussed. This book attempts to give you a feel for the correct principles and concepts that underlie any given set of rules for organizing and compiling genealogical records.

As a genealogist, you are a member of one of the largest and fastest growing American pastimes. Some authorities state that genealogy is the third most popular hobby in America. With many of us, however, genealogy is not just an enjoyable way to pass time, but a passion that we take very seriously indeed.

Introduction

Although many people consider genealogy to be dry and musty, and far removed from anything practical, nothing could be further from the truth. For genealogy is a living thing—or a living record if you will. It provides us with a glimpse of our most remote beginnings (insofar as we can be permitted to go) while at the same time it remains at the forefront of our daily lives. The process of birth and death has been in operation since the very beginning of life itself and will remain so until the last living thing passes from this sphere.

Therefore, genealogy is a part of the science of life, and as such, can never be finished. For no matter how much work is accomplished, there will always be more lines to work on in your past, as well as keeping up with the present and future generations.

Being a genealogist is like putting together a giant picture puzzle. We are trying to construct a vast mosaic starting with perhaps only a few little bits and pieces. As we proceed in our research—with each identification of a person, the picture becomes clearer and more detailed. Even though we will never see the entire picture, we can, nevertheless, complete many portions of it.

The compilation of a good genealogical record represents the accumulation of a great many little bits of information which must be logically organized to present as true a record as is possible with the information at hand. In this sense, genealogy is a science—although far from being cut and dried, it leaves much room for imagination and creativity which makes it also an art.

The matter of organizing all the little bits of accumulated information and their subsequent analysis and evaluation, however, is the most difficult part of the genealogical process. Thus, organization and record management is the foundation of all genealogical research and the subsequent preparation of family records. This concept is an axiom that cannot be over-emphasized.

Introduction

In the world of science, researchers publish scientific papers that describe the results of certain experiments or observations, measurements, and the conclusions drawn. Other scientists anywhere in the world can read the paper, repeat the experiments, and arrive at basically the same results, though conclusions may differ somewhat depending on the interpretation of certain data or the presence of unknown variables.

Some fields of sciences, such as mathematics, chemistry, or physics, may inherently be more precise than others. Thus, we would expect a higher degree of agreement or similarity in results as compared to other fields like biology or meteorology. In these fields, the number of variables and unknown elements would generally result in a wider divergence of observations, more anomalies in the process, and subsequent conclusions.

This general process is often referred to as "The Scientific Method" which is based upon the teachings of the great Greek philosopher Aristotle (384-322 B.C.). In Aristotle's philosophical system, theory follows empirical observation and logic based on the form of deductive reasoning, consisting of a major premise, a minor premise, and a conclusion. The compilation of a genealogy should follow the very same principles.

While genealogy can rarely be as precise as a scientific experiment, you should, nevertheless, approach it with the same mindset and dedication. If your research is broad enough and your sources accurate, you should be able to build a record that will stand the test of time. This should be the goal of every genealogist. No genealogy is ever perfect or complete, but you should strive to ensure that you are able to make your work as error-free as possible.

Introduction

COMPUTERS AND GENEALOGY

Though the use of a computer is not mandatory in genealogy, its benefits are overwhelming. To fully implement some of the principles and techniques that are described in this book does require a computer. In particular, the use of relational database and word processing applications are of inestimable value to the genealogist. But even if you don't have a computer as yet, many of the concepts and techniques that are described in this book can still be of great benefit to you.

GETTING STARTED

If you are going to do an ancestral genealogy, your starting point is different than if you seek to do a descendancy genealogy. An ancestral genealogy begins with yourself, or perhaps your children or grandchildren, and works back on all lines as far as you can go.

A descendancy genealogy usually begins with an early progenitor of a particular surname, or perhaps an immigrant ancestor to America, or it could begin with a not-so-remote pair of ancestors. In any case, a descendancy genealogy attempts to trace all the descendants of a given pair of ancestors down to the present day.

But before you actually begin doing anything, you need to answer some important questions such as: "How do you get started? How do you keep track of your research? How do you plan future research? What about the compilation of all your work into a family history? How will you organize and maintain your research notes and extracted data?"

A good way to help you focus on the foregoing questions is to utilize two very important tools: a Planning Log and a Research Log. While some people may assume these two to be the same thing, there are important differences. The Planning Log provides a convenient way for you to record your thoughts, ideas, and the general plan you wish to follow in accomplishing your genealogical goals. The Research Log is *Source-Specific*; in that it details the results of each specific source you consult for information.

Another way to compare these two documents is to liken the Research Log to an aerial photo of a region taken at a few hundred feet in elevation which shows great detail in the features below. Similarly, the Planning Log would correspond to a high-altitude photo, say 10,000 feet or more. While the lower level photo is more detailed, the high-altitude view covers a much wider range.

EVOLUTION OF A SYSTEM

To illustrate the evolution of some of the precepts that are presented in this book, I beg the reader's indulgence in the following story. When I first became interested in genealogy, I contacted a grand uncle who had been doing genealogical research for many years. He loaned me his big book of records, and I assiduously began copying everything. However, I soon noticed that many of his sheets had little or no references as to where the information was obtained. Many simply listed "Family Records" as the source. I soon began asking, "What family records?"

Later, when I visited a cousin who had a lot of records, I explained to her that I had some information that was not listed on her sheets. She always said: "Write it in." After thinking about this, I soon realized what a dangerous practice it was to accept someone else's information without the supporting evidence!

As I became more experienced and began doing my own research, I noticed that numerous points of fact were not in agreement between sources. At first I wasn't very organized as I encountered this situation, but I soon noticed that I was frequently returning to the same sources over and over again just to make sure of my facts.

It didn't take long before I came to the conclusion that the ideal genealogical system would comprise two separate sets of records. The first set would include all the researched and extracted data together with a Research Log and index. The second set of records, compiled from all the researched sources, would represent the sum total of all information thus far gathered.

Introduction

The compiled or composite records could include family group records, accompanying pedigree charts, or a printed family history. In the event I ever needed to recheck any data I used in the compilation, I need go no further than my original data extractions contained in the first set of records.

To put my "system" into practice, I had to take everything I had previously done and organize it accordingly. This required that I group all my researched data according to each specific source that had been examined. The next step was to number each source and paginate the extracted data using the Source Number as part of the page number. E.g., if Source Number 1 comprised three pages of data, it was numbered in the sequence 1-1, 1-2, and 1-3. After the pages were numbered, they were three-hole punched and put into a set of binders in simple numerical order. I called this first set of records my Source Extraction files.

Next, I prepared a straight-forward Research Log wherein I had a column for the number, followed by a description of the source, the date I examined it, what I was looking for, and any other pertinent details.

Then I went back to my compiled records and added the Source Number from the Research Log to the applicable source citations. Thus, if I had any questions as time went on, I only had to check my references and go immediately to the number in the first set of records (Source Extraction files) where I could quickly and easily re-examine the details, and if necessary, re-evaluate my conclusions.

From these beginnings, it soon became clear that developing a genealogy involved a very definite process or series of steps. I call these steps the "genealogical process."

THE IDEAL GENEALOGICAL PROCESS

The efficacy of the foregoing method depends upon extracting the information *exactly* as it is given in the source, even when you know it is wrong. A cardinal rule is: *Don't mix sources!* If you start combining sources together in your source extractions, you won't know who said what, and you will have introduced confusion into your record-keeping. Precision in your source extractions is a must.

Your compiled or composite records are the place to combine sources. Here, you have a forum to discuss and compare the information from the sources in question, the pros and cons of each, and your final conclusions. The more specific you can be in referencing your sources to an event, the more accurate your compiled record. If possible, the most important events (births, deaths, marriages) in each family record should be specifically linked with the source or sources for that information.

It is useful to break down the genealogical process into a few basic steps so you can better understand the basic principles. The following six steps summarize the genealogical process:

- Planning your genealogical project.

- Research and source extraction (obtaining information from various sources).

- Organizing and filing (storing) source extractions.

- Logging and indexing source extractions.

- Compilation of genealogical records (merging and comparing information from source extractions).

- Indexing and filing (storing) genealogical records.

Introduction

These six steps must be continuously performed as we progress in our endeavors because genealogy is an iterative (continuously repeating) process. The following is a brief description of these steps.

Planning Your Genealogical Project – First Step

One very important question to ask yourself at the beginning of a genealogical project is: "Why am I doing this?" The two most common reasons are: (1) you want to compile a family record for your children and future posterity, and (2) you are doing it just because you want to.

The fact is it doesn't really matter why you want to do it, but consider viewing it from the perspective of a future recipient. Sadly, many family records end up in the hands of someone who can't understand or decipher the information, and eventually it goes into the garbage or in a dusty box somewhere! I frequently see information that is nearly impossible to understand because it is so poorly organized and not logically arranged. If you want others to value and preserve the work you have done, organize and prepare it so that virtually *anyone* can understand it.

As already mentioned, a Planning Log is a genealogical tool that provides a simple and easy way for you to record your overall plans and objectives. Like most people, you will be starting and stopping your genealogical activities from time to time. The Planning Log will help you quickly get back on track after each period of inactivity.

Research and Source Extraction – Second Step

Strive to attain the highest degree of precision in extracting information from your sources to arrive at the most reliable and logical conclusions. In genealogy you often lack precise information. You may only have an approximated date instead of an exact date, or other incomplete information. Nevertheless, the same principles for the scientific method previously described, should be followed insofar as possible. If this is done, then it follows that your conclusions will more likely be reasonable and logical.

Organizing and Filing Source Extractions – Third Step

Once you start acquiring information extracted from various sources, organizational problems immediately arise. Good organization is perhaps the most difficult part of the genealogical process. You will usually find that after about three generations, the system begins to break down. This can happen even with the best of intentions and with the most careful attention to detail.

Many people end up with piles of cards, notes, lists, and group sheets, piled together in a spare drawer, bulging notebooks, or a shoe box somewhere in the house. This may sound ridiculous, but it may surprise you to learn how many people keep their records in this manner.

Get a computer you say and this problem will go away. Not so, sports fans! A computer is a truly wonderful tool, but the downside is that if you're not organized, a computer will probably only make things worse. This is because it is so easy to generate reams of paper and endless files. An old saying in the computer world that is apropos states: "Garbage In—Garbage Out!" What this means, of course, is that the computer can only give you back what you put into it.

Logging and Indexing Source Extractions – Fourth Step

Record every source you consult in a Research Log. You can buy forms, simple computer programs, or you can design your own. It's not really very difficult. Remember that the Research Log is *source-specific* whereas the Planning Log provides an overall plan for your work.

Introduction

Minimally, a Research Log should allocate a place for recording a unique number for the source, the exact title or description, the date and place where it was examined, by whom, and specifically what you were looking for. This last item is especially important, because often you may search a source for a specific name or other information; and then at a later time, you may have acquired other information that necessitates a return to that source. Be sure to record your thoughts, hunches, ideas for other searches, and latest results in your Research Log and Planning Log. Even when you find nothing in that source that you were investigating, be sure to record that fact. Using a unique number for each source facilitates the filing of all the source extractions.

When you first begin, you may think you're going to remember every source you consult. In actuality, after you've been through a few dozen books or films, you will find that you cannot recall them all from memory. The Research Log not only enables you to easily keeps track of every source you've consulted, but it can also be extremely helpful to someone else who may be interested in following after you, and continuing the work you have begun. They won't have to try and figure out what you've looked at and what you haven't seen. You might have long periods of time where you had to put your genealogical work aside to attend to other matters. The Research Log will be a great help in getting back up to speed and resuming work at the place where you stopped.

While it is recommended that you index all your source extractions, it becomes more imperative as you acquire large amounts of data. Some good examples might be census records or vital records where you could have a lot of names, dates and places. This is particularly true when you are compiling a descendancy genealogy and are attempting to account for all the descendants of a certain ancestor or everyone with a specific surname.

Compilation of Genealogical Records – Fifth Step

This step is where all your work comes together. Your compiled records should be based on as many sources as possible and should represent all the information that you have acquired about the particular family in question. As you merge extracted data from various sources, you will be creating a series of composite records called Family Group Records (FGRs). As you combine your extractions from various sources into FGRs, you will inevitably encounter differences or discrepancies between sources. It is at this point that the process of data analysis and evaluation will enable you to arrive at the most accurate and logical conclusions.

Sources may or may not overlap each other. Most often, they disagree only on certain details. You must carefully weigh the evidence given by each source (or lack of it), to arrive at the most logical conclusion. In this manner, you create a composite record. When you are comparing different sources, there are usually some minor discrepancies to be found, and in many cases, outright disagreement as to the facts. Many times you don't even have all the facts and have to make a guess or estimate based upon all the information you currently have at hand. It's OK to guess—but tell your reader that you guessed! Better still, describe the analytical process you went through in arriving at your conclusions.

If you are careful in detailing your methods of analysis, it greatly facilitates the addition of further information into the composite record. After a period of years, you or someone else may want to re-assess a family record to add new information or compare it to sources already examined. The completeness of your original analysis will be an invaluable benefit to you or any interested person who may want to revise or add more information to the record. In this manner, you or a successor can keep building upon what has been previously done.

Introduction

A most important part of the genealogical process that comes into play at this point is the concept of Unique Identification. Unique Identification is a process of acquiring sufficient information to identify each person in a genealogy such that he or she cannot be confused with any other person in the world. This process begins with the birth and continues on throughout that person's lifetime. This concept can be summarized in the phrase: "Who, what, when, and where?" This equates to correlating a person (who), with an event (what), a time (when), and a place (where). The *Genealogical Coordinate System*™ is a phrase that was coined to help you remember these key elements.

An integral part of the Unique Identification process assigns each person a simple but unique number. This number not only serves as a unique identifier, but it is also very useful in that it can be used to cross-reference FGRs to genealogical charts.

After birth, subsequent events and movements during a person's lifetime are monitored using the technique of jurisdictional tracking. Jurisdictional tracking focuses on civil or political divisions that create records. Probably 95% or more of all records you will ever consult in genealogical research are jurisdictional in nature.

Indexing and Filing Genealogical Records – Sixth Step

As you compile your FGRs, it is important for you to index and file them. As your collection of FGRs becomes more and more voluminous, the more important filing and indexing becomes.

GENEALOGICAL PROCESS SUMMARY

The derivation of the preceding six general steps evolved over a period of many years. Figure 1-1 graphically depicts the processes:

Introduction

Source Extractions

Planning ⇒ Research ⇒ Extraction ⇒ Organize ⇒ File ⇒ Index

Compiling Records

Source Extractions ⇒ Analysis ⇒ Identification ⇒ Compilation ⇒ Organize ⇒ File ⇒ Index

---

Figure 1-1. Process Comparisons, Sources, and Compiled Records

While these two groups show some similarities, they differ in one most important aspect. Because source extractions are all *source-specific*, each source which is to be examined involves all the steps.

Every family should be represented by an FGR that is compiled from the analysis and comparison of many different sources. The second group (Compiling Records) of steps pertains to the creation of the composite records (FGRs). The organization, filing, and indexing steps in this group are similar, but not identical to those used in the source extraction process. Each time new source extractions are obtained, the FGRs that are affected must be re-processed according to the steps in the second group.

Navigating through a collection of family group records can be greatly enhanced through the use of pedigree or descendancy charts. But, do not make the mistake of creating a family record solely on the basis of such charts. The foundation of all compiled genealogical records is the FGR which should contain all the information that is known about a family together with specific references to all the sources that were used in compiling it. The judicious use of pedigree and descendancy charts can provide useful supplements to the FGR.

Planning Your Genealogical Work 2

Good planning is essential in genealogy. A common error by many is to go to the library, pick up some books or films, and immediately start looking for names. When I was a beginner, I was struck by the sight of so many people furiously copying material out of books or films or waiting in line to use a copy machine. It's true that you want to work fast to get as much done as possible when you're at the library. But an important element in effective research is good planning beforehand. This means taking sufficient time to set some realistic goals for your library visit while at the same time allowing some time to follow up on promising leads.

TYPES OF GENEALOGIES

The type of genealogy you are going to create has a lot to do with how you get started. Most of the genealogies that people want to do are *Ancestral* which means tracing their direct lineages back as far as possible on all family lines. Less common are *Descendancy* genealogies. A descendancy genealogy attempts to trace all the descendants of an individual or couple, or perhaps all the people bearing a specific surname descended from some early progenitor of that name, often an immigrant to the new world. We often consult such books to see if the line we are working on is mentioned.

There are other books which we might call genealogical aids that do not deal with specific families or ancestors, but instead contain genealogical information that has been transcribed from various sources. Transcripts of census records, vital records, town and county land records, and indexes to various types of records are examples of genealogical aids. These books can be extremely valuable to genealogists because they can often save much time.

This book has been written for people doing either ancestral or descendancy genealogies. Theoretically, if we had a descendancy genealogy beginning with all the people living at the very dawn of civilization, we wouldn't have to do very much to extract an ancestral genealogy from it reflecting our own unique lineage. Of course, such a genealogy is impossible; it is only mentioned to illustrate the point that an ancestral genealogy is really a subset of descendancy genealogies.

It's important to know the differences because some of the principles that will be discussed later on may apply more to a descendancy genealogy than an ancestral genealogy, or vice versa.

An ancestral genealogy is usually characterized by the inclusion of a pedigree chart or group of charts that graphically depict a person's lineage. Pedigree charts are very useful tools that help us keep on track and are easily understood by those who know nothing about genealogy. Descendancy genealogies can include charts, but they are very limited in their scope because of the tremendous number of individuals that might have to be included. We often see such charts (greatly simplified) in historical novels or books about famous families. While not detailed, these charts can be useful for outlining major family lines of descent.

WHO IS YOUR AUDIENCE?

Most of us become interested in writing a family history that can be passed along to future generations. This is usually the objective when doing an ancestral genealogy. However, maybe you just want to do it because you enjoy it.

Those brave souls who endeavor to do a descendancy genealogy have a much bigger task to undertake and the reasons for doing it are usually different. Generally, these projects are done so that books can be placed in libraries for all to use. But many are valuable to other genealogists who have a major ancestral line contained therein. Most descendancy genealogies deal with a specific surname; i.e., all the descendants of a progenitor that bore this surname. These genealogies do not usually attempt to track down all the female lines because of the enormous number of people and different surnames involved, but focus mainly on the male lines.

For example, some descendancy genealogies may begin with a person's great, great grandparents and attempt to track down and document all descendants of this couple. Even this can be a very large undertaking. But if you begin with a progenitor several hundred years ago, the task of tracking every descendant on down would be a tremendous task, probably well nigh impossible.

But no matter what type of genealogy you are going to do, or for whatever reasons, approach it from the perspective that you are doing it for a specific audience, even if this audience happens to be members of your own family. Many genealogies have been done which eventually ended up in someone's possession who knew nothing about genealogy, and sadly, in many cases, cared nothing about it. It is probably safe to say that no matter why you are doing a genealogy, you want to see your work preserved or maintained.

There is really nothing you can do to guarantee that whoever inherits your material will appreciate or value it. But there is no question that if your work cannot be clearly understood and easy to follow, it will probably eventually end up in the garbage or at best, relegated to a dusty box in an attic. None of us likes to think about that possibility, but I have personally seen this situation take place numerous times.

ADVANTAGES OF ORGANIZATION AND PLANNING

While none of us can foresee or control what will happen to our work once we're gone, we do have the power to determine the content and quality of our work. If we leave behind jumbled piles of notes, files, and boxes of "stuff," it's a foregone conclusion that it won't last long. Remember that if non-genealogists have a hard time figuring it out, the chances of preservation are slim.

An illustration of this situation is appropriate. Some years ago, a distant cousin who had done a "lot of work" on the family surname sent me a copy of his work that he had done on a computer. It consisted of many pages of names, numbers, and dates. I was in shock when I realized I couldn't understand the organization of the information; and yet, I was an expert on those families! I recognized many of the names, but nowhere in his document could I get a sense of who belonged in what family. I knew many of the relationships from memory, but could not determine them as outlined in the material.

Since then, I have occasionally shown this material to various people (genealogists and non-genealogists alike), who have about the same reaction as I did when I first saw it. While I still have the material in my files, I have never attempted to use it because the time required to decipher it simply isn't worth it. So, if you prepare a genealogy that even an expert on the family has trouble figuring it out, how in the world will some poor non-genealogist deal with it?

So what can you do to ensure preservation? You can give it to a library and they will probably keep it, but your family members... Obviously, there are no guarantees. Take the time up front to really understand the correct way to organize and arrange your genealogical work. By doing so, you will greatly enhance the likelihood that your work will not only be preserved, but may even inspire someone else to carry on the work you have started after you are gone.

To take this one step further, ask yourself if you have often had long periods of time pass between genealogical pursuits. If you're like most of us, you have other demands in life which intrude upon your time. You may spend a few months or even years working intensively. Then, you put it aside and perhaps many months or even years pass before you are able to get back to it. How long did it take you to figure out where you were when you last quit? Can you even understand all those cryptic notes and scraps of paper with all that scribbling you left behind?

Correctly planning and organizing your work will not only benefit someone else who may inherit your work, but you will help yourself immeasurably! If you organize and document your work carefully, years could pass by before you get back to it. However, when you do return to it, you will find that you are able to easily understand what you were doing at the time you stopped. To be sure, it takes time to organize and write down the details of what you are doing. We are often so much in a hurry to do the research that we neglect to make careful notes as we go along, intending to do it later. In the long haul, the time spent up front will pay big dividends in the end.

USING A COMPUTER

Many people are now using computers to do all or part of their genealogical work. Computers are truly wonderful tools. Small laptop computers are now available that you can take to the library instead of having to write everything down in longhand.

Incredible as they are, computers cannot do everything, and they certainly can't do your thinking for you. What computers can do best is to store information. Whatever data you enter in and save is preserved for future updates and revisions. Sadly, if you're not organized on paper, it is doubtful that a computer can help you very much, and in fact, it may even make things worse. Computers can be misleading in that they make it so easy to generate reams of material. But quantity is not necessarily quality.

With a computer you need to be even more organized than you were in the old days before their advent. If you enter ambiguous information, vague notes, and allusions, the computer is not going to sort this out for you. You have to tell the computer what you want. It's just a machine, not a thinking entity.

There is no hard and fast rule in devising a system to organize data. What is important is that your system must serve you and your needs. Many times people develop systems or ways of doing things and then become slaves to that system. When that happens they are in trouble. Flexibility is always the desired goal. Devise a system and follow it, but don't be afraid to change if it will improve the way you work.

PLANNING GUIDELINES

One thing about genealogy is that it is never done. No matter how much work has been done, there will always be more to do. The more you do the more you will be wanting to do. For this reason, it is often a good idea to lay out some general guidelines for yourself because it is so easy to spread yourself too thin and lose focus.

For example, let us say you are working on your ancestral genealogy. Your father's family has been in America for a long time, but your mother's family are recent arrivals. This would mean that you would be doing a lot of research in other countries for your mother's lines and doing U.S. research for your father.

Depending on what available resources you have, it might be advisable to break the research down into "bite size" chunks. You might want to first focus on your paternal lines where you expect to make good progress. Your maternal lines will take longer to work on, and you will probably have many letters to write and relatives to contact which can be fairly time consuming. While you are waiting for responses from overseas, you can be working on your "local" lines.

Almost everyone has what are known as "stonewalls" in their ancestry. These lines can be extremely time-consuming (years) and discouraging. This is not to say that you shouldn't try to work on them, but perhaps at first it is best to concentrate on the areas where you can make better progress. If you ever run out of the easy lines, there will always be some of the hard ones to do.

Sometimes people become so obsessed with one particular line they neglect everything else. Sometimes you just need to cut it off when you have done everything you can think of and go on to other lines. Especially if your time is limited, it might be best to plan or prioritize what are the most important goals you want to accomplish. You may need to establish certain limits, otherwise genealogy can sometimes be very discouraging.

PLANNING LOG

As briefly introduced in the previous chapter, a Planning Log is a genealogical tool that will greatly assist you in addressing some of the issues that were discussed in the foregoing section. A well-designed Planning Log provides a simple and easy way for you to record your overall plans and objectives. If you are just starting out, it is a good place to put down your very first ideas and thoughts about what you want to accomplish and how you expect to begin. Later, your Planning Log can become more detailed, particularly as you gain experience and expertise.

Even if you are already an experienced genealogist, a Planning Log can be a very useful tool. Like most genealogists, you will be starting and stopping your genealogical activities as time goes by to attend to other matters. The Planning Log will help you quickly get back on track after each hiatus as it clearly details just what you were doing when you stopped.

While not as detailed as a Research Log, the Planning Log should at least contain the following basic elements:

1. **Date**. Always record the date you make an entry in your log.

2. **Place**. It's also a good idea to record where you were when you made the entry and perhaps even what you were doing at the time you got this new inspiration.

3. **Objectives**. The Planning Log need not be a formal document. Use it to write down your thoughts, hunches, and ideas as well as general and specific goals. There is no set way to do this because everyone should develop their own style. The main idea is to make the log serve as a record of your genealogical goals. Think of it as a special diary or journal.

    Sometimes when you doing research, you may suddenly get an idea about a whole new line of research or think of something to check out that you hadn't anticipated. When this happens, stop for a moment, and write down these ideas in your Planning Log, prefaced by the date and place.

    You can use your Planning Log anywhere; at home, the library, or on a trip. In any case, always have it with you, either in a special notebook or a file on your computer. Ideally, you should have long term goals as well as short term goals. The Planning Log is an excellent place to develop your ideas and goals.

4. **Results**. This section is a place to generally record the results of your planned goals, ideas, or leads you are going to follow up on. If you do check certain sources as planned, then you could record the Source Extraction Numbers from your Research Log. As a general recommendation, write down a brief summary of what you did or didn't find along with any ideas for further research, and so forth.

A few examples have been prepared to give you more of a "hands-on" feel for the kind of information that might appear in a Planning Log. These examples, illustrated in Appendix A, have been especially designed to illustrate different kinds of "typical" entries.

Source Extractions 3

Genealogical research consists of examining various sources for information that may relate to the individual or family you are investigating. You may ask, "What is a source?" A source can be a letter, a family bible, a picture, a book, a series of books, microfilms, civil records, church records, personal knowledge, or an oral interview, to name just a few. In short, a source can be any distinct entity which contains or provides information. Sources are generally classified into two major groups: Primary and Secondary.

Most sources that we will consult in our research are jurisdictional in nature. Technically, a jurisdiction can be any entity that creates records. *Family History For Fun and Profit* [originally published as*: Genealogical Research: A Jurisdictional Approach*], describes the jurisdictional concept very thoroughly. A jurisdiction can be a civil entity; organizations such as churches, fraternal groups, and insurance companies; institutions such as elementary and secondary schools or universities; companies or corporations, families, etc.

However, the most important jurisdictions that you will be working with are civil entities such as a state, territory, province, county, district, township, or town to name a few. Some records are not specifically jurisdictional. A family Bible, for example, may only list names and dates and moves around with the family. Even if localities are cited in a Bible record, the Bible itself is not a civil jurisdiction; it is a source created by the family which is actually a jurisdiction of its own. The weakness in a Bible record is that many times the information contained in it cannot be verified against another source. Of course, the places mentioned can be very valuable in searching the appropriate jurisdictional records.

Family genealogies and articles in periodicals are other examples of non-jurisdictional sources. However, I estimate that probably 95% of all sources you consult will have been created by civil or political jurisdictions.

PRIMARY SOURCES

A primary source is an original record such as a birth certificate, marriage certificate, a deed, a family Bible, a court record, or a baptismal record. Primary sources are generally considered to be superior to secondary sources. If you can access the original records, you should make every effort to do so.

However, don't make the mistake of thinking that just because it's a primary source that it's infallible. Most of the records that we consult in search of genealogical data were not set down by the members of the family or someone that really knew the facts, but by some clerk in an office. Many clerks did a poor job and some did well. There is no question that many records that should be filed in some state or county archive simply aren't there. For whatever reason, they were omitted, lost or destroyed.

Mistakes and carelessness occur everywhere and have been happening ever since the first stone tablet was chiseled. Names are spelled incorrectly or inconsistently, dates are wrong and so forth. Original records such as birth, marriage, and death records are probably the least accurate public records. Of these three, birth records tend to be more reliable than marriage or death records. If the record concerns money or property, you can be pretty sure that the degree of accuracy is going to be higher.

SECONDARY SOURCES

Secondary sources are generally compiled works. Sometimes primary sources are copied verbatim (supposedly), but the copies are still considered secondary sources. A published family history, a book listing all the marriages in a region, an index to vital records, and census indexes, are examples of secondary sources. Many secondary sources contain errors that were introduced when the author compiled his material from various sources, perhaps including personal knowledge of individuals living at the time. The biggest problem with secondary sources is that most of them do not precisely define the sources the author used in compiling the work.

Many works, especially those published in the nineteenth century, are notoriously inaccurate and contain little if any specific information as to where the author actually got the information. If you don't know the authority for the information you are using, it's value is considerably lessened. This is not say that it's worthless; but remember in our endeavors to be as scientific and precise as possible, we must account for each bit of information. The best that such works can give us are probably some clues as to where to look.

Nevertheless, even with their inherent defects, secondary sources can be very useful and valuable for several reasons. Many primary sources are unavailable or located in such remote places that it is simply not feasible to examine every one first hand—to say nothing of the considerable costs that might be incurred in traveling to various archives and repositories to examine the originals. The tremendous increase in genealogical research at public archives has also caused many original records that are very fragile and in poor condition to be made unavailable to the researcher.

Microfilming has been an enormous boon to the genealogical researcher because original sources such as county and state archives, land records, census records, probates, and vital records, can be made available anywhere in the world. All you need is a microfilm reader to look at them.

Source Extractions

Occasionally, though, even microfilmed records can be deficient. Perhaps the film operator was careless and pages or papers were omitted in the filming, or the condition of the originals together with inferior photographic techniques rendered portions of the original records difficult if not impossible to decipher. Sadly, this has happened in the filming of many of the records in our national archives. For example, many of the 1900 census volumes and their corresponding Soundex card files were poorly filmed and the originals destroyed soon afterwards, making it impossible to ever go back and refilm or recheck!

In a few cases, it is possible that a secondary source can be equal or even superior to the primary source. This situation can occur when the compiler takes meticulous pains to proofread everything and even to discover and correct inaccuracies in the primary records such as ambiguous pagination or records not grouped properly. Some secondary sources have significantly clarified the primary sources whose condition was so poor as to render an accurate translation difficult, if not impossible to decipher. Just because it's a secondary source doesn't automatically make it inferior.

For example, many years ago I was trying to locate the record of a Los Angeles County marriage that took place in the 1870s. I found the marriage recorded in the original index, but when I checked the index reference, the record was not there. A daughter of this couple had previously searched in vain for this record and never found it, encountering the same problem. I did finally find the record by systematically going through every marriage record on file for the years 1872-1876 which proved to be a large undertaking. In the end, the error was found to be in the County Clerk's index. A secondary source transcribing these records might well document this and other such errors in the original records.

Source Extractions

As you become an increasingly competent genealogist, you will gain expertise in judging the materials you examine. Document your perceptions! For example, you soon realize that Aunt Katie's records are frequently wrong. This doesn't mean that you should throw all her records in the trash. As you accumulate data, you will have more sources with which to compare; and if most or all other evidence is contrary to Aunt Katie's records, you can make the logical assumption that in this case she was wrong. Nevertheless, her records still may contain many valuable clues to other facts which may not be available anywhere else. Never throw any information away, but instead organize and file it properly as it may eventually be of great benefit.

The more sources that you can examine or use to build a Family Group Record (FGR), the better. Generally, each separate source contributes some unique aspect, even though much of it may appear to duplicate information contained in another source.

Source extraction actually encompasses three major steps: (1) recording or otherwise identifying the source, (2) extracting or copying desired information from the source, and (3) indexing the extracted information in a specific genealogical format. The first step is easily implemented by the use of a Research Log. The actual data copied or extracted from a source comprises the Source Extraction file for that source.

RESEARCH LOG

Because your compiled records depend solely upon the information gathered from various sources, it follows that you need some way of keeping track of your sources. Many genealogists call this a Research Log. The Research Log is the key that binds all of your source extractions together and is *source-specific*, whereas the Planning Log covers an entire range of sources, ideas, or objectives for general lines of research.

Source Extractions

A research log can be much more than just a summary of all your data extractions. Properly designed and implemented, it can serve as a powerful index to your data while at the same time, providing an easy way to store your notes and files.

A Research Log can be designed in various ways, but as a minimum, it should contain the following elements:

1. **Source Number**. Each source that you consult should be given a unique, sequential number which will allow you to file all source extractions in simple numerical order. This method does have the absolute requirement that you maintain an index to the assigned numbers to preclude duplication. But, this is a small price to pay for the ease and simplicity of what you are doing. The following section, Source Extraction Number, describes this subject in more detail.

2. **Title or Description of Source**. You should record the complete title of the source together with all publication information (publisher, city, year, edition). Many sources you may consult will not be published materials, but original documents, including such public records as deeds, wills, births, deaths, marriages, and privately recorded events.

    Sources such as personal diaries, letters and family Bibles, may be in the possession of private individuals or in a manuscript collection of some institution such as an historical society or university. Whatever the source is, you need to fully describe it so that someone else can easily locate it. (See *Library Call Number* and *Repository or Location* items following.)

3. **Date**. Record the date every time you examine a source. If you consult the same source at different times, the log should always record the date and what it is you were looking for at the time. You should also record the name of the person who made the data extraction. Maybe this person will always be yourself. In cases where several people are working together on a research project, it is important to know who did what and when.

4. **Library Call Number.** Record the library call number and/or film number for each source consulted at a library or institution. Not only is this a good research practice, but it can save you (or someone else) valuable time, particularly if you need to return to this source at a later time. Many institutions or record repositories such as government or state offices may have special numbers or methods of identification for each item in their custody. Be sure to record this information in lieu of a library call number if you are at such a repository.

   In some cases, you may have both a library call number and a special identification number. In this event, you should record all such information. Public records such as land records, probates, and vital records, are usually identified according to the standards of the agency. A good film operator always inserts any special accession numbers and other important information about the records at the beginning of the film.

5. **Repository or Location.** It is very important to record where you consulted the source in question. This is particularly true when the source in question is a very rare or unique item that has never been duplicated. If you examined the source at a library, be sure to record the name of the institution and its address.

   When you consult original documents such as Bible records, civil records, or church records, be sure to record where you saw or examined them. Unique records such as family Bibles, personal diaries, journals, or old letters are often in someone's personal possession. In this case, you should give the name and address of the person who had possession of the records at the time you copied or examined them.

Source Extractions

6. **Objective of Search**. It is very important to be as specific as possible in recording the main objective of your search in a particular source. Often, you may consult a source for only a single name or a specific family. Then, at some future time, you may want to again consult this very same source because you have since obtained further information that warrants the search. This is the reason for recording the date in your Research Log each time you consult a source.

7. **Comments/Notes**. Sometimes a source may raise more questions than it answers! There may be inferences or references to other sources or information that may directly affect your final conclusions. You should also note the condition of a source when you examine it. Many ancient civil records or Bible records are in such poor condition that an accurate transcription or even a photocopy will not clearly reproduce all details. Thus, its subsequent translation may always be suspect.

Sometimes microfilms are of inferior quality. There may be portions of them that are either impossible to read, or so poorly reproduced that you can never be sure of what you are trying to decipher. Be sure to note these observations in your Research Log.

Sometimes, you will get a "hunch" or intuitive feeling about a source. There will also be instances where you either know for sure or suspect that a source is not accurate. Record your thoughts and feelings! One word of caution however: *Always transcribe a source exactly as it is given*. Do not change information in a source extraction even if you know it is wrong.

There may be areas in your Research Log where you suspect a problem. In this event, be sure to add notes to sufficiently explain your concerns. The place to make the corrections and draw your final conclusions is in your *compiled record* (FGR) with sufficient supporting evidence.

SOURCE EXTRACTION FILES

The Source Extraction files contain the actual information that you copy or extract whereas your Research Log identifies and generally describes each source you examine. Each file corresponding to a specific source is identified and paginated by the Source Number as recorded in your Research Log. The Source Extraction files can be kept in a series of folders, a sequential set of 3-ring binders or other suitable filing system. As you continue your research you will be continually adding new sources to your Research Log, and a corresponding page or pages to your Source Extraction files. Because your Source Extraction files are always going to be sequentially filed in simple numerical order, you will never have to worry about repagination.

In many cases, particularly if you want to save time, you may want to photocopy entire pages or sections of material from a book or microfilm. These whole pages can be incorporated into your source extraction records by adding your source extraction number to each page of the photocopies, or by mounting the copies on standard size pages and then numbering them.

SOURCE EXTRACTION NUMBER

As previously mentioned, each of your source extractions are identified by the Source Number as recorded in your Research Log. Because the Source Number is unique, the extractions from each can be filed in simple numerical order. The number of pages for each source extraction can vary widely. Using the Source Number in conjunction with the page numbers will greatly simplify the pagination.

It is recommended that you use one or two letters as a prefix to the Source Number. Your initials might be a logical choice for a Source Number prefix. For example if your initials are BC, then you could prefix each Source Number with "BC;" i.e., BC1-1, BC1-2, BC1-3, and so forth. If there were several people in your family doing genealogical work, the letter prefixes would be a useful way of distinguishing your source extractions from others. However, using prefix letters is optional, and they can be entirely arbitrary and don't have to mean anything.

Source Extractions

The Source Extraction Number is a very important element when indexing your extractions. (See the following section, *Indexing Your Source Extractions*.) Using letter suffixes in conjunction with your Source Extraction Number provides an added enhancement to your indexes. Thus, the Source Extraction Number comprises four separate elements, or subfields; a letter prefix, the Source Number, the page number of the extraction file, and a letter suffix.

Figure 3-1 depicts these four components for a typical example.

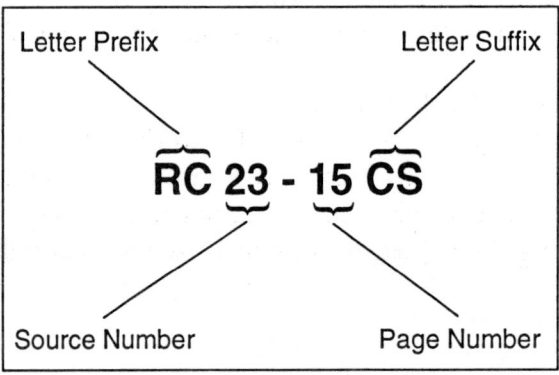

Figure 3-1. Elements of a Source Extraction Number

Subfield 1 **Letter Prefix**. In this example, the letters "RC" represent the initials of the person who did the source extraction.

Subfield 2 **Source Number**. Because all your Source Extraction files are arranged in simple numerical order, you can immediately access any given file should the need arise.

Subfield 3 **Page Number**. In this example, the designation "23 - 15" indicates this is Page 15 of the Source Extraction file No. 23. The hyphen appearing between the Source Number and the page number is only used as a separator to enhance clarity and readability.

Subfield 4 **Letter Suffix.** This subfield is only necessary when the Source Extraction Number is being used in an index entry. In this example, "CS" denotes that the source is a census record. Predefining a few letter suffixes enhances your index by providing an indication to the type of source. This is a technique that can not only save you time, but is very easy to use, requires little space, and is especially useful when you have a large index.

One word of caution, however. If you have too many suffixes, you won't be able to easily remember them. This will detract from the efficiency of your index.

INDEXING YOUR SOURCE EXTRACTIONS

The last step of the source extraction process is to index your data extractions. The importance and necessity of indexing the names you have extracted depends somewhat upon their bulk. However, it is recommended that you index all your extractions, regardless of how many names you have. The experience you will gain from doing it will give you a good foundation for more advanced work later. Obviously, indexing is a must if you are doing a descendancy genealogy and are collecting information about everyone with a particular surname.

To correctly index name extractions for genealogical data is not like building an index to a book, although many people approach it in the same manner. They are not the same!

How many times have you consulted an index to a genealogical book or periodical and only find a list of names and a page number? Because this kind of index doesn't tell you anything about the person, you have to look up all those pages to see if the person in question is of interest to you. This can be very time-consuming and unrewarding.

There is no question that the proposed method of indexing to be described will require additional time, good planning up front, and definitely more space. But, these considerations are insignificant in view of the big dividends it will pay in the end. Just think of all the time it would save you if the index were sufficiently detailed so that you would rarely have to look up the entry to know if you are interested.

Either too little or too much information can diminish the value of this kind of index. The usual index which consists of only a name and a page number is frustrating because it tells you absolutely nothing meaningful about the person. On the other hand, you can make the mistake of trying to include too much information in an index. If you try to include too much data, you defeat the purpose of the index. Thus, a good genealogical index lies between these two extremes.

Essential Elements for Genealogical Indexing

A good genealogical index provides sufficient information to help you quickly find someone who fits the criteria you have in mind. The following items are submitted as being essential components of an "ideal" genealogical index:

1. Given name(s) and/or initials and surname.

2. Jurisdictional hierarchy. This term refers to the town or township, county, state or province, and country (as applicable) which existed on the date given in Item 3. The jurisdictional hierarchy should always be as complete as possible.

3. Date (a single year).

4. Gender or sex of individual.

5. Race of individual (if given in source).

6. Source Extraction Number.

7. Era Correlation Key (symbol or letter).

Names

When extracting names from various sources, you will usually encounter many variations in spelling. This is not only true for given names and surnames, but in place names as well. Just as with personal names, many place name spellings have changed over the years. To optimize the efficiency of your index, consider using standardized spellings. In the case of place names, use the spellings found in a modern atlas whenever possible.

In your source extractions for personal names you should note the various spellings found and specify what spellings (if any) you intend to use in your index if they differ from the original record. As previously stated, never, never change anything in your source extractions. Always copy your source extracts *exactly* as given, but include some notes in your source extraction record if you intend to use another spelling in your index. When you merge or incorporate such information into your FGR, you can change or modify them to suit you (with sufficient explanations so your reader will know what you have done and why).

Sometimes sources may show a personal name spelled in such a distorted fashion or with such an unusual abbreviation that you cannot be absolutely sure what name it really is. In this case, you should leave the spelling as it is found.

Sex or Gender

When indexing your Source Extractions, you can usually be sure if a name belongs to a man or woman. But there are many exceptions. Also, keep in mind that in many cases, ancient vital records do not give the sex of a child. For example, a birth or death record might give something like, "child of Ezekiel and Ann." In addition, sources sometimes give the sex designation incorrectly, which can be very misleading.

Source Extractions

Using "M" and "F" for male and female, respectively, are simple and obvious designations. In a situation where a person is only referred to as "child," the use of "C" is a good choice. What may not be obvious is that indexing females is more involved than for males. This is because a female's surname often changes during her lifetime. When you encounter a woman's name in a source, you often will have no clue as to whether or not she is married or unmarried, widowed or divorced.

Another potentially ambiguous situation involving females is when a woman marries a man with the same surname as her maiden name, or even her previous surname (if she was a widow or divorced). This can be an especially important issue when working on a descendancy genealogy.

Many of the sources you consult may not give marital status information. Nevertheless, it is useful to have a simple method in place to indicate marital status, should the source give this information. An easy way to accomplish this is to have another letter designation available to indicate a woman's marital status.

There is no hard and fast rule here. You could use some letter other than "F" for married women, such as "W," for example. If you choose to only use the "F" designation for females, you must always remember that the females in your Source Extraction Indexes may be married or unmarried.

However, a Source Extraction index need not describe every possible situation regarding females, because it is only an index. Its purpose is not to make genealogical connections, but merely to help you quickly locate people that you are attempting identify as belonging to a specific family.

Race

In some sources a person's ethnic origin may be given which can provide an important clue in the identification process. Particularly if you are doing a descendancy genealogy, you may be gathering information on everyone with the same or similar surname. In many cases, the ancestors of present-day persons of African American descent who were slaves, assumed the surname of their plantation owners or chose an arbitrary Anglicized surname. For this reason, your index should be capable of recording this information.

You could predefine a few single letters to denote general racial information; i.e., use "B" for Black, "W" for White (or "C" for Caucasian), "M" for Mulatto, "O" for Oriental, and so forth. As you may sporadically encounter other races to be indexed, you could choose a single letter to represent them.

For simplicity, you may wish to have a blank (no information) represent the predominant race in your genealogy. For example, if your genealogy primarily concerns those of White or Caucasian descent, then leave the Race entry a blank; if you are mostly involved with the Black race, then define it as a blank, and so forth.

Era Correlation Key

The Era Correlation Key (ECK) is the name given to a special character that is associated with a date and a place. That is, what does the association of a person with respect to a date and jurisdiction represent? The purpose of the ECK is to add more information for a record while requiring minimal space. Using the ECK is optional but recommended.

The ECK is nothing more nor less than a simple, special character that can add a bit more precision to your index. Think of it as a kind of shorthand. Table 3-1 lists the five suggested ECK characters, their notational form, and general interpretation. These characters, while arbitrary, were chosen because of their dissimilarity with each other and any alphanumeric character.

Source Extractions

Table 3-1. Era Correlation Key Characters and Interpretation[1]

ECK	Notational Forms	Interpretation
Hyphen (-)	1803 -	Fairly certain beginning of a time period.
Forward Slash (/)	1803 /	Approximate beginning of a time period.
Asterisk (*)	1715 *	Indicates the person died during the indicated year.
Greater-Than (>)	1715 >	Indicates the person died after the indicated year.
Less-Than (<)	1715 <	Indicates the person died before the indicated year.

SOURCE EXTRACTION EXAMPLE

The following example has been prepared to illustrate the Source Extraction process. Let's say you want to check the 1790 census for Massachusetts in search of an ancestor, John Chamberlin. You don't know in what town or county he might have lived. All you know is that he was said to have been born in Massachusetts, and lived there until his first child (a son) was eight years old, after which he removed to New York. Because you have other information which gives this son's year of birth as 1787, you are expecting to find him living with his father at the time of the 1790 census.

---

[1] Mathematically the format for the < and > symbols is incorrect because the character should precede the year. However, these symbols were chosen for simplicity and convenience and are not used mathematically.

Like many, you would probably first consult the printed volume, *Heads of Families at the First Census of the United States in 1790 For the State of Massachusetts*. This is a secondary source prepared by the Bureau of the Census in the early part of the twentieth century. Because this is a secondary source, you may want to eventually verify any extracted information against the original census microfilms.

Let's say you find seven John Chamberlins, six of whom, from the meager information given, could be the man you're seeking. Figure 3-2 shows a typical Research Log summary for this source (Source Number 1). An example letter prefix of "BC" is used to denote the initials of the person who did the research and source extraction.

Source Extractions

NO.		
1	Title	Heads of Families at the First Census of the United States Taken in the Year 1790 for the State of Massachusetts. Published by the U.S. Government Printing Office, Washington, D.C., 1908
	Call No.	974.4 x2 1790
	Location	Family History Library, 35 North West Temple, Salt Lake City, Utah
	Date: 15 June 1995	
	Objective	I was looking for any heads of families named John Chamberlin.
	Result	Found eight heads of families named John Chamberlin (Chamberlain, Chamberlin, Chamblain) were found and extracted onto one page numbered BC1-1 (BNC).
	Date: 6 Sep 1995	
	Objective	Index extracted data.
	Result	Indexed all extracted names and added the information as an additional page, numbered BC 1-2. RefCode Suffix: CS (BNC).

Figure 3-2. **Research Log Example**

Figure 3-3 shows how the Source Extraction file might represent the extracted information.

Heads of Families at the First Census of the United States Taken in the Year 1790 for the State of Massachusetts. Published by the U.S. Government Printing Office, Washington, D.C., 1908

Family History Library, 35 North West Temple, Salt Lake City, Utah

Call No. 974.4 x2 1790

15 June 1995:

The index contained the following entries for John Chamberlin (and other surname variations):

Chamberlain, John, 93
Chamberlain, John, 144
Chamberlain, John, 218
Chamberlain, John, 233
Chamberlain, John, 245
Chamberlin, John, 166
Chamberlin, John, 178
Chamblain, John, 205

Looked up the these names from the preceding page number references:

Page	County	Town	Name	Age Groups
P. 93	Essex	Salem	John Chamberlain	1-2-1-0-0
P. 144	Middlesex	Hopkinton	John Chamberlain	2-1-1-0-0
P. 165	Plymouth	Bridgewater	John Chamberlin	1-2-1-0-0
P. 178	Plymouth	Plympton	John Chamberlin	1-1-5-0-0
P. 205	Suffolk	Roxbury	John Chamblain	2-1-2-0-0
P. 218	Worcester	Dudley	John Chamberlain	1-2-2-0-0
P. 233	Worcester	Royalston	John Chamberlain	1-0-1-0-0
P. 245	Worcester	Worcester	John Chamberlain	4-3-4-0-0

The John Chamberlain of Royalston, in this list, can probably be eliminated as his family age groups do not contain any males under the age of 16 years. The John Chamberlain we are looking for was known to have had at least one son born before 1790. However, until we have more information, this man will be listed in the index.

BC1-1

Figure 3-3.   Source Extraction Example

Source Extractions

In this example, the extraction is very straight-forward and everything fits on a single page. There will be other cases when you should record additional information or observations you may have made while going through the source. Note that your Research Log entry merely identifies the source and summarizes the results of your search, but the Source Extraction file contains all the information you deemed pertinent to copy or extract.

Figure 3-4 shows how a good genealogical index might appear. In this example, the indexed section has been appended to the Source Extraction file and paginated as page BC1-2.

Given	Surname	Town	County	ST	Year	ECK	S	R	Source
John	Chamberlain	Salem	Essex	MA	1790	/	M		1-001CS
John	Chamberlain	Hopkinton	Middlesex	MA	1790	/	M		1-001CS
John	Chamberlin	Bridgewater	Plymouth	MA	1790	/	M		1-001CS
John	Chamberlin	Plympton	Plymouth	MA	1790	/	M		1-001CS
John	Chamblain	Roxbury	Suffolk	MA	1790	/	M		1-001CS
John	Chamberlain	Dudley	Worcester	MA	1790	/	M		1-001CS
John	Chamberlain	Royalston	Worcester	MA	1790	/	M		1-001CS
John	Chamberlain	Worcester	Worcester	MA	1790	/	M		1-001CS

BC1-2

Figure 3-4.   Source Extraction Index Example

SOURCE EXTRACTION SUMMARY

Even though the methods of data extraction are essentially the same for all sources, different types of sources may require a somewhat different approach for clarity.

In Chapter 8, *Using a Database*, you will learn why computer databases are so eminently suited to implement the principles of genealogical indexing that have been described.

Appendix B, *Source Extraction Examples and Exercises,* contains additional examples to further illustrate the three elements associated with Source Extraction process. The last section in this appendix provides several exercises to give you some practice in genealogical indexing.

Unique Identification 4

Following the Source Extraction process is the compilation of a Family Group Record (FGR). Because a family always consists of at least two people, it follows that each individual in your FGR needs to be identified. We could say that the goal of every genealogist should be to: *Uniquely identify each person in his or her genealogy*.

Essentially, the process of unique identification involves the correlation of an *event* with a *name*, *time* and *place*. The combination of these elements is called the *Genealogical Coordinate System*™ (GCS). The GCS is a phrase that will help you remember these elements by likening them to coordinates or dimensions. Another way to remember them is the phrase: "Who, what, when and where." The importance of precision in these four elements cannot be over emphasized. If your data is incomplete or vague, the identification you make may be faulty.

Unique identification begins with a person's birth and continues until death. Unique identification means that you have acquired enough information to clearly establish a person's identity separate and distinct from anyone else in the world. The more precisely you can do this, the more your work will stand the test of time, as it provides the bedrock for any subsequent data analysis and evaluation.

Continuing the unique identifications process after birth is not only more difficult, but in some cases, impossible. Nevertheless, the goal is to account for all periods of time in each person's life.

This chapter focuses on the key elements required for unique identification, using the birth event as a model. Chapter 5, *Jurisdictional Tracking*, continues the unique identification process with the events following a person's birth.

NAME

Always attempt to obtain the full name given at birth. Use the most complete information available and avoid initials if the middle name(s) are known. In many cases children were given initials that stood for no name. A good example is former President Harry S. Truman. The "S" did not stand for a specific name. Two of his grandparents had names beginning with "S," but President Truman never adopted either of them. In a few cases, you may find some people identified only by initials. This can present a much more difficult challenge.

It is important to know if a person did not go by the name given at birth. For example, a man might go by J. Reuben Clark instead of James R. Clark or James Reuben Clark; women named Mary often went by the name "Polly." In many cases, particularly in the past century, people often were given nicknames when they were children. Many of these nicknames have found their way into the records.

Even if a person did not use these nicknames as adults, it is important to record nicknames a person may have used. In many other instances, men, particularly in later life, were often identified with titles such as Dr., Rev., Lt., Capt., Col., Hon., Esq., and so forth. Sometimes titles used in conjunction with a name can help in the identification process, but be aware that they can be misleading as they often changed throughout a person's lifetime.

Moreover, most people generally don't have titles after their name, unless the person is of royal birth. Of course, men who are named after their father usually have titles such as "Jr.," "II," or "III," "2nd," "3rd," following their names. In a few cases, some ancient records have recorded a "Jr." after a daughter that was named after her mother.

As we go back into history, before 1800, for example, middle initials or middle names were uncommon. For example, if you're looking for someone with a common name like John Smith or Joseph Brown, and had little else to go on, it would be very difficult indeed to be sure that the person with that name is the one you are seeking. Of course, if a person had a unique name it would be more significant, but this only happens rarely, and even then you would need other corroborating data. Obviously you require much more information than just a name.

SPELLING

For the most part, spelling is more important today than it was formerly. Names can appear in a great many possible spelling variations. In my opinion, many people are unnecessarily concerned about the spellings of names in ancient records and often attempt to make positive identifications based solely on this criteria. Only in the last two or three generations or so can you rely with any certainty on the spelling of a name. Before that, the degree of literacy in the average family was just not that high.

Moreover, it is believed that most of our ancestors were just not that fussy about spellings. Remember too, that most entries in the original records were not made by the person or family in question, but by someone outside of the family, usually a clerk or recorder. It is a common fact that in ancient records, names are frequently spelled in several different ways in the same document.

A study of the linguistics principles involved in the derivation of various sounds and spellings is beyond the scope of this discussion. However, we can make several generalizations that will apply and may be useful.

1. **Literacy**. A high degree of literacy was not present among most families before 1900. Many families did not know the exact spelling of their name and certainly most of the clerks who kept the records knew even less. Moreover, most people were probably not that concerned about it anyway. If it sounded alright, they were satisfied.

2. **Reproduction of Sounds**. The ability for a person to hear sounds and correctly reproduce them varies widely. Thus, we have another margin of error introduced by the varying ability of people to hear a sound correctly and accurately translate it into written language. The letter "r" is a good example. Many people, especially as children, have great difficulty in hearing and reproducing the "r" sound correctly.

   For example, in a fair number of instances, I have found the variations of Chambelin and Chambelain intended for Chamberlin and Chamberlain respectively. The varying inability of people to correctly reproduce sounds may be a major reason for the subsequent evolution of language changes and variations over past millennia as people migrated to other places.

3. **Long Names**. The longer a name is, the more likely it will undergo spelling changes. This is because we are more aware of the beginning sounds of a word and least aware of the way it ends. If a name is long, people tend to miss the ending syllable or syllables.

4. **Vowels**. Generally, the vowels are most susceptible to change and the consonants the least likely. Thus, many variations in spelling are caused by the change or omission of a vowel or vowels.

5. **Name Compression**. Name compression is the term I have given to the effect of forcing writing to be done in a small space. This effect most often only applies to long names. Particularly in census records (and any record using a form), you might find handwriting that begins in normal size letters and spacing, but which end up being quite cramped or distorted.

   This effect was probably caused by the writer suddenly realizing the form would not allow them to continue writing at the same size and spacing. As a result, the writing becomes smaller and more squeezed together. In a number of cases, the last remaining letters were often omitted entirely.

In conclusion, don't be misled by odd spellings or take them too seriously! While this discussion mainly focuses on surnames, the same principles also apply to given names. We see many instances where people see a certain spelling of a name not in general usage and insist on using it throughout their documentation. This doesn't necessarily make that decision wrong, but it can be misleading later. Of course in your Source Extractions, be sure to record all names exactly as given. When you build your FGR, you can elect to use standard spellings.

Using standard, consistent spellings for all names, including names of jurisdictions or political divisions is of paramount importance, particularly if you are using a computer in your work. A computer does not easily deal with spelling variations. The important thing is to be sure and record your spelling preferences and usages in your FGR.

BIRTH DATE

The birth date, together with the place of birth, is the probably the most important information for a person because it will be the point of reference for everything else that follows. The exact birth date is often difficult to obtain before the early 1900s, and you may have to content yourself with an approximation made from other information such as baptismal records, christening records, censuses, and age at marriage or death.

When a precise birth date is not available, you must estimate it as accurately as possible, based upon solid evidence (the more the better). For at least the past 50 or 60 years, birth certificates also record the time of birth, which adds further precision to the birth date.

Unique Identification

All the required elements of the GCS will be established once the location of the birth event has been added to the name and date information. Think of an ancestor for which you have a name, exact birth date, and precise geographical location. What is the probability that another person with an identical name would have the same exact birth date and geographical location? For example, you could have two or more mothers with the same surname located at the same hospital where the only difference would be in their room number or floor.

Even in this hypothetical scenario, each mother would have to have a child born at the exact same time with the exact same name, and so forth. In reality, the mathematical odds against this scenario are enormous. The biggest problem in the identification process is the lack of precision in available records.

LOCATION

Because of the commonality of many names, having only the name and date are insufficient to establish a unique identification. It is surprising and sad that many printed genealogies mostly consist of only names and dates. This is not to say that they are entirely worthless, but their value is significantly diminished without the correlation to a precise location with respect to a name and event. The reason being that anyone desiring to review this information has no idea of where to look for corroborating evidence.

Because ours is a finite, physical world, we have used certain measurements to establish physical locations on the globe since time immemorial. Hundreds of years ago, the system of latitude and longitude was developed primarily for seafarers to enable them to successfully navigate on the great oceans of the world. On land, our methods were generally not as precise where we used measurements of distance such as miles, rods, furlongs, feet, paces, and kilometers, together with general directions such as north, east and southwest.

Unique Identification

Ancient land records often used references to unusual features of the landscape or to a nearby neighbor to describe a parcel of land. Today, such property descriptions are not acceptable. In fact, in certain areas of the eastern United States, title companies and county governments are still finding significant errors originating from the ancient surveys that affect present-day owners.

Actually, it would be ideal if we had the exact latitude and longitude for every important event because it would give us such a high degree of precision. Today, with our modern maps such information is readily available.

But even superior to maps are electronic devices developed by the Global Positioning System (GPS) technology. The GPS technology was originally developed for military purposes by the Department of Defense. Small hand-held GPS devices, about the size of a TV remote, communicate with satellites circling the globe to obtain latitude and longitude information, probably accurate to within a few feet of the absolute.

Commercial versions of these devices are readily available. While they not as accurate as their military counterparts, they can still determine latitude and longitude data to an accuracy within a hundred yards or so of the absolute. These devices could be of great use to a genealogist who is trying to locate the accurate position of "the old homestead" or other landmark of genealogical significance without the need for an expensive survey or intensive study of maps.

Thus far, when speaking of locations, we have only concerned ourselves with geographical locations in physical terms such as latitude and longitude. Generally speaking, the geographical features of our planet have been in a constant state of change for millions of years. In terms of our human life spans, these changes are occurring so slowly that we are not usually aware of them except in specific cataclysmic events such as earthquakes and volcanic eruptions or violent storms of wind and rain that cause widespread destruction or changes to the physical landscape. In terms of our own individual lives we can say that physical geography is relatively stable.

Superimposed on the physical geography of our planet are human political divisions that were first created thousands of years ago and which have been evolving ever since. Unlike the slow physical geographic changes that are going on, political divisions have undergone many dramatic and even violent changes within relatively short periods of time.

Civilizations have risen, flourished for hundreds of years, and then crumbled into oblivion from forces within or by destruction from natural events or conquest from other nations. Acquisition of new territories through war and conquest, or by colonization and the systematic destruction of cultures is a story as old as the human race.

As civilization grew and advanced, political divisions or entities were created to govern people. We generally call these political entities *jurisdictions*. As in all things, jurisdictions have been and are constantly changing.

The settlement of America began with colonization by different European countries, principally England, Holland, France and Spain. Colonization was often based upon land grants given to groups of people forming a company or business venture, such as the Massachusetts Bay Colony or the Virginia Colony. States were formed with counties or districts and communities. Gradually as the country was settled, new states were formed from older states and new territories. New towns and counties were formed in a similar manner.

As stated earlier, it is estimated that at least 95% of all genealogical source materials are jurisdictional in nature. Every jurisdiction has the potential of creating records. Of course, there are jurisdictions other than the political or civil ones that are described here.

If the jurisdiction in effect at the time of an event is known, you know where to look for information, and knowing where to look is the key. There is an old prospector's proverb which states: "Gold is where you find it!" The same adage is true in genealogy; if you have a good idea of where to look, you can generally save a great deal of time. Because time is of the essence in genealogy, making your time count is of paramount importance. Of course, just knowing the correct jurisdiction doesn't guarantee that you will find what you are looking for.

It is a sad but true fact that many records that should be there aren't. Moreover, not every jurisdiction created records. Over a period of hundreds of years, fires, floods, acts of God, and particularly human carelessness and vandalism, have caused many records to be lost or destroyed, be incomplete, or even never to have been created in the first place.

One of the worst mistakes made in recording a genealogical event is to not state the *correct jurisdiction in effect at the time of the event*. Thus, we might postulate an important genealogical axiom: *Always give the correct jurisdictional hierarchy in citing an event*. Many genealogical works fail to do this. Never forget that jurisdictions have been and always will be changing. If you don't know the correct jurisdiction, you'll be looking in the wrong place and wasting time.

There are thousands of examples. For instance, many early Vermont records are not found in Vermont at all, but in New York state because of disputed territory between these states at about the time Vermont became a state. The current atlas says that Hingham, Massachusetts, is in Plymouth County. Suppose you want to check the county records for information relating to Hingham in the early 1600s. If you consulted the records in Plymouth County, you wouldn't find a thing. This is because Hingham was in Suffolk County from 1644 until 1803, when it then came under the jurisdiction of Plymouth County.

Incorrect jurisdictional hierarchies are given in numerous works, including the enormous International Genealogical Index™ (IGI) created by The Church of Jesus Christ of Latter-day Saints. If a jurisdiction you are working in has changed over the years, you should note this information in the FGR.

Concerning the previous example, with the town of Hingham in Massachusetts, you could have a note in the applicable FGR that states:

> "Hingham was part of Suffolk County from 1644 until 1803, when it became part of Plymouth County."

PROVING AN IDENTIFICATION

Up to now we have described an identification process built upon the evidence of various records to establish our facts. But are they facts? Many people spend years in establishing a pedigree, supported by a long list of references and copies of original certificates. The truth is that none of these certificates or records can provide *incontrovertible proof*.

To illustrate this point a bit further, let's assume you are applying for a social security number. You show up at the appropriate office and fill out an application. In most cases, you will be given a social security number on the basis of your birth certificate as evidence. The trouble with this scenario is that just having a birth certificate in your possession doesn't prove that you are the person on the certificate.

One very good way that a certificate could really prove who you are is for it to have had your fingerprints put on it when you were born. Then it would be a simple matter to compare those prints with your fingerprints. A sample of your DNA could provide the same degree of certainty if it was in a form that could not be separated from the certificate portion of the record.

Birth certificates, marriage licenses, and death certificates (to name a few examples) only establish that the event thus described took place. They do not prove that a person who has these documents, or has the same name, is the very same person described in the document. Sadly, it is this very fact that has led to the unfortunate abuse of records by various people obtaining multiple social security numbers, or creating fraudulent records, certificates, driver's licenses, and so forth.

Most often, the people who have successfully engaged in this illegal practice simply find birth records for people who were known to have died young. Then they obtain a copy of that person's birth certificate which is quite simple when you know the main facts. Once they have the birth certificate, they can fraudulently obtain a driver's license or some other form of ID.

Besides the illegality of this practice, these people have made it very difficult for legitimate genealogists and researchers to even have access to vital records (particularly births). Many states have closed off public access to all vital records in an attempt to stop this practice. Today's society has mandatory vital record registrations, social security cards, employment and medical records, as well as federal and state government records, and the like. The multiplicity of various forms of ID have helped proliferate the problem.

In view of these facts, it is entirely likely that this practice, in some form, is nothing new, and has probably happened in at least some degree in ages past. Of course, there is no way to know for sure, and hopefully it was not as common then.

But even assuming that you can prove that someone is the person on the certificate, another question must be asked: "How do you know that all the information on the certificate is true?" The answer is that you don't know. Unfortunately, people often lie (for various reasons) or just make an honest mistake when they give information that is to be recorded.

Unique Identification

An actual case in my own family research illustrates this latter point. I was looking for information relating to my great, great grandfather, James Andrew Brown, who was born 12 Feb 1829, Mentor, Geauga Co., Ohio, whom the family lost track of in the 1870s. We found a death record of a James Andrew Brown who died 17 Nov 1909, at Lordsburg (later La Verne), Los Angeles Co., California. The death certificate for this man stated that he was born 12 Feb 1836 in New York state. The month and day matched but the year was off as was the place of birth. The question before me was to determine if the man who died in 1909, was the same man who was born in 1829.

As it turned out, in 1959, I was able to locate the person (a lady, fortunately still alive) who gave the death certificate information in 1909. (This lady was the daughter by a second marriage of the man who died in 1909.) After we had compared notes and other important evidence, we knew beyond any doubt that her father and my great, great grandfather were the same man. She told me that when her father died in 1909, the family was uncertain as to his actual age and only knew that he mentioned living his early life in New York. The information she gave was based upon some honest guessing. This is a good example of a primary source being incorrect.

The whole point of this discussion is that you should know there is always going to be a *degree of uncertainty* in any pedigree, no matter how well it is documented. Because so little can actually be proven, you instead have to rely upon the *preponderance of evidence* to draw your conclusions. This is why the concept of precision Source Extraction, followed by a thorough analysis and evaluation in your final compilation is so frequently emphasized.

To pursue this subject further, it is recommended that you read *Genealogical Evidence*, by Noel C. Stevenson, a very interesting, useful, and extremely well-written book.

LINKING FAMILIES

It is of the utmost importance to have a method or system in place whereby we can logically link families to each other. Because all families are theoretically related (no matter how distantly), a system should be capable of accommodating this eventuality. The best way to do this is to start out by first uniquely identifying each individual within a given family. The following simple equation/definition illustrates this basic concept.

Unique Father + Unique Mother = Unique Offspring (name, time & place)

This definition is not affected by a situation in which there are no children by a given set of potential parents. A pedigree chart provides an easy way to grasp this concept as it visually shows the links between parents-to-child and child-to-parents. However, a pedigree chart can only conveniently show one child per set of parents, who may have had other children. Consider a theoretical situation in which each parent of a child (or children) has been married twice and has had children by each marriage as depicted in the following simple diagram:

Unique Father (No. 1) + Unique Mother (No. 1) = Unique Offspring
Unique Father (No. 1) + Unique Mother (No. 2) = Unique Offspring
Unique Father (No. 2) + Unique Mother (No. 1) = Unique Offspring
Unique Father (No. 2) + Unique Mother (No. 2) = Unique Offspring

This diagram illustrates a case in which each of the four children depicted have a unique set of parents. And, of course, one or both of these parents could have had more than two marriages. The principle point to remember here is that once each person has been uniquely identified, he or she can be linked back one generation to his or her parents and forward one generation to his or her own children (if any). This process can be repeated indefinitely.

As individuals are identified in your genealogy, you will need an easy way to keep track of them. Many genealogists assign numbers to each person for this purpose and there are quite a few numbering systems in general use, each with advantages and disadvantages.

Before we discuss the subject of genealogical numbering, let's first pose the question: "Why use numbers at all?" The one great virtue of a number is that it is unique. For example, take the integer one. This simple, single digit number cannot be confused with any other number.

Unlike numbers, names lack uniqueness, because they are always subject to spelling variations, and many people (particularly as you go back in time) often have identical or very similar names. Names can also be quite long (given, middle and surname), and you have to deal with name changes, like when females marry, to cite one example. In other cases, names may be incomplete or entirely absent; i.e., "Mr. Jones, Miss Smith, Mrs. (—?—)."

Most people dislike being identified by a number, probably for the reason that it seems demeaning and impersonal. However, in our modern societies with ever-growing populations, the use of numbers to positively identify different people is not just desirable, it is a necessity. For example, in the United States, it is now a federal law that every person must have a social security number, and even newborn babies are given one.

Men and women who have served in the military are given unique service numbers that serve much the same purpose. Inmates in prison are identified with numbers. Every driver's license has a number. Corporations and companies assign each employee a number. The list could go on and on. In all these examples, numbers are used for simplicity and unique identification.

Numbers are used in genealogy for the very same reasons. Unfortunately, the subject of numbering is perhaps the least understood and neglected element in genealogy. The plethora of articles and new systems on the subject have not improved the situation. An important point that must be made is that if the number isn't simple and easy to use, we are defeating one of the main reasons for using it in the first place.

Numbering Systems

Assuming that by now you agree that numbers are necessary, the next question that arises is, "What kind of numbers?" As in everything else, there are many ways to use numbers. Some systems propose unwieldy numbers or alphanumerics in some obscure fashion to indicate a relationship or connection from one person to another, from one family to another, or having the number indicate the birth order in the family, or someone on a pedigree chart. While the use of alphanumerics is not necessarily bad, it can (and usually does) add a significant level of complexity to your work.

There are those that propose using hexadecimal or binary numbers instead of decimal numbers because numbers using base 2 and 16 are so compatible with genealogical relationships. The biggest drawback to hexadecimal and binary numbers is that they are quite awkward and difficult for most people to use.

Some systems require you to calculate or derive the numbers you will use. This requirement will always carry with it the risk that you will eventually make a mistake. Remember the genealogical axiom which states that it is very important for non-genealogists to be able to understand your material. In other words, "Keep it simple!"

One recent article had the author extolling the virtues of being able to look at a number and know the person's relative place in the family. This poses the obvious questions: "Why is it important for a number or alphanumeric to convey a relationship?" "Is it important?" If you're really interested in someone, why not just check that person out and have access to the whole record?

Unique Identification

Numbering systems in general use today apply to either an ancestral genealogy or a descendancy genealogy. If you have genealogical charts in your genealogy, how do you reference your FGRs to your charts? You can't use a descendancy genealogy numbering system because those numbers are only valid for a specific line of descent from a particular progenitor. Similarly, numbers derived from a pedigree chart are only valid for the ancestry of a specific person (and their full siblings, if any). Thus, numbers derived from either of these systems are only meaningful for a specific domain. The subject of chart numbering is fully discussed in Chapter 7, *Numbering and Genealogical Charts*.

Absolute Numbers

A new system has been developed to eliminate the difficulties and deficiencies of the systems thus far described. In this system, each person in your genealogy is identified by a simple integer, called a *LifeNumber*™ or LN. The assignment of the LN is entirely arbitrary, and it can be used for both ancestral and descendancy genealogies. In fact, the LN system is really not a system at all because there is no need to figure out relationships, or try to maintain some specific sequence, or to perform any calculations. There is no set pattern or implied relationships to be derived from the number itself. Once assigned, the LN never changes, and it cannot be used for more than one person. In essence, this is an *absolute* numbering system.

To briefly illustrate the use of the LifeNumber™ system, again consider the previous diagram with one child per marriage, but with LNs assigned to each person as follows:

> Father (LN 1) + Mother (LN 2) = Child (LN 3)
> Father (LN 1) + Mother (LN 4) = Child (LN 5)
> Father (LN 6) + Mother (LN 2) = Child (LN 7)
> Father (LN 6) + Mother (LN 4) = Child (LN 8)

In this example, there are two different fathers, two different mothers, and four children; a total of eight people. Thus, it only required eight numbers to uniquely identify these individuals.

There is no need to try and draw any conclusions from the numbers themselves as they have no function other than to merely be numbers. The fact is that the LN system is ideal for people who don't like numbers! You do not have to calculate anything or try to derive some cryptic information from the number. It is merely a placeholder.

Having each person identified with a unique number greatly facilitates keeping track of this person. The LNs for each person in a given family may or may not be in any kind of order, but this is not a problem because all information about each person can be filed in simple numerical order.

An easy way to grasp the principle embodied in the LifeNumber™ system is to imagine the numbers as addresses; say like a post office box. Extend this concept to imagine and visualize that every person who has ever lived or who will be born has their own unique post office box number. Putting this another way, you have the data itself and the address (or place) where the data is located or stored.

The same relationship could be applied to each person and his or her number; that is, mail (data) is to an address as a person is to a number. Think along the same line to grasp this concept. Think of the number as only an address, and you can forget that it has to have some esoteric meaning.

Let us make a simple comparison. In a computer environment, all data is assigned, and thereafter is always associated with a unique address or location within a defined domain or structure. With this definition as a given, a computer always "knows" where everything is located.

Sometimes errors occur in a computer program which result in a conflict between addresses. This situation will always have the effect of "crashing" the system, or at the very least, terminating the operation of the program that caused the problem. By its very design and construction, a computer cannot tolerate a duplication or conflict between addresses. This very same principle must be the goal in a genealogical numbering system. The LifeNumber™ system meets this goal.

Example

How do you identify someone in your ancestry that you know existed (no question about it), but whose name you either don't know at all or only partially? In the real world of genealogy, there are going to be numerous instances in which your information becomes very sketchy and incomplete. In light of the material at the beginning of this chapter, you may be wondering by now how you can uniquely identify someone about whom you know nearly nothing.

Let's take an actual case. There was a man named William Brown, whose daughter Anne Brown, married a John Chamberlin, 19 May 1653, Boston, MA. How can you uniquely identify this man when all you know about him is this marriage record of his daughter? There isn't a birth date for him, there is no information about where he was born, and nothing is known about his parentage. The given name William and surname Brown are among the most common of names.

Even in 1653, there may well have been a number of William Browns in the Massachusetts Bay Colony, of an age to have a daughter marry. So, how can we uniquely identify this man, which is the whole idea here? Based upon this meager amount of information, it would seem that we are at an impasse.

However, we can still assign this man a unique number and proceed to do some estimating. I.E., if we assume that his daughter Anne was of an average age (21 years), and that her father was probably some 25 years older than she, we can derive an estimated birth date for him as occurring about the year 1607. We might further assume, at least for the time being, that his birth occurred in England because most colonists in New England at this time were of English ancestry.

While these assumptions be may be in error, they can always be corrected later. The important thing is that we now have the required essential elements for our starting point (name, number, birth date, and jurisdiction) identified with a number. Once a unique number has been assigned, that person has been uniquely identified.

Because the number never changes, the identification already made will be unaffected. Revising your information to reflect the results of further research is an ongoing process and the lack of data need not prevent you from making the identification.

The Chapter 5 section, *Jurisdictional Tracking Format*, illustrates the use of the LN in jurisdictional tracking records which continues the process of unique identification after birth.

Jurisdictional Tracking 5

It is assumed that you have read and understand the material described in Chapter 4, *Unique Identification*. Once a person has been identified at the time of birth, the process continues on throughout subsequent events during his or her lifetime. By continuing this process you will build a chronological record of various jurisdictions with which the person has been identified. The goal is to account for all periods of time during a person's life.

Jurisdictional tracking is a very powerful and yet simple method that will enable you to easily correlate jurisdictional hierarchies with respect to a time period for individuals that you are tracking. As described in Chapter 4, the correlation of a name together with a jurisdictional hierarchy and a time comprise the GCS (*Genealogical Coordinate System*™). Not only is this method very precise and reliable, but perhaps more importantly, it can save you much time.

Most of the records you will ever consult in your research are jurisdictional in nature. Thus, it is logical that a system which helps you to more quickly and easily identify jurisdictions will be of great value to you.

In the Chapter 3 section, *Indexing Your Source Extractions,* you were introduced to a few basic principles about genealogical indexing. Examples were given to show you how easily information could be presented in a simple format yet convey a wealth of data. Jurisdictional tracking uses a very similar format to genealogical indexing.

EVENTS

Compiling a person's life history can best be done by first connecting many chronologically recorded incidents in life which are called *events*. Various events comprise the framework of our lives which can be fleshed out with individual personalities, knowledge, and accomplishments. As a minimum, every person has two events in their lifetime: birth and death. An event can be virtually any incident in a person's life that can be related to a time and a place.

Other events in our lives include marriage, births of children, graduation from schools, military service, social security records, employment records, medical records, and so forth. There is virtually no limit as to the number of events or incidents that can be linked to a time and place. Thus, most of the sources that you will usually consult in your search for genealogical information will include vital records (births, marriages, deaths), church records (baptisms, christenings, marriages, memberships), and other civil records such as land transactions, wills, probates, and census enumerations.

There will be many sources, such as diaries, letters, and personal knowledge that may not correlate with a specific event, but which provide information of great interest and value in a narrative record. But, you are unlikely to find these kinds of sources recorded within a jurisdictional entity. You should be primarily interested in events that have a high degree of probability of having been recorded, because they are occurrences that are the most easily tracked during a person's lifetime. As you gain genealogical expertise, you will develop a good feel for what records are likely to be found during a given time period and jurisdiction. Don't spend a lot of time looking for events that have little probability of having been recorded. Always use the GCS concept to correlate each event with a name, time and place.

Modern society provides a much larger array of potential records than were available in decades past. There are so many more organizations and jurisdictional entities now than formerly. So, as you proceed back in time, you will find fewer and fewer sources for recorded events. Once you have become expert in using the jurisdictional tracking technique, it will significantly improve the way you approach all your genealogical research.

Elements of Jurisdictional Tracking

To begin, let us construct an elementary tracking record in a format which contains the following elements:

1. Given name(s) and/or initials and surname.

2. Jurisdictional hierarchy. This term refers to the town or township, county, state or province, and country (as applicable) which was in effect corresponding to the date given in Item 3. The jurisdictional hierarchy should always be as complete as possible.

3. Date (a single, specific year or range of years).

4. Gender or sex of individual.

5. Notes or remarks to supplement the data in items 1-4.

Note the close similarity between these elements and the ones discussed in the Chapter 3 section, *Essential Elements for Genealogical Indexing*. The similarities and differences will be more obvious later, but for now consider the following record format:

Given	Surname	Town	County	ST	S	Era	Remarks
Joseph	Chamberlin	Forked River	Monmouth	NJ	M	1812-1850	Born 1812.

Jurisdictional Tracking

In this and subsequent examples, a single line of data is referred to as a record. The individual columns or discrete areas of information within the record are referred to as fields. This particular record tells us that a Joseph Chamberlin lived in Forked River, Monmouth Co., NJ, from 1812 until 1850, and that he was born in this place in the beginning year of the indicated time span. Also note that the time period is called an Era, because the data in this field may only consist of a single year or a span of years.

Now let us add an additional record after the first one so that our tracking information for this person now comprises the following:

Given	Surname	Town	County	ST	S	Era	Remarks
Joseph	Chamberlin	Forked River	Monmouth	NJ	M	1812-1850	Born 1812.
Joseph	Chamberlin	Forked River	Ocean	NJ	M	1850-1853	County change.

The second record indicates that the county jurisdiction changed from Monmouth to Ocean in the year 1850, and that this man lived there until 1853. Again, another record is added to the previous ones as follows:

Given	Surname	Town	County	ST	S	Era	Remarks
Joseph	Chamberlin	Forked River	Monmouth	NJ	M	1812-1850	Born 1812.
Joseph	Chamberlin	Forked River	Ocean	NJ	M	1850-1853	County change.
Joseph	Chamberlin	Salt Lake City	Salt Lake	UT	M	1853-1879	Died 1879.

This last record tells us that this man lived in Salt Lake City, Utah, from 1853 until 1879, when he died. This simple example represents a complete jurisdictional history for this man.

This is a very straight-forward and simple example, but there are many others that are more complex. You might note that in this example there is no specific correlation to an event. The one event, not related to any one person, is the change in county jurisdictions which occurred in the year 1850 for this town (Forked River).

Jurisdictional Tracking

Let us now assume that we have a Family Group Record (FGR) for this person and his family from which the following data was extracted:

```
Date              Jurisdictional Hierarchy        Event
12 May 1812       Forked River    Monmouth   NJ   Birth Event
19 Oct 1835       Toms River      Monmouth   NJ   Marriage Event
23 Sep 1837       Forked River    Monmouth   NJ   Child's Birth Event
27 May 1839       Forked River    Monmouth   NJ   Child's Birth Event
 4 May 1841       Forked River    Monmouth   NJ   Child's Birth Event
 8 May 1843       Forked River    Monmouth   NJ   Child's Birth Event
12 Jan 1845       Forked River    Monmouth   NJ   Child's Birth Event
13 Mar 1847       Forked River    Monmouth   NJ   Child's Birth Event
11 Jan 1849       Forked River    Monmouth   NJ   Child's Birth Event
11 Feb 1851       Forked River    Ocean      NJ   Child's Birth Event
19 Sep 1852       Forked River    Ocean      NJ   Child's Birth Event
-- Sep 1853       Salt Lake City  Salt Lake  UT   Arrived in Utah
11 Aug 1854       Salt Lake City  Salt Lake  UT   Child's Birth Event
10 Jun 1856       Salt Lake City  Salt Lake  UT   Child's Birth Event
 3 Aug 1860       Salt Lake City  Salt Lake  UT   Child's Birth Event
18 Apr 1879       Salt Lake City  Salt Lake  UT   Death Event
```

From this information you can derive certain general conclusions. This man lived in Forked River, NJ., from the time of his birth until 1853, when he removed to Utah. He continued living in this place until the time of his death in 1879.

You can easily see how the information for the previous tracking records were derived by combining and simplifying the data given in the preceding list of events. Notice how all the essential facts reduce to only a few lines of information. This list also reveals that the jurisdiction of Toms River was omitted from our tracking record for this man.

Jurisdictional Tracking

To incorporate this information, the tracking record now comprises the following five records:

Given	Surname	Town	County	ST	S	Era	Remarks
Joseph	Chamberlin	Forked River	Monmouth	NJ	M	1812-1835	Born 1812.
Joseph	Chamberlin	Toms River	Monmouth	NJ	M	1835	Married
Joseph	Chamberlin	Forked River	Monmouth	NJ	M	1835-1850	
Joseph	Chamberlin	Forked River	Ocean	NJ	M	1850-1853	County change.
Joseph	Chamberlin	Salt Lake City	Salt Lake	UT	M	1853-1879	Died 1879.

Note that adding the new record only required a few minor changes to the Era field for the records immediately preceding and following the new record. In constructing a jurisdictional history, the goal is to account all periods of time.

Just because an individual is associated with a given jurisdiction, it doesn't necessarily mean that he or she resided in that place. A person may live in one place yet travel to other places to transact business, or engage in other activities which may get their name into the local records. In the preceding example, this man went to another town to get married. A person may leave home to go to school, serve in the military, take a trip, and so forth. In our present-day society, such movements are the order of the day.

This point is particularly important for those people doing descendancy genealogies, in which they are trying to identify all individuals of a given surname. In this example, we were able to show all the jurisdictions that this man was associated with during his lifetime. In many cases, you will encounter periods of time for which you cannot positively determine a specific jurisdiction or at best, only a general jurisdiction.

In other cases you may know the jurisdiction, but not the exact time frame. In dealing with any of these situations, you can still make an educated guess which can be reflected in the jurisdictional tracking record. These situations will be discussed in more detail later.

By now you should have a fairly good idea of the jurisdictional tracking concept. If you don't, go back and review this material until you feel comfortable with it. While the jurisdictional tracking format is very similar to the one described in Chapter 3, they are not the same. The most important difference is that Source Extraction indexing is *source-specific,* and is neither designed nor intended to show family connections or relationships. Conversely, jurisdictional tracking only applies for identified individuals in a family.

While the preceding format is a good start it still has some deficiencies. Adding just a little bit more information and making some slight modifications will greatly enhance the record format.

Era Correlation Key

The Era Correlation Key (ECK), used in conjunction with the date, was introduced and discussed in the Chapter 3 section, *Indexing Your Source Extractions*. The same characters are also used in jurisdictional tracking records where their function and interpretation is very similar. In Source Extraction indexing only a single year is used to denote a date whereas jurisdictional tracking may use a single year or a span of years.

You might be tempted to increase the repertory of special characters for the ECK, but the downside is that you might end up with too many of them. Thus, instead of keeping things simple, they would only compromise the simplicity of the format. Also, someone not familiar with this notation would have more difficulty in interpreting them.

Table 5-1 lists the five suggested ECK characters, their notational forms, and general interpretation for use in jurisdictional tracking.

Jurisdictional Tracking

Table 5-1. Era Correlation Key Characters and Interpretation

ECK	Notational Forms	Interpretation
Hyphen (–)	1790 – 1803	Fairly certain that the person was associated with the stated jurisdiction for the indicated span of years.
	1823 –	Fairly certain that the person was associated with the stated jurisdiction beginning with the indicated year and remained there for an indeterminate time.
	– 1684	Fairly certain that the person was associated with the stated jurisdiction as late as the indicated year but could have been there earlier.
Forward Slash (/)	1864 / 1871	An approximation of the span of years the person was believed to be associated with the stated jurisdiction.
	1712 /	An approximated year the person was believed to have been <u>first</u> associated with the stated jurisdiction.
	/ 1876	An approximated year the person was believed to have been <u>last</u> associated with the stated jurisdiction.

Table 5-1. Era Correlation Key Characters and Interpretation (Continued)

Asterisk (*)	1778 * 1840	The person was associated with the stated jurisdiction for the indicated span of years but died during the <u>ending</u> year of the span.
	* 1902	The person was associated with the stated jurisdiction for an indeterminate time and died there during the indicated year.
Greater-Than (>)	1669 > 1688	The person was associated with the stated jurisdiction for the indicated span of years but is believe to have died <u>after</u> the ending year of the span.
	> 1856	The person was associated with the stated jurisdiction and is believed to have died there <u>after</u> the indicated year.
Less-Than (<)	1656 < 1668	The person was associated with the stated jurisdiction for the indicated span of years but is believe to have died <u>before</u> the ending year of the span.
	< 1757	The person was associated with the stated jurisdiction and is believed to have died there <u>before</u> the indicated year.

Jurisdictional Tracking

Genealogical records or references often use notations such as "died after...," or "died before...," or "died between...(two years given)...." While the greater-than symbol is a mathematical character, it is a very simple character that serves a very useful function for the ECK. Like the greater-than character, the less-than character serves a similar purpose, but somewhat in reverse.

Jurisdictional tracking records showing various usages of the ECK characters are shown and described in more detail in the following section.

JURISDICTIONAL TRACKING FORMAT

As described in the Chapter 4 section, *Linking Families,* the use of an absolute number such as the LifeNumber™ (LN) to positively identify each person in your genealogy is also helpful when used in connection with jurisdictional tracking records. Adding another field to the jurisdictional tracking record will provide the place for the LN. Let us again, consider the jurisdictional tracking format previously discussed, but this time incorporating both the LN and the ECK within the Era (span of years) as follows:

Given	Surname	Town	County	ST	S	Era	LN
Joseph	Chamberlin	Forked River	Monmouth	NJ	M	1812-1835	53
Joseph	Chamberlin	Toms River	Monmouth	NJ	M	1835/	53
Joseph	Chamberlin	Forked River	Monmouth	NJ	M	1835-1850	53
Joseph	Chamberlin	Forked River	Ocean	NJ	M	1850-1853	53
Joseph	Chamberlin	Salt Lake City	Salt Lake	UT	M	1853*1879	53

By comparing this set of records with the previous set, it is easy to see that the changes are quite minor. The modified record format, while still simple, nevertheless serves its purpose quite well. It's true that more fields could be added to show other information. However, keep in mind that an index is just that; an index, and jurisdictional tracking is a special kind of index. Too little or too much information is not desirable.

Jurisdictional Tracking

Consider the following group of tracking records:

Given	Surname	Town	County	ST	S	Era	LN
John	Adams	Roxbury	Suffolk	MA	M	*1679	701
James	Becket		Niagara	NY	M	<1843	345
Anne	Brown			EN	F	1628-	901
Anne	Brown	Boston	Suffolk	MA	F	1653/	901
Anne	Chamberlin	Boston	Suffolk	MA	F	1653*1662	901
Peleg	Chamberlin	Newport	Newport	RI	M	1666>1722	292
William	Chamberlin	Boston	Suffolk	MA	M	1661-1663	213
William	Chamberlin	Providence	Providence	RI	M	1663-1682	213
William	Chamberlin	Shrewsbury	Monmouth	NJ	M	1682<1717	213
Mary	Thurston	Gloucester	Essex	MA	F	1786/1802	201
Elizabeth	Worden	Chicago	Cook	IL	F	1850>	127

Spend a few minutes studying these tracking records, paying particular attention to the use of the ECK character in the Era field. (Refer to Table 5-1, *Era Correlation Key Characters and Interpretation*.) Remember that the information given in your jurisdictional tracking records can only reflect the information you have at hand, based upon known facts and logical assumptions. As you continue your research and add data, you will need to constantly update your jurisdictional tracking records to reflect the latest information.

Jurisdictional Hierarchy

Note that some jurisdictions are incomplete in that they lack information for either the town or county or both. You will undoubtedly encounter this situation many times during your research. You may only have a family tradition that your so-and-so ancestor came from a certain state or country or a certain county in some state. However meager, it is a starting point, and can always be changed or updated as required.

Jurisdictional Tracking

Name Changes

The change of surnames for females in an important event to track. From the preceding examples, take the case of Anne Brown (LN 901). Her first record merely gives her name (Anne Brown), jurisdiction (EN) linked to the Era: "1628-". Because this is her earliest record, the year 1628 can be her inferred birth date. Next, she is associated with the jurisdiction of Boston, Suffolk Co., MA, for the Era: "1653/."

The forward slash (/) is used to indicate an indefinite or approximate period of time. In this case, the notation tells us that she could have been in this jurisdiction some time before the year 1653. In the next record, her surname changes to Chamberlin (year of marriage to John Chamberlin), same jurisdiction, and the Era is: 1653*1662. This record indicates that she bore the surname of Chamberlin until 1662, when she died. See also the record of Mary Thurston in the preceding list for an example of using the forward slash.

Incomplete Time Periods

There are several records in the preceding list that depict incomplete or partial time periods. The ECK characters used in the Era field are especially useful for clarification and brevity in this situation.

Two years separated with the greater-than character (>) denotes that the jurisdiction is valid for these years and that the person is believed to have died there after the ending year. For example, take the case of Peleg Chamberlin (LN 292) who is only represented by a single record that links a jurisdiction with the Era: 1666>1722. Interpreting this record says he was born in 1666 and lived in the stated jurisdiction until he died at an unknown time after 1722.

Two years separated with a less-than character (<) denotes that the jurisdiction is valid for these years, and that the person is believed to have died there before the ending year. For example, take the case of William Chamberlin (LN 213) in the listing for the jurisdiction of Shrewsbury, NJ. The Era gives: 1682<1717. Interpreting this record says he lived in this jurisdiction from 1682, and died there at some unknown time before the ending year 1717.

A less-than character (<) or greater-than character (>) with only a single year in the Era field is interpreted somewhat differently than if two years are given. For example, if an Era gives: "1632>, it means that the person was born that year and died young. If an Era gave; "<1725," it means that the person died before the stated year. It does not define how long the person may have been associated with this jurisdiction. See James Becket and Elizabeth Worden in the preceding list.

An asterisk preceding a single year in the Era field denotes that the person was associated with the indicated jurisdiction for an indeterminate time, but did die there during the stated year. The tracking record of John Adams (LN 701) illustrates this combination.

Obviously, the more you practice using this technique, the easier it will be to construct these database records and understand the notation therein. Characters other than alphanumerics were chosen for the ECK to minimize the possibility of confusing them with the characters in the adjacent fields. A more sophisticated example of jurisdictional tracking is described in the Chapter 8 section, *Jurisdictional Tracking*.

Jurisdictional Tracking

EXERCISE

Let's assume you have identified a woman in your ancestry whose parentage still remains unknown. Her name is Elizabeth Ross, and she married your great, great-grandfather Ebenezer Watkins on 25 Apr 1853, at Cleveland, Cuyahoga Co., Ohio. The marriage record gives her age as 23, and formerly a native of New York. A few months after their marriage, they moved to farm in an area of Hamilton County near the village of Delhi. They were living here until she died in July 1859. Assuming her LifeNumber to be 36, prepare jurisdictional tracking records for this woman based upon the foregoing information and compare your results with the following:

Given	Surname	Town	County	ST	S	Era	LN
Elizabeth	Ross			NY	F	1830-	36
Elizabeth	Ross	Cleveland	Cuyahoga	OH	F	1853/	36
Elizabeth	Watkins	Cleveland	Cuyahoga	OH	F	1853-1853	36
Elizabeth	Watkins	Delhi	Hamilton	OH	F	1853*1859	36

Do not worry too much if your answers differ slightly from the ones given here. There will be some cases where there may be more than one way to do it. Additional exercises have been prepared to give you more practice in creating jurisdictional tracking records. You don't need a computer to do these exercises. Just take a sheet of paper and mark off some areas that correspond to the rows and columns that have been shown in the previous material. The exercises and answers are contained in Appendix C, *Jurisdictional Tracking Exercises*.

The Family Group Record   6

The basic principles involved in consulting various sources and copying selected data into Source Extraction files were discussed in Chapter 3, *Source Extractions*. This chapter deals with the merging of data from your Source Extraction files into Family Group Records (FGRs).

Nearly everyone who has done genealogical work have used a form called a "Family Group Sheet" or some similar name. I prefer to call this document an FGR as it may comprise not one, but many pages of information. Because the FGR is a compiled or composite record, it should represent the sum total of information that was extracted from the various sources.

As you merge data from various sources, you may encounter differences or discrepancies. When this occurs, you must analyze and evaluate the conflicting information from the sources in question to arrive at the most logical conclusion.

A thorough understanding of the *Unique Identification* concept introduced and described in Chapter 4 is essential to fully assimilating the material in this chapter. If you don't feel that you really understand the *Unique Identification* concept at this time, go back to Chapter 4, and review it until you do feel comfortable with the material.

The material in Chapter 5, *Jurisdictional Tracking*, is one of the most useful tools you can utilize—both in your researches and in the compilation of your individual FGRs.

While pedigree charts are useful visual aids, they are not a substitute for a FGR. The FGR must be the foundation of every genealogy. Even the development of a written family history in a narrative form should still be compiled from individual FGRs.

Pre-printed "Family Group Sheets" only provide limited space to record the bare statistical facts for a given family which makes them an inadequate medium for a FGR. A FGR could be prepared manually (handwritten or typed), but a computer word processing application is strongly recommended.

Genealogy is a never-ending process of revision and updating. One of the greatest advantages of using a computer word processing program is that you don't have to retype or re-enter unchanged data when revising your records.

The FGR is the focal point where all your information for a given family comes together. There could be some discussion as to what constitutes a family, but this book will define it as any specific set of parents and their offspring (if any).

If you are doing an ancestral genealogy, you will want to compile FGRs on all your direct ancestors. As you proceed farther and farther back in your ancestry, you will eventually come to a family where you will not have sufficient information to go any further back, or at least not enough information to compile another FGR. In the case of a descendancy genealogy, you may start with a couple at some point in time and proceed forward by compiling FGRs for all their descendants.

RECOMMENDED CONVENTIONS AND GUIDELINES

Certain recommended conventions and guidelines have been prepared to help you attain clarity, consistency, and precision in recording information in your FGR.

Incomplete, Missing, or Ambiguous Names

In many instances, complete names are often unavailable or are not given in the records. For example, you may encounter events recorded in a manner similar to the following:

> "Son of Samuel & Betsey Brown, was born...."
> "Daughter of Dea. Nathaniel Avery, was baptized..."
> "Child of the widow Abigail Howe, died..."

The question then arises, "How do you identify these people in your compiled records?" The easiest way is to use the conventions as suggested in the preceding example. If the sex of the person is not known, use "Child" in lieu of the name. When the sex is given but with no name, just use "Son" or "Daughter" in lieu of the given name in your records, and assign them unique numbers. If, in the future, you are able to establish a name or initials, you can easily revise your records to reflect this information.

Many times marriage records cannot be found, but the wife's given name may be obtained from other sources. When the marriage event is documented in your FGR, you could show the wife's name as "Mary —?—," or "Jane —?—," etc. Sometimes, you will be unable to find any name for a wife. In this case, the notation "Miss —?—" will serve for the time being. Using "Miss" in lieu of a given name infers that she was not previously married, which may or may not be correct. However, if and when you are able to establish this fact, you can change it. If you find that she was indeed previously married, you can change "Miss" to "Mrs. —?—."

The Family Group Record

Using correct notation for women's names is very important. A woman's full name should always include her maiden name (whenever known). For example, if a man marries a woman who has been previously married, the following notation is recommended: "John Smith married Mrs. Elizabeth (Anderson) Hobart, …" If her maiden name were unknown, then this example would read: "John Smith married Mrs. Elizabeth (—?—) Hobart, …" Sometimes you will encounter a notation similar to "Mary Ann Smith, née Adams…." The word née is a term of French derivation that is used to denote the maiden name of a married woman.

Less common is the absence of the man's name, but it does happen. In this case, you can always safely use the notation "Mr. —?—," or "Mr. Jones," as appropriate. The uncertainty involved in using the various notations in lieu of actual exact names is virtually eliminated when you have identified that person with a number that will never change such as the *LifeNumber*™ (LN) which was described in the Chapter 4 section, *Absolute Numbers*. You can never lose track of these people and their names and other information can be corrected as appropriate without having to change anything else.

Marriage Anomalies

There will be instances in nearly every family (more common in the last few decades) where you will encounter couples that had children, but who were never legally married. In this case you will not have a date and place of marriage. However, it is recommended that in lieu of a marriage date, you record a date that approximates the year that the people in question began living together preceded by the letters "NM" (*Never Married*) or another suitable acronym of your choice, followed by their place of residence (complete jurisdictional hierarchy) at the time.

In the case of people who have married more than once, the question arises as to how you will compile your FGRs. You could have one FGR per marriage, but there are some good reasons not to do this. First, it is redundant in that you are copying information from a spouse on one FGR to another FGR for the other marriage or marriages.

The Family Group Record

Secondly, if you have to update your information for this person, you will have to do it for multiple FGRs. This procedure carries with it the risk of making an error so that the information about this person is not the same from one FGR to the other. Or, you may inadvertently neglect to update the other FGRs. Thirdly, depending upon how you file your FGRs, the multiple FGRs for a single person may not be in one place, which may add another level of inconvenience and possible error to your records.

If you are doing an ancestral genealogy, it is best in the long run that you keep all marriages for a given ancestor on a single FGR. This is because you won't usually be compiling FGRs on the children of these other marriages. However, if you are doing a descendancy genealogy, there may be cases where it will be best to have a given person appear on more than one FGR, because of progeny from different marriages.

Recording Dates

The most reliable way to record a date is by day, month, and year; e.g., 15 January 1824 or 15 Jan 1824. (Standard convention uses the first three characters of the month for the correct abbreviation.) The year is always given in full. Never use such notation as 12/9/1798, as it can be misunderstood as to which is the day and which is the month.

When recording dates, it is appropriate to mention "double-dating," a system of expressing dates prior to 1752 (in America and the British Colonies) within the period of January through March 24th. A date occurring within this period was often expressed in the following form: 22 Feb 1732/33, 19 Jan 1697/98, 15 Mar 1743/44, and so forth. It is best to always record double-dates exactly as they are given.

The changes brought about by the adoption of the Gregorian calendar in 1582, and the constant changing of the first day of the year, particularly in Great Britain and her colonies before 1752, can affect the accuracy of your Source Extractions. For example, many secondary sources, particularly the printed vital records for New England, inconsistently converted double-dates. In some cases, this can give rise to the wrong year for an event.

For this reason, if you are extracting information from secondary sources with dates occurring between January 1st and March 24th, you should always verify them against the primary sources (if possible). Note that different countries in Europe and Asia adopted the Gregorian calendar over a period of centuries from 1582 until 1918, as well as possibly changing the first day of the year. (See *Calendar* and *Double-dating* in the Glossary for further details.)

Baptisms and Christenings

Some people may want separate entries for baptisms or christenings, because in many cases, you may be able to obtain dates for these ordinances in lieu of birth dates. Certainly in the absence of the actual birth date, they can provide very useful information. But don't be misled into thinking that they are equivalents. They aren't.

Baptisms and christenings were generally done when a person was an infant, but you can't count on it. Often these baptisms or christenings were done many months or even years after the person's birth. It would be nice and neat if baptism and christening records always gave complete information on the person in question; such as the person's age at the time and their place of residence (if different from where the ordinance took place). It is true that occasionally this information is recorded, but not often. Baptisms especially were often done when the person was a half-grown child or an adult.

The reality is that most records of these events give little information other than the person's name, the names of their parents, and the date when the ordinance was performed. The place where these ceremonies were performed may have been many miles away from where the person was actually born. If baptism or christening dates are all you have, do try to obtain other information to arrive at either an exact date or a reliable estimate for a birth date. It cannot be over-emphasized that precise statistical data for every individual provides a bedrock foundation for your genealogy.

Abbreviations

As a general rule, use abbreviations sparingly. Some of the more common genealogical abbreviations are: *Aff* (Affidavit), *Bp* (Baptized), *Chr* (Christened), *Int* (Intention), *Inv* (Inventory), *Lic* (License), *Adm* (Administrator or Administration), to name a few. If you want to make frequent use of abbreviations, it is best that you either provide a place in your FGR that defines their usage or create another document where you can record your usages and notational conventions.

Latin phrases or abbreviations are often used in quoting or citing genealogical events. For example, in many genealogical works, particularly those written in the last century, it is common to find the use of such Latin terms as *Circa* (or *Ca.*), *Ante, Ibid* or *Ibidem, Op. Cit, q.v, sic, s.p,* or *d.s.p.*

When plain English will suffice, there is no reason to use an obscure Latin word or phrase such as *circa* in place of the English *about*. Again, remember that you want anyone, particularly non-genealogists, to be able to read and comprehend your material. Of course, in formal scholarly papers, Latin phrases may be more appropriate.

Event Modifier

A very common situation arises in most genealogies when there is some question as to the date and/or cited jurisdiction. It would be nice if you always had a complete date and a precise location, but as you proceed back in time, it doesn't always happen. The result is that genealogists often have to estimate dates and/or suggest the most likely place for an event.

The goal is to convey the most precise meaning to your records that you are able to do with the data you have at hand. Event Modifier is the name given to the use of predefined words or special notations that are used with an estimated date and/or presumed jurisdiction. Two kinds of Event Modifiers have been developed: date modifiers and jurisdictional modifiers.

The Family Group Record

The following date and jurisdictional modifiers are ones that have been developed and refined over a period of many years. There is no universal "accepted standard" of usage in this area. Though their use is optional, using event modifiers judiciously will add another degree of precision to your records.

DATE MODIFIERS

Date modifiers are only recommended for use with three major events: birth, marriage, or death.

The use of the words *about, before, after,* and *between*, are commonly found in genealogical literature. Of these, the word *about* is the most effective and meaningful when used in connection with a specific date (year).

The use of *before, after,* and *between* are generally discouraged because they are so imprecise. Occasionally, the use of *after* and *before* can be used with either a marriage or death date. They are definitely not recommended for the birth event because a specific year for the birth date must be given as either known or estimated. The use of *between* is not recommended at all. Frequently this term is used in conjunction with the date a testator made his or her will and the date that it was proved. In these instances however, the time between these two dates could be a period of many years which is very imprecise. Thus, it is much better for you to estimate a date.

The word *about* is commonly used when citing an uncertain date. However, the word *about* followed only by a year isn't enough. A reader might ask: "Is this date based upon some solid information, or is it more or less just a guess?"

To add a bit more precision when using the word *about*, the following notation and general definitions are suggested:

"About 1793, ..." A reliable estimate based upon solid evidence with a margin of error within a range of 2-4 years or so.

"About 1804 (?), ..." An "iffy" guess based upon some tangible evidence, but with a margin of error within 5-9 years.

"About 1827 (??), ..." A "wild" guess with a margin of error probably exceeding 10 years.

Suggested abbreviations for date modifier terms are:

Term	**Abbr.**
About	Abt
After	Aft
Before	Bef
Between	Bet

JURISDICTIONAL MODIFIERS

The modifier *probably* preceding a jurisdiction is a good word to indicate a good degree of certainty; that it is definitely based upon some solid tangible information. The word *perhaps* preceding a jurisdiction is useful in denoting a lesser degree of certainty; i.e., the cited jurisdiction is more of a possibility than a probability; an "educated" guess. The word *near* can serve in situations to indicate a close proximity to a known jurisdiction. Occasionally, it is appropriate to use the word *Of* as a modifier to denote that the person in question was associated with the cited jurisdiction, but not necessarily connected to it for the specific event in question.

Suggested abbreviations for jurisdictional modifier terms are:

Term	Abbr.
Probably	Pr
Perhaps	Per
Near	Nr
Of	Of

Some typical usages of date and jurisdictional modifiers are shown in the examples referenced throughout the remainder of this chapter.

Family Numbering

Many genealogies often use two general types of numbers for each family; generation and birth-order numbers. These numbers have no relationship to the numbers used for identifying individuals or for numbering genealogies.

GENERATION NUMBERING

In particular, descendancy genealogies commonly use generation numbers to indicate the number of generations removed from a progenitor who is also an immigrant ancestor. Generation numbers are small superscripts usually appearing immediately after the given name of each descendant.

For example, assume the progenitor is a man named Samuel^1 Johnson. The small superscript "1" indicates he is the first generation. A great granddaughter (fourth generation) might be Esther^4 Johnson, and so forth. Some genealogies introduce a degree of possible confusion by using the generation numbers for descendants of female lines which bear a different surname. It is best to keep generation numbers separate for each surname.

Some authorities suggest using alphabetical characters to denote the pre-American ancestors of the immigrant, such as "A" for his father, "B" for his grandfather, and so forth. For example, assume that Samuel^1 Johnson's father was William, his grandfather was Nicholas, and great-grandfather was Thomas. Thus, his line of descent could be stated as: Samuel^1 (William^A, Nicholas^B, Thomas^C). In the long run, it would be more practical to use negative superscripts to denote pre-American ancestors. Using the preceding example, the same line of descent would be expressed as: Samuel^1 (William^{-1}, Nicholas^{-2}, Thomas^{-3}).

BIRTH-ORDER NUMBERING

Many genealogies also use small lower-case Roman numerals to denote the birth order within each family. When there are children by more than one wife, the birth-order numbering can be chronological for all children or it can be independent of each wife. Their use is optional, and you may decide not to use them as they contribute little.

FGR STRUCTURE

Because the FGR contains different types of information, each section should be individually optimized for presentation, clarity and precision. An outline view of a simple FGR with five major sections in a suggested order is shown in Figure 6-1.

A brief description of the sections outlined in Figure 6-1, is as follows:

1. **Parents**. Primary statistical data for husband and wife.

2. **Children** (if applicable). Children that have their own FGR still need to have their primary statistical data recorded in this section within their parent's FGR. Children who do not have an FGR of their own should have their own biographical information (if any) included in this section.

The Family Group Record

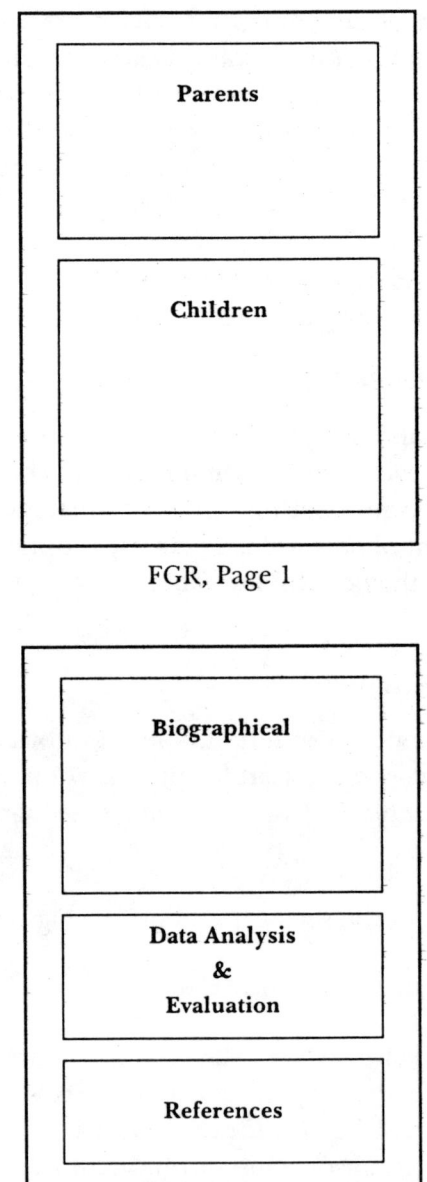

Figure 6-1. Family Group Record (FGR) Outline

3. **Biographical.** Biographical data can include (but is not limited to) the following types of information for the family as a whole (but focusing on parents):

    General family history including property transactions and probate records.

    Personal journals, diaries, family letters, etc.

    Places of residence over the years.

    Occupations and notable accomplishments.

    Physical description of family members.

    Health history (including causes of death for family members).

    Religious preferences.

    Pictures, drawings, maps, etc.

4. **Data Analysis & Evaluation.** This section is the place to record your conclusions after analysis and resolution of discrepancies between sources. It is also the best place to list remaining questions, leads to be followed, notes to yourself, comments, hunches, and ideas for future research.

5. **References.** In this section you list all the sources (Source Extraction files) that you used to compile the FGR.

Parent's Section

Each FGR should begin with the primary statistical data for husband and wife which includes:

1. Number.

2. Given Name(s) and/or initials and surname.

3. Key Events.

4. Parentage of each spouse.

NUMBER

As discussed in the Chapter 4 section, *Absolute Numbers,* the assignment of a number is essential to the process of unique identification for each person in a genealogy. The *LifeNumber*™ (LN) is used throughout this chapter to demonstrate its effectiveness as a numbering system.

NAME

Each parent's given name and/or initials and surname, as complete as possible is necessary. Female spouses should always be identified by their full maiden name (if known).

KEY EVENTS

Key events are defined as birth, marriage(s), death and burial or cremation. Each of these events must be accompanied by a date and place. The date should be as precise as possible. The place of the event should include the jurisdictional hierarchy (city or town, township, county or province, state, and country) as completely as possible, and *as it was at the time of the event.*

If known, the address of the home or residence, name and address of the church, institution, mortuary, cemetery, mausoleum, or hospital (as applicable) where the event took place should be recorded. This information will add another degree of precision to your records.

While burial, cremation, or interment information is generally not as important as the death data, it is very useful information nevertheless. In many instances, burial information is given in lieu of death data; and in this case, it would be considered primary data. So, while you may have to guess about the place of death, the burial information always provides solid proof of at least "the final resting place" and a very definite jurisdiction.

Special emphasis must be given to the birth event. Every person, *as a minimum*, must have either a known or estimated birth date and a corresponding jurisdiction (known or speculated) recorded on the FGR. Even if this information later turns out to be inaccurate, it is absolutely necessary to have a date here.

Because birth is the starting point for every person, the absence of this information will make it impossible to correlate any data about the person. Without a birth date you have no point of reference. Thus, in the absence of definite information for the birth date, you must derive an estimated date based upon what information you do have at hand.

Similarly, you may need to make an "educated guess" in the matter of the jurisdiction associated with the birth event. A complete jurisdictional hierarchy is always the desired goal. In absence of anything definite, you should have at least the state or country as a minimum. As you obtain further data, you can always go back and revise your FGR accordingly.

If one or both parents had other marriages, it is important to record the name of the other spouses along with the date and place for each marriage. In addition, you may want to include the primary statistical data for other spouses. However, this is your choice.

PARENTAGE

Each spouse (husband and wife) must have a place to record the names of their own parents and corresponding LN. As previously mentioned, each parent's given name and/or initials and surname should be as complete as possible. Females should always be identified by their full maiden names (if known).

The Family Group Record

PARENT SECTION EXAMPLE

Figure 6-2 shows the details of a typical Parent's section.

```
                                                              LN
HUSBAND:  John Allen Bartlett                                 69
    Father:   Samuel D  Bartlett                              33
    Mother:   Elizabeth Anne Worden                           34
Born:   10 June 1834, Philadelphia, Philadelphia Co., PA
Died:   21 Nov 1903, Chicago, Cook Co., IL
Buried:  — Nov 1903, Evergreen Cemetery, Chicago, IL
Married:   12 Apr 1856, Danville, Dodge Co. WI
Other Marriages:  None


                                                              LN
WIFE:       Eliza Jane Adams                                  119
    Father:  William Lane Adams                               203
    Mother:  Betsey S  Dale                                   204
Born:   3 Dec 1836, Lyons, Wayne Co., NY
Died:   14 June 1916, Corona, Riverside Co., CA
Buried:   19 June 1916, Holly Cemetery, Riverside, CA
Other Marriages:  None
```

Figure 6-2.   FGR Typical Parent's Section

Standard convention generally has the husband or male at the beginning of the record, followed by the wife or female. This system works well if you are doing an ancestral genealogy. However, if you are doing a descendancy genealogy, it is best to put the parent who is the descendant at the beginning of the FGR, regardless of whether it is a man or woman.

The numbers in the right margin opposite the parents and their parents (in the examples) are their LNs. As a personal preference, you might wish to add subheadings, such as "Place" or "Where" after each of the event headings. The goal in this and other examples is not to imply that this is the only way to do it, but to merely illustrate the type of information that should be recorded.

Generally the examples typify minimal verbiage. If you're not using a computer, you'd probably want lines under each category. Use what's comfortable for you as long as the data being presented cannot be misunderstood. Two additional typical FGR Parent's sections are shown in Figures D-1 and Figure D-2, in Appendix D, *Family Group Record Examples*.

Children's Section

Figure 6-3 shows the details of a typical Children's section. (The children's LN number precedes their names.)

		CHILDREN
M	218	Benjamin J Bartlett, b. 17 Nov 1857, Danville, Dodge Co., WI. Married Cynthia Alice Sayer, 22 June 1884, Plainfield, NJ. Died 23 Feb 1924, Corona, CA. +
F	219	Betsey Anne Bartlett, b. 29 Aug 1859, Cincinnati, Hamilton Co., OH. Twin of Mary. Attended public schools in Chicago, and after graduation, she attended the Eliza Smith School for Girls. Never married. She became a school teacher and taught for many years in the Chicago public schools. Died 18 Dec 1929, Chicago, IL.
F	220	Mary Samantha Bartlett, b. 29 Aug 1859, Cincinnati, Hamilton Co., OH. Twin of Betsey. Died young, 3 Oct 1859, Cincinnati, OH. Buried in the All Saints Cemetery, Cincinnati, OH.
M	221	William Allen Bartlett, b. 30 May 1862, Chicago, Cook Co., IL. When a young man he was employed on the railroad and eventually settled in San Francisco, CA. Eventually, he became a newspaper reporter and when he retired in 1931, he was managing editor of a publishing firm. Never married. Died 12 Apr 1940, San Francisco, CA.

Figure 6-3.   FGR Typical Children's Section

The Family Group Record

What has already been said in the parent's section applies to each child in a family. When constructing an ancestral genealogy, most people are generally less concerned about siblings of an ancestor. But remember that the more complete your information is, the better your work will stand the test of time. There are many instances wherein tracing collateral lines brings to light certain crucial information that may not be available elsewhere. You need all the information you can get to be sure of arriving at the most precise and logical conclusion.

As shown in Figure 6-3, you will note that each child's entry contains a brief summary of his or her key events (birth, marriage(s), if any, and place of death (if known). A handy notation places a plus sign (+) at the end of each child's record to indicate each has his or her own individual FGR. This convention is particularly useful when doing a descendancy genealogy, or tracking various collateral lines in an ancestral genealogy.

It is true that this proposed format results in a little overlap between FGRs, but it is very helpful because it enables your readers to tell at a glance if they are interested in proceeding further on a line. Many descendancy genealogies only give a child's name and date of birth in the parent's record. This requires you to have to look in another place to find out if there is any more information about this person. How frustrating and what a waste of time! This is a good example of minimizing verbiage and maximizing inefficiency.

Note that the family surname is shown with each child's name, which at first glance appears to be redundant because it is already given in the Parent's Section. However, there are many instances where children (usually sons) have chosen to use a different spelling of the family name, or even to change it. This was a particularly common occurrence when people migrated from other countries.

If you are doing an ancestral genealogy, you could indicate your direct ancestor by having the child's name in bold type or underscored. You may also wonder why the example has the jurisdictional hierarchies spelled out in full for each child, even when they are the same. Many genealogical compilations will make some statement like: "The first four children were all born in…, the next two were born in…, etc." This notation, while not actually incorrect, is not recommended because it is too easy to make a mistake when recording it in this fashion.

Moreover, if someone else (unfamiliar with family) is perusing your material they could have difficulty or err in trying to figure out where each child was born. In citing these important events, it is better to have a little redundancy than to economize on verbiage and risk making a critical error.

The line just following the *Children* heading is often a good place to preface the section with a concise subheading when there are questions about the birth order of the children, or their completeness. You could use phrases like: *Perhaps Others, Probably Others, Order Uncertain*, or *Perhaps not in Order*, to name a few.

Another example of an FGR Children's section is shown in Figure D-3 of Appendix D, *Family Group Record Examples*.

Biographical Section

We might say that an FGR is roughly analogous to a human being in that while the statistical data is the skeleton, the biographical data is the flesh and blood. The flesh and blood part of our organism cannot function properly without a skeleton, but not many people are going to be interested in a collection of skeletons. Like everyone else, genealogists like to have more than just a skeleton in their closet! Most people, especially non-genealogists, are much more interested in biographical details about their ancestors rather than just a collection of names and dates.

The Family Group Record

Biographical data can include photographs, narratives of family events, occupations of family members, education, religious background and beliefs, notable accomplishments, personal details such as what people liked to do, what they believed in and did, their physical characteristics, genetic traits, health history, and so forth.

As you go further back in your ancestry, this detailed type of information generally becomes difficult, if not impossible to obtain. You may have to be content with only being able to rough out a simple narrative of a family or person's movements during their lifetimes. Biographical information is best derived from sources such as wills, land records, personal diaries, journals, letters, interviews, and personal knowledge.

This section may also be used to list or describe nicknames, titles, or aliases that may have been used by family members, especially the parents. For example, men were often referred to by their name and a title such as: "Lt. Samuel Smith," "Col. William Chamberlin," Rev. Thomas Crosby."

In many instances, people were often identified with nicknames or aliases instead of their actual names. Women were often referred to as "Polly" instead of Mary, or "Betsey" in place of Elizabeth, to name two examples. Often, the nicknames or aliases have no similarity or relationship to given names. Whenever you encounter these situations, be sure to record the facts as you know them.

Some people may be surprised that biographical data should be included in the FGR. Many times, various clues gained from biographical details can be crucial in arriving at correct conclusions. There is no question that this section will always be of the most interest to anyone that is reading your material.

It is recommended that biographical data specific to a child be included in the Children's section (as shown in Figure 6-3), rather than putting it in this section. This is especially recommended if you do not intend to create an FGR for that child. However, this is your choice.

Figure 6-4 shows the details of a typical Biographical section. Figures D-4 and D-5 in Appendix D, *Family Group Record Examples*, illustrate other kinds of information that could be put in a biographical section.

BIOGRAPHICAL

John Bartlett spent his early years in Philadelphia, PA. When he was 18 years old, he found employment with a local freighting firm which had connections in other cities. In due time, he was given an opportunity for advancement which required that he move to the state of Wisconsin. While working in Wisconsin, he met his bride-to-be, Eliza Jane Adams, the daughter of one of his firm's leading shippers. About a year later, they were married at her parent's home in Danville, WI, with many relatives and friends joining in the festivities.

Physically, John Bartlett was of medium build, standing about 5 feet, 8 inches in height and weighed about 165 pounds in his youth. He had fairly heavy eyebrows, deep blue eyes and brown hair. His wife Eliza Jane, was said to have been about 5 feet 3 inches in height and very slim. She had brown eyes and very long blonde hair which she usually kept in braids all her life. [Etc.]

Figure 6-4. FGR Typical Biographical Section

Data Analysis & Evaluation Section

In this section you can include notes to yourself for further research, as well as hunches or conclusions, and so forth. Here you can discuss and explain your rationale in drawing certain conclusions about the information that you have recorded. Many times, your conclusions will bring out details that are not readily obvious from the individual sources themselves.

The FGR is the focal point where all your information from various sources comes together. Thus, it is the logical place where the data analysis and evaluation process should take place.

The Family Group Record

Obviously, you cannot start any comparisons until you have at least two differing points of fact. The best way to begin is to take the data from your first Source Extraction file and build an FGR (or FGRs) based only on the information from this one source. When this has been done, proofread everything you have done before proceeding.

Take the data from your next Source Extraction file and integrate it with the information you already have in the FGRs. As you do this, very carefully compare each bit of data with what you already have recorded. Information from the second Source Extraction file that is new can be added as given. The citation for the source can be added to the References section.

As you proceed, you will inevitably encounter points of fact between your sources that appear to conflict. When this happens, you must begin an analytical process to decide which source appears to be the most logical and accurate. You may even decide that neither of them seems correct. Sometimes, with only two sources to compare, you may be unable to decide which one you prefer. Obviously, differing points of fact cannot both be correct and you must look further.

The process just described must be repeated for every Source Extraction file you have that pertains to the FGR or FGRs you have already compiled. Each and every time you acquire information from a new source, you must repeat this process.

As you gain expertise and experience in processing and evaluating the information from various sources, you will come to know their strengths and weaknesses. Figure 6-5 shows how the Data Analysis & Evaluation process might be performed. Additional examples are shown in Appendix D section, *Data Analysis & Evaluation*.

> Sarah Anne Elston married Robert W. Helm, but no record of their marriage has been found, nor her own birth record. Sarah and Robert had 12 children. Their first child was born in 1838; the last child was born in 1866. Robert Helm was born on 10 July 1803, according to a family bible record. In the 1850 census, Sarah's age was given as 31 years and Robert's age was given as 45 years; in the 1860 census, her age was given as 54 years and Robert's as 65 years. Obviously, either one or both of the census records are incorrect with respect to their ages. The issue here is to derive an estimated birth date for Sarah.
>
> **Analysis and Result.** At first glance, it seems there is very little to go on. However, we do know that Sarah's first child was born in 1838 and her last child in 1866; a span of some 26 years. As a general rule we could state that it is uncommon for a woman to bear children after the age of 50, although there are exceptions.
>
> Let us first assume Sarah was about 21 years old at the time she married, and had her first child about a year later in 1838. Subtracting 22 from 1838 yields an estimated birth year of 1816. If we subtract 1816 from 1866 (the year her last child was born), we obtain 50 as her estimated age at this time. Now let us assume she was younger than 21 years at the time of her marriage, say about the age of 17. Using the previous assumptions as applicable, her age in 1866 would now be about 44 years, definitely more probable than 50. Of course, it is possible (but highly unlikely) she could have married at an even younger age.
>
> Thus, it would be fairly safe to say that her birth year occurred no earlier than 1816 and probably no later than 1824, with the average of these two dates being about 1820. Under this assumption, she would have been about 30 years old in 1850, which closely correlates with her age given in the 1850 census (31), but way off in the 1860 census which stated she was 54 years old. Thus, her estimated birth date will be given as: "About 1820...," which indicates a probable margin of error within 2-4 years.

Figure 6-5. FGR Typical Data Analysis & Evaluation Section

References Section

The References section is often the most neglected part of an FGR. Be as complete and consistent as possible when recording the sources you used when compiling the FGR. You should also include the Source Extraction file number with each source you have cited. This will enable you to instantly retrieve this file for further examination or re-evaluation should the necessity arise.

This section should actually comprise three important subgroups as follows:

1. **PREPARATION OF THIS RECORD.** This heading followed by a "standard" paragraph is important because it tells the name of the compiler who put the FGR together, along with his or her name and address. The date the FGR was prepared could appear after the compiler's name, or in another place. My personal preference is to place this date as part of a running footer at the bottom of each page. Every time the FGR is updated or changed, the date should change accordingly.

2. **References.** Each and every source you consulted in the compilation of the FGR is listed in this section. Following each item, be sure to cross-reference your Source Extraction file. While this section is often just a "laundry list," it can be much more than this. As a minimum, it is recommended that all important events such as births, marriage(s), deaths, or burials be specifically linked to the applicable source.

   There are several ways this can be accomplished. You may wish to use footnote citations (numbers) throughout your FGR to provide a link to a specific source. However, rather than use some arbitrary sequence of footnote numbers, it is easier and more logical to use the Source Numbers themselves.

   In either case, footnotes should identify the specific source in the reference section. This will save you a lot of time if you want to review specific information from the source in question.

3. **DISK ID**. This subgroup is used when you are using computer files for your FGRs. Each FGR should be stored in its own computer file. This is another case where using the LifeNumber™ (LN) system is very handy.

Each FGR file can be prefixed with "LN" followed by the number of the father or male parent. (In the case of descendancy genealogies, use the LN of the descendant which can be either a male or female.) For example, assume you have an ancestor, Thomas Madison, LN 25. You could identify his FGR computer file as LN00025.DOC (suffix assumes a word processing file). The leading zeroes are useful if you want to be able to sort your files in simple numerical order. Other conventions are possible of course, but this one is as good as any.

Figure 6-6 shows the details of a typical References section. In this example, the references are not listed in any specific order. The number in square brackets following the citation is the Source Extraction file number denoted by "SE."

Figure D-6 of Appendix D, *Family Group Record Examples*, shows the same list, but with the Source Number appearing in a column opposite the description of the source. Figure D-7 in the same appendix, shows an FGR Parent's Section using the Source Extraction Numbers as footnotes to link a source to a specific event as recommended in Item 2 of the preceding list.

SUMMARY

It is hoped that by now you have a good understanding of just what an FGR should be. Because of the relatively small size of the pages in this book, a "page view" of an entire FGR could not be shown with any clarity or detail. However, by illustrating and describing its major sections separately, it is hoped that the characteristics of each major section are more obvious and easier to understand.

The Family Group Record

PREPARATION OF THIS RECORD

This record was prepared by James H. Jones, 134 S.W. Adams Street, Peoria, IL 61602, using data obtained from various sources as listed. Comments and additional information are welcome. This FGR last updated on 10 Jan 1996.

References

History of the Town of Hingham, MA. Published by the town, 1893; three volumes in four; Library Call No. 974.482/H1. Vol. 3, pp. 178-182   [SE 31]

Monmouth County, New Jersey, Deeds, Vol. M, 1800-1802. Maintained and housed at the Monmouth County Clerk's Office, Freehold, N.J.; Family History Library (35 North West Temple, Salt Lake City) Film No. 0592651, pp. 387-93. [SE 104]

Essex County, Massachusetts, Records of the Probate Court, 1638-1881; Essex County Court House, Register of Probate, Salem, MA; Index to the Probate Docket, Vols. 9-12, K-Ri, 1638-1840. Family History Library (35 North West Temple, Salt Lake City) Film No. 0860478, pp. 138-39. [SE 42]

Letter to Samuel D. Tompkins from Andrew C. Moore, Jersey City, N.J., 18 July 1872, in possession of Mrs. Laura L. Anderson, Route 3, Box 139, Talent, OR 97540 (1989).   [SE 28]

Gravestone Inscriptions, Old Waretown Cemetery, Waretown, N.J., copied by Donald F. Gray, 401 Dowd Avenue, Elizabeth, N.J. 07206, 21 May 1984.   [SE 17]

U.S. Federal Census, Licking County, Ohio, Hartford Twp., National Archives Microcopy, M-19, Roll. No. 134; Family History Library (35 North West Temple, Salt Lake City) Film No. 337,945, P. 486   [SE 69]

Personal Knowledge of Mrs. Lucille S. Young, 492 North 13th Street, Red Bluff, CA 96080 (1990).   [SE 13]

Family Bible of William F. Thomson, in possession of Mr. Robert S. Evans, 2495 East Bates Avenue, Denver, CO 80210 (1978).   [SE 5]

[DISK ID LN25]

Figure 6-6.   FGR Typical References Section

Genealogical Charts and Numbering 7

Charts are very useful tools in genealogy because they graphically illustrate various family structures and lines of descent. Not only are they valuable guides for the experienced genealogist, but they are generally very easy to understand by non-genealogists as well. There are two different kinds of genealogical charts: ancestral (or pedigree) and descendancy.

The benefit of using numbers to cross-reference Family Group Records (FGRs) and genealogical charts is obvious. It is important to have the capability of choosing an individual from a chart and quickly locate the FGR that describes that person's family in more detail. Similarly, you might want to take an individual from an FGR and see his or her relationship in the context of a chart.

ANCESTRAL OR PEDIGREE CHARTS

An ancestral chart is usually called a pedigree chart or just a pedigree. A pedigree begins with a specific individual and graphically depicts that person's direct ancestors on all lines back as far as possible, insofar as available information permits. Because every person always has two parents, a pedigree fits a very standard format that is quite easy to lay out from a graphical standpoint.

Genealogical Charts and Numbering

A pedigree may comprise anywhere from just one to a great many pages. Because each page can only contain just so much information, it is necessary to have a method of organizing and numbering the pedigree charts so they can be linked to each other. The number of ancestors or generations contained on a single chart has a direct bearing on the numbering scheme being used. While pedigree charts come in all sizes and shapes, the de facto standard is generally considered to be the four-generation chart, hereafter referred to as the *Standard* pedigree chart which is shown in Figure 7-1. The standard chart is often and erroneously called a five-generation chart.

The first chart of a pedigree differs from all succeeding charts in that the name of the first person in the pedigree is not duplicated anywhere else. A person in the last generation on any given chart becomes the first person on the extension chart for that line. Except for the first chart, one generation is always duplicated as you move back. This overlap of generations applies to all pedigree charts of a linked series, regardless of the number of generations for which it is designed.

It is true that the first chart does show five generations if you count the person for whom the pedigree applies, but therein lies the error. The dictionary defines pedigree as: *a chart of an individual's ancestors*. This definition distinguishes between the individual and the individual's ancestor's. According to this definition, a pedigree should begin with the parents of any given person. Thus, my point that the standard chart terminating in 16 ancestors is a four-generation affair.

Pedigree charts are not limited to showing four generations as they could be designed to show two, four, eight, 16, or theoretically any number of generations. Because the number of ancestors double for each generation, you soon come to a practical limit for page size. The fact is, that the standard pedigree chart which shows four generations remains the most practical size.

Genealogical Charts and Numbering

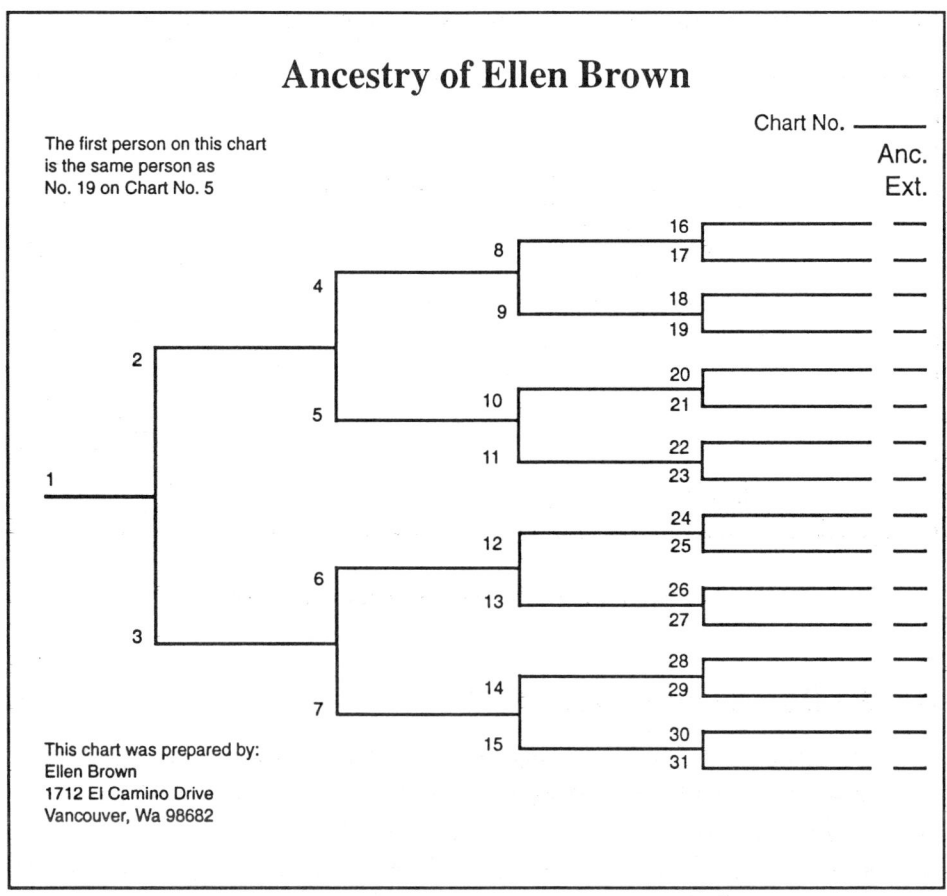

Figure 7-1. Four-generation Pedigree Chart

Figure 7-2 depicts the linking from one pedigree chart to another.

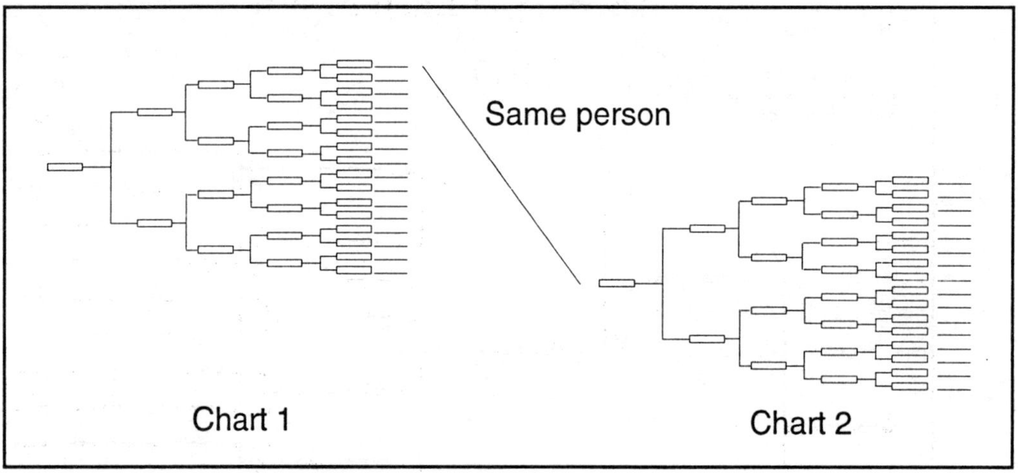

Figure 7-2. Pedigree Chart Linking

Numbering Considerations

As shown in Figure 7-1, the standard (four-generation) pre-printed pedigree chart numbers each person. Similarly, the first chart in a pedigree is usually identified as No. 1, and succeeding charts are numbered in consecutive order for each generation. The rule is that all possible charts must be allocated a number even if they don't exist. This is because at some future time, ancestral lines may be extended, and you will want to have the correct numbers available.

Because all ancestors will be outlined and connected using the same type of chart, it is easy to see that the numbering scheme for all linked pedigree charts is a function of the powers of two; i.e., two parents, four grandparents, eight great grandparents, and sixteen great, great grandparents, and so forth. The number of ancestors in any given generation is always equal to 2 raised to a power corresponding to that generation. The total sum of ancestors out to any given generation is equal to the power series $2^1 + 2^2 + 2^3 + 2^N ...$, where N = the generation number.

Because the number of ancestors is always a function of the power of 2, there are some who propose using binary or hexadecimal numbers for pedigree numbering. Most people would find these numbering systems very awkward and difficult to use. However, the Appendix E section, *Numbering Systems,* provides a brief explanation of these alternate numbering systems for those interested in learning more about them.

Due to the fact that the number of ancestors double for each generation, it doesn't take very long before an interesting situation occurs. Suppose that you would like to know how many ancestors you have in your fortieth generation (equal to the expression, 2^{40}). Two raised to this power equals 1,099,511,627,776 which rounds off to the tremendous number of *1.1 trillion* people! And this only represents the theoretical number of ancestors in that *one* generation.

This number enormously exceeds the total population of the planet for that period in time (about the year 1,000 A.D.). In fact, this number is much, much larger than the total number of all human beings (homo sapiens) who have ever lived. (As a general rule, we can assume about four generations per century which equates to about 1,000 years for 40 generations.)

This example seems absurd and impossible, and is in fact, a paradox. Fortunately, it is one that is easily explained. The fact is that if you could go back far enough on all your ancestral lines, you would quite soon start finding many of the same ancestors in more than one place on your pedigree. In actuality, you have far fewer ancestors than the theoretical numbers indicate.

From a more realistic perspective, assume you are using the standard charts and are able to trace your ancestry back 16 generations on all lines. The first four generations only require a single chart; generations five through eight would require 16 charts; generations nine through 12 would require 256 charts, and generations 13 through 16 would require 4,096 charts, for a total of 4,369 charts! The total number of ancestors contained in these 4,369 charts would amount to 131,118!

Pedigree Chart Numbering

The standard pre-printed four-generation pedigree depicted in Figure 7-1, shows pre-assigned numbers for each individual on the chart starting with 1 and ending with 31. According to this design, the first person on the chart, who can be either a male or female, is No. 1. The two parents are numbered 2 & 3, the four grandparents are numbered from 4 through 7, the eight great grandparents are numbered from 8 through 15, and the 16 great, great grandparents are numbered from 16 through 31. Note that in this scheme all males are even-numbered and females are odd-numbered.

However, according to definition, the pedigree should begin with the parents of the first person on the first chart. In the standard four-generation chart, there are a total of 30 ancestors. For this reason, the first person on each chart should not be numbered. If you follow this rule, the last number on the chart will be 30 which is in agreement with the fact that 30 ancestors can be shown on a four-generation chart.

This modification would allow all males to be odd-numbered and all females to be even-numbered. Not only is this arrangement more logical, but it is esthetically compatible with the universal Law of Gender. i.e., the masculine element originates or initiates; the feminine element executes or complements. Thus, in every pair of consecutive integers, two is the complement of one, four is the complement of three, 6 is the complement of five, and so forth. Making this numbering change is not only more correct, but it will greatly simplify all subsequent chart numbering.

Pre-printed pedigree charts usually have a statement (Figure 7-1) that references the first person on any particular chart to the correct ancestral extension line on another chart (Figure 7-2) as shown in the following example:

>   No. 1 on this chart is the same person as
>   No. 19 on Chart No. 5

The following statement would be more suitable in that it could be used whether or not you choose to number the first person on the chart (recommended):

> The first person on this chart is the same person as No. 19 on Chart No. 5

The Ancestral Extensions (Figure 7-2) provides a place to record the chart number for ancestral lines being continued.

Computing Pedigree Chart Numbers

Standard convention identifies the first chart in a pedigree as No. 1, which requires that the charts for the 16 ancestral extension lines be numbered consecutively from No. 2 through No. 17. Even though you always have an even number of ancestors, your charts will always end in an odd number which does not logically correlate. In addition, having the first chart identified as No. 1 adds a slight level of complexity to all subsequent numbering.

Instead, it is more logical and convenient to identify the first chart as No. 0 (zero) instead of one which simplifies the mathematics when computing chart numbers. Because chart numbering is always a function of the powers of two, it is quite easy to calculate any chart number even if there are many missing charts between existing ones. This rule is valid for any size pedigree chart.

Table E-1 in Appendix E, *Pedigree Chart Numbering*, gives the equivalents of the powers of 2 for a selected range of values. Tables E-2 through E-5 enable you to find the correct numbers for all charts up to 4,353 which will suffice for up to 16 generations. Few people have lines extending further than this, and if they do, the numbers for these charts can be easily calculated. Explanatory text in the appendix describes the use of these tables.

Genealogical Charts and Numbering

If you don't mind doing a little elementary math, you can forget about the tables. Using a simple formula, you can easily calculate the correct chart number for any ancestral extension.

The following general formula will allow you to compute the ancestral extension numbers for a pedigree chart of any size:

(1) $2^{\alpha}(C-1) + 2 = N$

     Where C is a positive integer ≥ 1, and equivalent to the number of the chart you are working on, and

     α is a positive integer $\neq 0$, equivalent to the number of ancestral generations shown on the chart, and

     N = the chart number for the first extension line,

     Note: The variable $\alpha = 3$ for a three-generation chart; 4 for the four-generation (standard) chart; 8 for an eight-generation chart, and so forth.

If you are using the standard chart (four generations), formula (1) reduces to:

     $2^4(C-1) + 2 = N$, or

(2) $16(C-1) + 2 = N$

Formulas 1 and 2 assume that your first chart is identified as No. 1. However, if your first chart is identified as No. 0 (recommended), then formula (2) becomes even simpler:

     $2^4C + 1 = N$

(3) $16C + 1 = N$

For example, let's say you are using standard charts (with your first chart identified as No. 0), and are currently working on Chart No. 23. You want to compute the chart number for the fourth ancestral extension. Using Formula (3):

     16 x 23 + 1 = N,

     368 + 1 = 369 (the number of the first ancestral extension).

Because you are only extending the fourth line, you need to add 3 to the previous result, or just simply count down three, thus:

369 + 3 = 372, the correct chart number for the fourth ancestral extension.

If your first chart was identified No. 1 in the previous example, the calculations using Formula (2) would be:

16 (23-1) + 2 = N,

352 + 2 = 354 (the number of the first ancestral extension).

354 + 4 = 358 (chart number for the fourth ancestral extension).

Pedigree Numbering Systems

While a pedigree chart is a very useful tool in genealogy, it does have certain limitations that are important to understand. A pedigree chart cannot conveniently show more than one child of any pair of ancestors who may have had other children, and there is no easy way to number other relatives on collateral lines. Some authors have proposed various schemes to address the inherent difficulties of this requirement, but none are satisfactory as the suggested computations are confusing and subject to error.

The most important thing to know about a pedigree is that it presents a *relative* picture. It is *relative* because the position of any person on a given chart can change. This doesn't mean that the lineage has necessarily changed; it just means the *relative position* of any given ancestor is subject to change. Every pedigree chart begins with some individual whose ancestors are shown as occupying certain positions throughout the set of charts comprising the pedigree.

Let's say that you have built a pedigree based on yourself; that is, you are the first person on the first chart. Now, assume that some years have passed and you'd like to give an interested granddaughter a copy of your work. However, you want the pedigree to begin with her.

Genealogical Charts and Numbering

The chart you have used for yourself would now only represent one-fourth of her pedigree. This means that you would either have to prepare a whole new pedigree or give her a copy of your pedigree and leave the remaining three-fourths of her lineage undone. In this example, you can readily see that any person's position in a pedigree is always relative. Your position in your granddaughter's pedigree is not the same as it was when you were the person with whom it began. If you cross-referenced your FGRs with your pedigree chart numbers, they would all have to be changed as well.

The two most popular numbering systems for ancestral genealogies are the standard numbering system and the Ahnentafel system.

STANDARD NUMBERING SYSTEM

The so-called standard numbering system simply uses the numbering scheme as previously described for the standard chart in conjunction with the number printed on the chart. Thus, a person identified as No. 27 on Chart 56 could be referenced as 56-27. This number can also be used to cross-reference the FGRs supporting the pedigree. However, remember that such numbering is only valid for a specific pedigree. The pedigree cross-reference numbers for your FGRs would probably be invalid for anyone else.

AHNENTAFEL SYSTEM

The Ahnentafel system, also called the Sosa-Stradonitz system, is a pedigree numbering system widely used by many genealogists. Ahnentafel is a German word meaning *ancestor table*. The Ahnentafel number is used to denote an ancestor on a pedigree chart. From the first person on a pedigree chart who is No. 1, the Ahnentafel number for that person's father is simply twice the value of the preceding number; the Ahnentafel number for the mother is twice the value of the preceding number plus one. The best feature of Ahnentafel is that the numbers on each chart do not overlap from one chart to another, and they can also serve as a cross-reference to the applicable FGR.

While the Ahnentafel number does have the virtue of being unique and easily computed, it suffers from other defects. First, you have to compute the numbers and will always run the risk of making a mistake. Second, if you wanted to build a new pedigree from a different person on the existing pedigree, you have to re-compute all the numbers. Thirdly, if you can trace your ancestry back far enough, you will find the same ancestors appearing in different places on your pedigree. In this case, you will have different numbers for the same person which will be confusing at best.

Proponents of Ahnentafel claim that this system eliminates the problem of chart numbering. However, this really isn't true. If you have only a few charts comprising your pedigree it would not be hard to find someone on them. But a good-sized pedigree could easily comprise several hundred charts. Regardless of what numbers you use to identify any given chart, you still need some easy way to locate a specific person and this will involve some system of chart numbering. So, when all is said and done, are you any better off using Ahnentafel over standard numbering? Of course, that decision is up to you. At least on the standard pre-printed charts the numbers are already there so you won't have to compute them.

The Ahnentafel numbering rules will not work if you follow the recommendation of not numbering the first person on each chart. However, you can still incorporate the basic motif of the Ahnentafel numbering system by modifying the rules somewhat. On the first chart, you would number the first person's father as 1 and the mother as 2. From then on the computations would be somewhat reversed from the Ahnentafel numbering rules in that all subsequent males would be twice the previous person's number, plus one; all females would require you to first add one to the previous person's number and then double it.

PEDIGREE NUMBERING COMPARISONS

Table 7-1 shows comparisons between the Standard pedigree numbering and the Ahnentafel system. This table is based on the first chart being identified as No. 1. Assume an ancestral line which begins with Ancestor 23 on Chart No. 1 and extends to Chart No. 9. From Chart No. 9, Ancestor 28 extends to Chart No. 142. Note that on the standard chart, Ancestors numbered from 16 through 31 are the ancestral extension lines. Refer to Tables E-2 through E-5 in Appendix E, *Pedigree Chart Numbering*, to confirm these chart extension numbers.

Ancestor No. 23 on Chart No. 1 is also Ahnentafel 23, which is the same Ahnentafel number on Chart No. 9. Ancestor 28 on Chart No. 9 is Ahnentafel 380 which is the first person on Chart No. 142. The connecting ancestral lines are shown in bold face type with the applicable table cells shaded to emphasize the interconnections.

DESCENDANCY CHARTS

A descendancy chart is much more restricted in scope than a pedigree chart because of practical considerations. The enormous number of people that might have to be included could easily exceed all practical dimensions for even the largest printed page after only a few generations.

Of course, a descendancy chart could be customized in such a way as to separate it into smaller sections that could conveniently fit on a standard page, or it could be manually written out on huge rolls of paper which could extend for a considerable distance. But this is not something you would want to do on a regular basis. Unlike a pedigree, every descendancy genealogy has a different pattern. There is no standard chart that could be designed to fit every family, except on a most general basis.

Genealogical Charts and Numbering

Table 7-1. Pedigree Numbering Comparisons

Standard	Ahnentafel	Standard	Ahnentafel	Standard	Ahnentafel
1-1	1	9-1	23	142-1	380
1-2	2	9-2	46	142-2	761
1-3	3	9-3	47	142-3	762
1-4	4	9-4	92	142-4	1520
1-5	5	9-5	93	142-5	1521
1-6	6	9-6	94	142-6	1522
1-7	7	9-7	95	142-7	1523
1-8	8	9-8	184	142-8	3040
1-9	9	9-9	185	142-9	3041
1-10	10	9-10	186	142-10	3042
1-11	11	9-11	187	142-11	3043
1-12	12	9-12	188	142-12	3044
1-13	13	9-13	189	142-13	3045
1-14	14	9-14	190	142-14	3046
1-15	15	9-15	191	142-15	3047
1-16	16	9-16	368	142-16	3048
1-17	17	9-17	369	142-17	6080
1-18	18	9-18	370	142-18	6081
1-19	19	9-19	371	142-19	6082
1-20	20	9-20	372	142-20	6083
1-21	21	9-21	373	142-21	6084
1-22	22	9-22	374	142-22	6085
1-23	23	9-23	375	142-23	6086
1-24	24	9-24	376	142-24	6087
1-25	25	9-25	377	142-25	6088
1-26	26	9-26	378	142-26	6089
1-27	27	9-27	379	142-27	6090
1-28	28	9-28	380	142-28	6091
1-29	29	9-29	381	142-29	6092
1-30	30	9-30	382	142-30	6093
1-31	31	9-31	383	142-31	6094

For these reasons, descendancy charts are not used very often; when they are, they are generally restricted to key lines of descent, perhaps only showing males lines or specific selected lines. Historical novels often contain simple descendancy charts to graphically depict important members of a family that are discussed in the text.

Figure 7-3 show an outline view of a typical descendancy chart arranged in a vertical style. It could also be arranged in a horizontal fashion or even in a combination of both. Each style has its advantages and disadvantages.

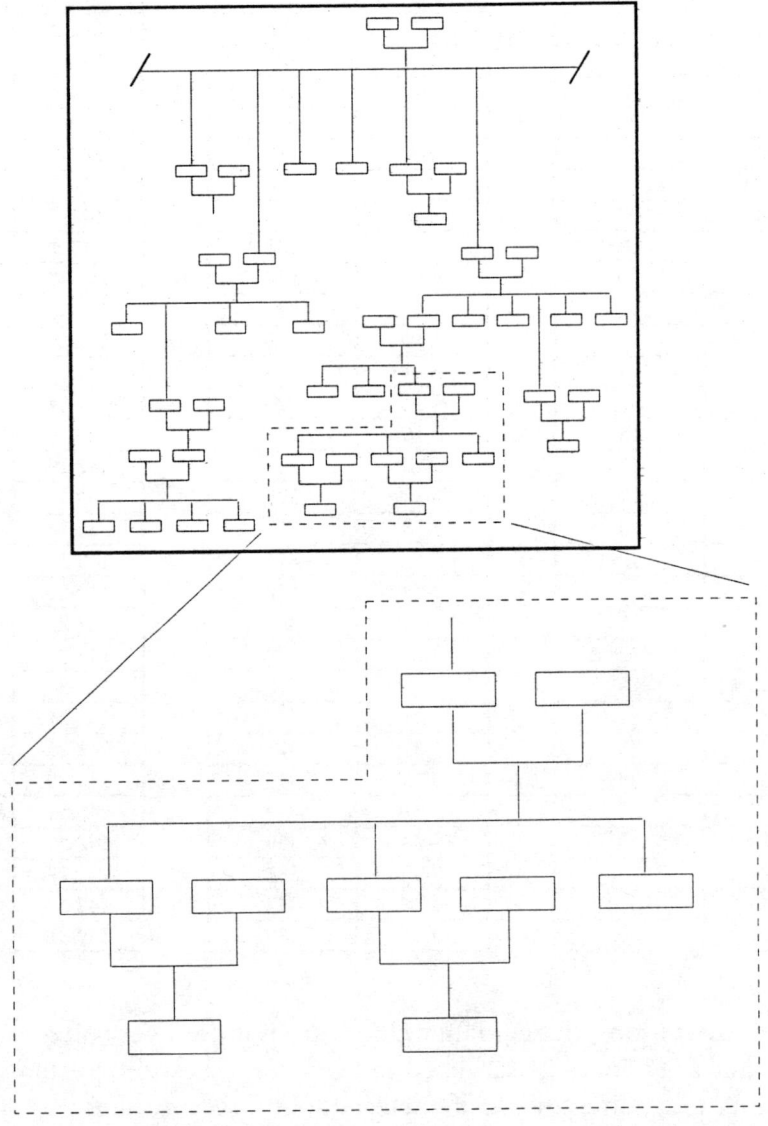

Figure 7-3. Typical Descendancy Chart Outline

Figure 7-4 shows the details of a selected portion (dashed-line box) of the outline depicted in Figure 7-3. Note that only the descendants bearing the surname Adams are identified with a generation number.

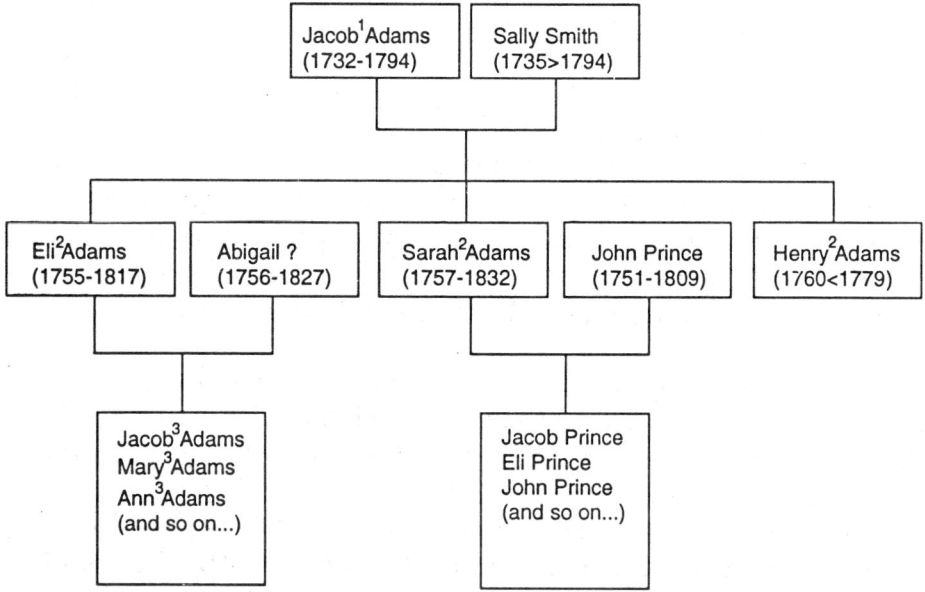

Figure 7-4. Typical Descendancy Chart Detail

Descendancy Numbering Systems

The New England or Register System and the Modified Register System are probably the two most popular descendancy numbering systems in general use today. Two other systems, the Index and Henry systems, which are virtually identical, are less frequently used. A general drawback to all of these systems is that the derived numbers are only valid for that particular descendancy genealogy. A person could be a descendant in as many descendancy genealogies as they have surnames in their ancestry. Thus, they would have another and entirely different number for each descendancy genealogy in which they might be listed.

THE INDEX AND HENRY SYSTEMS

The Index system was devised in 1900 by a man who adapted his system from the Dewey Decimal Classification System, a confusing methodology that was developed for use in libraries. In the Index system, every person's number is based on the birth order of his or her ancestor in the direct line.

If there are more than 10 children in a given family, the author proposed using an "x" for the tenth child, an "a" for the eleventh, a "b" for the twelfth, and so forth. The problem is that after only a few generations you can have huge numbers or alphanumerics. For example, suppose you are a descendant in the ninth generation from an immigrant ancestor. You could easily have a number such as 13462x1ab. If you were in the fifteenth generation you could have a number like 16347a1x93b39x4!

The Henry system only differs from the Index system in that a 10th child is denoted by (10), the eleventh by (11), the twelfth by (12), and so forth. While this eliminates the confusion of the Index system alphanumerics, the parenthetical numbers are clumsy. Without the parenthesis, the numbers can easily be misinterpreted; i.e., is 11 an eleven or two one's? With this system you could have numbers such as 13462(10)1(11)(12) for a ninth generation descendant or 16347(11)1(10)93(12)39(10)4 for a fifteenth generation descendant. Difficulties abound when using either the Index or Henry systems.

Suppose that you have researched and generated a descendancy genealogy and then discover a new child somewhere back in the early generations. In this event, you would have go back and renumber everyone that has been affected by this change. Depending on the extent of your genealogy, this could be a mammoth undertaking. Conversely, suppose you discover that a child does not belong in the family. Again, you would be faced with the same task. These problems may never happen to you, but the potential for them is always a possibility. In any case, you need to make a decision as to which system to use before embarking on a project.

There are other variations and attributes in these systems, but the purpose here is to only acquaint you with their essentials.

THE NEW ENGLAND OR REGISTER SYSTEM

The New England system, often called the Register system, is one of the better descendancy numbering systems in general use. As the name suggests, this system was developed by the New England Historic Genealogical Society in 1870. This system starts with a male progenitor and assigns him the number 1. From then on only the those descendants whose lineage is to be carried forward are numbered.

Generally, many printed genealogies using the Register system rarely number the females or attempt to carry them forward. In any case, not numbering females is technically incorrect. Every person has just as many female lines as male lines; thus, it is logical that each person, male or female, has a number. Moreover, in days past, children of unmarried females were often given their mother's maiden name. If you are trying to track all the descendants of a specific surname how would you deal with this situation when the mother has no number?

Each child of the progenitor who is to be carried forward is numbered in chronological order, beginning with the next number. Thus, the first child is 2, the next child is 3, and so forth. In the third generation, the children of the first child carried forward from the second generation are numbered first; then the children of the second child in the second generation are numbered and so on. All numbers are sequential from the progenitor.

While this system has the virtue of using simple, unique numbers, it suffers from other deficiencies. Because the numbering is based on chronological order of descendants, it is subject to the same problems as previously discussed for the Index and Henry systems. If the birth order of the children were to change, or children are subsequently added or omitted, you would have to renumber all previously numbered descendants affected by the change. Having to be constantly faced with the possibility of renumbering your records is a good example of working hard but not smart.

THE MODIFIED REGISTER SYSTEM

The Modified Register system, also referred to as the NGSQ system, was adapted from the Register system by the National Genealogical Society in 1912 when they commenced publication of their quarterly periodical. While the two systems are very similar, I believe the NGSQ system is the better system as it does correct one of the most serious problems of the Register system in that it numbers each child in a family whether or not it is to be carried forward in the genealogy.

As in the Register system, each child of the progenitor is numbered in chronological order, beginning with the next number. The numbers are always sequential for each generation. Thus, the first child is 2, the next child is 3, and so forth. In the third generation, the children of the first child carried forward from the second generation are numbered first; then the children of the second child in the second generation are numbered and so on. The two systems also disagree in certain stylistic conventions unrelated to numbering which need not be elaborated on here.

Because the NGSQ numbering is based upon the chronological order of descendants like the Register, Index, and Henry systems, it is subject to the same basic problems. All of these systems depend on accurate chronological birth order to maintain the original numbering assignments.

Genealogical Charts and Numbering

There are few genealogies so complete and perfect that the first few generations will never change. Unfortunately, it is the vagaries of the early generations that cause the most trouble with chronological numbering systems.

The Register and Modified Register Systems were specifically developed for use in genealogical periodicals, and for this medium they are quite adequate. It is in the creation and maintenance of comprehensive descendancy genealogies where their inherent deficiencies cause the most problems.

DESCENDANCY NUMBERING COMPARISONS

In the Chapter 4 section, *Absolute Numbers*, the advantages of the LifeNumber™, an absolute numbering system were discussed. A special example has been prepared to illustrate the differences between the Index, Register, NGSQ, and LN systems for descendancy genealogies.

Suppose there was a man named Jacob Adams, who married and had eleven children, four sons and seven daughters. Table 7-2 lists Jacob^1 Adams, his children, grandchildren, great grandchildren, and a few of his great, great grandchildren. Each generation is listed in assumed chronological order.

For the sake of brevity, only the names are given with their generation indicated in a superscript. The last three columns show how all these people would be numbered according to the Index, Register, NGSQ, and LN systems for descendancy genealogies. The first three columns are given to help you differentiate the various lines of descent from Jacob^1.

Now suppose that further research has revealed that Jacob had another son, Samuel^2, whose birth had been overlooked. The newly discovered birth record showed that Samuel was born between Sarah^2 and Eli^2. In the Index, Register, and NGSQ systems you would have to go back and renumber everyone beginning with the second generation. If you were using the LN system, all you would have to do is assign a LifeNumber™ to Samuel and proceed as if nothing had happened.

Genealogical Charts and Numbering

Table 7-2. Original Descendancy Numbering Assignments

Antecedents	Parent	Name	Index	Register	NGSQ	LN
		Jacob¹	1	1	1	1
	Jacob¹	Jacob²	11	2	2	2
	Jacob¹	Sarah²	12		3	3
	Jacob¹	Eli²	13	3	4	4
	Jacob¹	Thomas²	14	4	5	5
	Jacob¹	Mary²	15	5	6	6
	Jacob¹	Anne²	16		7	7
	Jacob¹	Dorothy²	17	6	8	8
	Jacob¹	William²	18		9	9
	Jacob¹	Abigail²	19	7	10	10
	Jacob¹	Elizabeth²	1X		11	11
	Jacob¹	Rebecca²	1A		12	12
Jacob¹	Thomas²	Sarah³	141		13	13
Jacob¹	Thomas²	Henry³	142	9	14	14
Jacob¹	Thomas²	Jacob³	143	10	15	15
Jacob¹	Thomas²	Nabby³	144		16	16
Jacob¹	Thomas²	Hannah³	145	11	17	17
Jacob¹	Thomas²	Nathaniel³	146	12	18	18
Jacob¹	Thomas²	Thomas³	147	13	19	19
Thomas²	Henry³	Anne⁴	1421		20	20
Thomas²	Henry³	Betsey⁴	1422	14	21	21
Thomas²	Henry³	Thomas⁴	1423	15	22	22
Thomas²	Henry³	Martha⁴	1424		23	23
Thomas²	Jacob³	Joseph⁴	1431	16	24	24
Thomas²	Jacob³	Jane⁴	1432	17	25	25
Thomas²	Jacob³	Sarah⁴	1433		26	26
Thomas²	Jacob³	Hannah⁴	1434	18	27	27
Thomas²	Jacob³	William⁴	1435	19	28	28
Thomas²	Nathaniel³	Elizabeth⁴	1461		29	29
Thomas²	Nathaniel³	John⁴	1462	20	30	30
Thomas²	Nathaniel³	Nathaniel⁴	1463	21	31	31
Thomas²	Nathaniel³	Robert⁴	1464	22	32	32
Thomas²	Nathaniel³	Joan⁴	1465		33	33
Thomas²	Nathaniel³	Agnes⁴	1466	23	34	34
Thomas²	Nathaniel³	Hannah⁴	1467	24	35	35
Thomas²	Henry³	Thomas⁴	Jonathan⁵	14231	25	36	36
Thomas²	Henry³	Thomas⁴	Anna⁵	14232		37	37
Thomas²	Henry³	Thomas⁴	Ebenezer⁵	14233	26	38	38
Thomas²	Henry³	Thomas⁴	Martha⁵	14234		39	39
Thomas²	Henry³	Thomas⁴	Eleazar⁵	14235	27	40	40

Genealogical Charts and Numbering

Table 7-3 shows the same comparisons after changes in the genealogy necessitated changes in numbering caused by having to add the son Samuel^2. Shaded cells highlight the numbers that had to be changed.

From these comparisons one can see the value of the LN system. Consider another situation in this hypothetical family. In this case, one of the grandsons of Jacob^1, whom we thought was a son of Thomas^2, was in fact a son of Jacob^2 whom we thought had no issue. Again, as in the previous variation, you would have to do a lot of renumbering in the Index, Register, and NGSQ systems.

In the LN system, this is a very minor problem. The FGR for Jacob^2 is revised to list this son, but still retains the original LN assigned to him when we thought he belonged to Thomas^2. Once assigned, the LN never changes. Everything else can change, but not the number.

Imagine another case where we find that a child in one of the families turned out to be identical with another child and was mistakenly thought to be two different people. Again, the Index, Register, and NGSQ systems would require renumbering. In the LN system, you would just eliminate one number which can either be discarded or made available to be used again. There is no requirement that all numbers have to be accounted for. The only rule is that no number can be used more than once.

In this example, the numbering requirements for spouses of the descendants was not addressed. None of the descendancy numbering systems assign numbers to spouses. Because you may be only tracking the surname and not every person in a descendancy genealogy, it may indeed be simpler to only number the persons that bear the surname.

In the LN system, however, spouses of people bearing the surname could either have their own LN or a composite LN related to that spouse. For example, from the list of descendants in Table 7-2, locate Henry^3 Adams, LN 20. Suppose he was married twice and had children by both wives. You could number his first wife 20.1 and his second wife 20.2. You could also do the same thing for spouses of female lines.

Genealogical Charts and Numbering

Table 7-3. Revised Descendancy Numbering Assignments

Antecedents	Parent	Name	Index	Register	NGSQ	LN
		Jacob[1]	1	1	1	1
	Jacob[1]	Jacob[2]	11	2	2	2
	Jacob[1]	Sarah[2]	12		3	3
	Jacob[1]	Samuel[2]	13	3	4	41
	Jacob[1]	Eli[2]	14	4	5	4
	Jacob[1]	Thomas[2]	15	5	6	5
	Jacob[1]	Mary[2]	16		7	6
	Jacob[1]	Sarah[2]	17	6	8	7
	Jacob[1]	Dorothy[2]	18		9	8
	Jacob[1]	William[2]	19	7	10	9
	Jacob[1]	Abigail[2]	1X		11	10
	Jacob[1]	Elizabeth[2]	1A		12	11
	Jacob[1]	Rebecca[2]	1B		13	12
Jacob[1]	Thomas[2]	Sarah[3]	151	9	14	13
Jacob[1]	Thomas[2]	Henry[3]	152	10	15	14
Jacob[1]	Thomas[2]	Jacob[3]	153		16	15
Jacob[1]	Thomas[2]	Nabby[3]	154	11	17	16
Jacob[1]	Thomas[2]	Hannah[3]	155	12	18	17
Jacob[1]	Thomas[2]	Nathaniel[3]	156	13	19	18
Jacob[1]	Thomas[2]	Thomas[3]	157		20	19
Thomas[2]	Henry[3]	Anne[4]	1521	14	21	20
Thomas[2]	Henry[3]	Betsey[4]	1522	15	22	21
Thomas[2]	Henry[3]	Thomas[4]	1523		23	22
Thomas[2]	Henry[3]	Martha[4]	1524	16	24	23
Thomas[2]	Jacob[3]	Joseph[4]	1531	17	25	24
Thomas[2]	Jacob[3]	Jane[4]	1532		26	25
Thomas[2]	Jacob[3]	Sarah[4]	1533	18	27	26
Thomas[2]	Jacob[3]	Hannah[4]	1534	19	28	27
Thomas[2]	Jacob[3]	William[4]	1535		29	28
Thomas[2]	Nathaniel[3]	Elizabeth[4]	1561	20	30	29
Thomas[2]	Nathaniel[3]	John[4]	1562	21	31	30
Thomas[2]	Nathaniel[3]	Nathaniel[4]	1563	22	32	31
Thomas[2]	Nathaniel[3]	Robert[4]	1564		33	32
Thomas[2]	Nathaniel[3]	Joan[4]	1565	23	34	33
Thomas[2]	Nathaniel[3]	Agnes[4]	1566	24	35	34
Thomas[2]	Nathaniel[3]	Hannah[4]	1567	25	36	35
Thomas[2]	Henry[3]	Thomas[4]	Jonathan[5]	15231		37	36
Thomas[2]	Henry[3]	Thomas[4]	Anna[5]	15232	26	38	37
Thomas[2]	Henry[3]	Thomas[4]	Ebenezer[5]	15233		39	38
Thomas[2]	Henry[3]	Thomas[4]	Martha[5]	15234	27	40	39
Thomas[2]	Henry[3]	Thomas[4]	Eleazar[5]	15235	28	41	40

The LN system is in essence an *absolute* numbering system. Suppose in the distant future there is an enormous computer system or network with every known person identified with a number. All genealogists of that day will merely obtain the correct numbers for the identified people in their genealogy. Those people not already in the computer will be assigned a number once sufficient supporting evidence of their existence has been presented and accepted. The result of such a system is that a person who may be listed in any number of genealogical works will always have the same number no matter where they appear.

Of course, this is a theoretical and fantastic example, and it is only mentioned to demonstrate the advantages of using absolute numbering. As a start towards this mythical goal, large family organizations devoted to the research and maintenance of records pertaining to a particular surname could begin by implementing the absolute numbering system on a family surname level. This has already been accomplished for the Chamberlin/Chamberlain (and other variants) surname in America and Canada.

FGR Numbering Example

An example that is pertinent to this discussion and a true story, concerns a man named Henry Chamberlin, who first appeared in America at Hingham, MA., in 1638/39. Later, he was of Hull, MA, where he died in 1674. The ancient records of the day called him both a blacksmith and a shoemaker. His "supposed" family record has appeared in many, many genealogies over the past decades.

In 1985, an article was published that conclusively proved that there were two men named Henry Chamberlin, both of Hingham, MA, and living there at about the same time, 1638/39. One was a blacksmith and the other a shoemaker.[1]

Figure 7-5 delineates an abridged record of the family structure of Henry Chamberlin before it was known that there were two men of the same name and that both families had been merged into one. This family outline also shows the unique numbers (LifeNumbers) that had been assigned to the family members.

This example is not intended to give all the information known about these people, because the focus here is only on the numbers. Their names along with their estimated or known date of birth have been included for clarity. The purpose of the example is to show how separating the "original" family into two different families affects the LN numbering. Figures 7-6 and 7-7 show the family structures of Henry Chamberlin the blacksmith and Henry Chamberlin the shoemaker, respectively.

As it turned out, the children, Nos. 2, 3, 4, 7, 8 and 9, remained in the blacksmith's family. The children, Nos. 5, 6, 10, 11, 12, and 13, went to the shoemaker's family. The shoemaker, his wife, and three children who were not in the original (supposed) family structure were assigned LifeNumbers.

The LifeNumbers already assigned were not changed, and the subsequent effects upon the descendants of both men were unaffected. A few new LifeNumbers had to be assigned and other relatively minor changes were made to complete the revision. View these examples only from the perspective of how the original LifeNumber™ assignments remained unchanged by subsequent changes in family structure. This example clearly illustrates some very definite advantages of using LifeNumbers.

---

[1]. See "The Two Henry Chamberlin's of Hingham, Massachusetts: 1638-1649," by David Conrad Chamberlin, Sr., *The New England Historical and Genealogical Register*, Volume CXXXIX, April 1985, pp. 126-138.

				LN
HUSBAND: Henry^1 Chamberlin "Blacksmith & Shoemaker"				1
Born: About 1592 (?), ...				
				LN
WIFE: Jane				99
Born: About 1595 (?), ...				

CHILDREN

F	2	Susanna^2, b. About 1616, ...
M	3	Henry^2, b. About 1619, ...
M	4	William^2, b. About 1623, ...
M	5	Daniel^2, bp. 15 May 1632, ...
F	6	Mary^2, bp. 15 May 1632, ...
M	7	John^2, bp. 15 Nov 1633, ...
F	8	Ursula^2, b. About 1634 (?), ...
F	9	Faith^2, b. About 1636 (?), ...
M	10	Daniel^2, bp. 17 May 1639, probably a son, ...
F	11	Sarah^2, bp. 26 Sep 1641, perhaps a daughter, ...
M	12	Nathaniel^2, bp. 26 Nov 1644, perhaps a son, ...
M	13	Ebenezer^2, b. About 1646, perhaps a son, ...

Figure 7-5. FGR Numbering Example 1

			LN
HUSBAND: Henry¹ Chamberlin "Blacksmith"			1
Born`: About 1592 (?), ...			

			LN
WIFE: Jane			99
Born: About 1595 (?), ...			

CHILDREN
(Perhaps others)

F	2	Susanna², b. About 1616, ...
M	3	Henry², b. About 1619, ...
M	4	William², b. About 1623, ...
M	7	John², b. About 1626, ...
F	8	Ursula², b. About 1634 (?), ...
F	9	Faith², b. About 1636 (?), ...

Figure 7-6. **FGR Numbering Example 2**

			LN
HUSBAND: Henry¹ Chamberlin "Shoemaker"			1259
Born: About 1603 (?), ...			

	LN
WIFE: Grace	1260
Born: About 1607 (?), ...	

CHILDREN
(Perhaps others)

M	5	Daniel², bp. 15 May 1632, ...
F	6	Mary², bp. 15 May 1632, ...
M	1261	John², bp. 15 Nov 1633, ...
M	1262	Robert², bp. 15 Mar 1635/36, ...
M	1263	Henry², bp. 15 Mar 1635/36, ...
M	10	Daniel², bp. 17 May 1639, probably a son, ...
F	11	Sarah², bp. 26 Sep 1641, perhaps a daughter, ...
M	12	Nathaniel², bp. 26 Nov 1644, perhaps a son, ...
M	13	Ebenezer², b. About 1646, perhaps a son, ...

Figure 7-7. FGR Numbering Example 3

Using a Database 8

A computer database is one of the most useful tools available for a genealogist. To fully implement some of the techniques and principles described in Chapter 3, *Source Extractions,* Chapter 5, *Jurisdictional Tracking,* and the material in this chapter without a computer would not only be very difficult, but impractical. Even if you don't have a computer as yet, the material in this chapter will not only give you valuable insights into the advantages of using a database, but also a deeper view of the genealogical process. There may be some terms in the following material that will be unfamiliar to you. Please refer to the Glossary for definitions of special terms.

In a very broad and loose sense, a database can be virtually any collection of information, such as files in a file cabinet, books, papers, notebooks or computer files. However, the types of databases we will be considering do not fit very well into this generic description. The dictionary defines a database as "a collection of data arranged for ease and speed of search and retrieval." This definition makes it clear that the organization of the data within the database is of paramount importance. Thus, databases must be designed to optimize and implement the principles of Data Storage & Retrieval. Just as this name implies, a well-designed database provides the means to quickly and efficiently store various types of data and conversely, to be able to easily retrieve such data in nearly any kind of organization or profile.

Since the advent of personal computers, the capabilities of database applications have been enormously enhanced. The tremendous advances in computer application software and mass storage devices such as very large hard disk drives, CD-ROMs, and magneto-optical devices, now allow a computer user to have the equivalent of an entire library available at his or her fingertips.

Using a Database

There are literally hundreds of books and dozens of technical journals devoted to the design and implementation of computer databases that are available if you wish to pursue the subject further. The purpose of this chapter is only to acquaint you with some of the most elementary characteristics and capabilities of databases, but at same time give you an idea of just how useful a database can be in the genealogical environment.

TYPES OF DATABASES

All computer databases contain one or more tables. In essence, a database table is nothing more than a series of rows and columns of information. For example, consider your address book. If you were to organize your address book into single lines of information in a table, you would probably have as a minimum, each person's name, followed by their street address, city, state, zip code, and telephone number. Figure 8-1 shows how a few lines of a table like this might appear:

Name	Street Address	City	ST	Zip	AC	Telephone
Jane Thomas	1121 E. Topeka Ave.	Kansas City	KS	66102	913	572-7495
John Smith	204 S. Main St., #5	Forest Grove	OR	97116	503	395-2938
Ellen Brown	1712 El Camino Drive	Vancouver	WA	98682	360	594-9261

Figure 8-1. Simple Database Table

Note that the information within each row appears to be in a column or discrete area within the line as indicated by the headings. In database terminology, each line or row of information is referred to as a *database record* and the columns are referred to as *fields*. A simple correlation between the assumed address book information and the fields in this example should be readily apparent.

There are two basic types of computer databases; flat-file and relational. A flat-file database essentially consists of one or more tables such as the one just described. A relational database also contains tables, but its design allows the tables to be interconnected or linked together and to work in conjunction with other database objects and structures.

Flat-file Databases

A flat-file table like the one shown in Figure 8-1 could be constructed manually with just a typewriter or pencil and paper, but once created there is little more that you can do with it except to add more rows of information. Computer word processing applications or spreadsheets can also be used to create flat-file tables which can usually be sorted by their various fields. According to the capabilities of the application, other types of operations may be possible as well. Depending on your requirements, such tables may be entirely adequate for the task at hand.

There are three major disadvantages of using flat-file tables in a computer environment. First, there is no convenient way to connect or integrate the information from these tables into a cohesive structure to enhance the capabilities and performance of the database as a whole. Second, such tables are generally very inefficient in the use of available mass storage. Thirdly, depending on the size of your table, the overall performance of your database could be quite mediocre because the more data the computer has to process, the longer it will take to execute a specific procedure.

Suppose you want to add an additional field for fax numbers to the table shown in Figure 8-1, and that you want this field to be able to contain up to a maximum of 15 characters or digits, and that you have 150 people in your address book. These conditions would require space to accommodate 2,250 (150 × 15) characters or bytes of information. (In computer terminology, each character is referred to as a *byte*.) Even if you have no information in a particular database field, the space must still be set aside or reserved.

Now let's say that only ten of the people in your address book have fax numbers. The remaining 140 database records would contain no information in the fax number field which means that you have 2,100 (140 × 15) bytes of storage space that are not being used—a small amount of space in this example.

Using a Database

But, suppose you have a large table consisting of say ten thousand records with many fields. If one of these fields were designed to hold 100 bytes, the total reserved space for this one field in the table would amount to 1,500,000 bytes (1.5 Megabytes). From this example, you can see how easy it is to waste a great deal of mass storage space if your table fields are not carefully chosen and effectively designed. As a general rule, flat-file tables contain much redundant information, and they do not efficiently use mass storage space because every record has to allocate space for all fields whether or not they contain any data.

Another problem with a table of this design is that it can significantly impact the performance or speed of your program. Fast as they are, even a computer requires a certain amount of time to do every operation. It should be quite obvious that the more records there are in a table, the more time it will take to search its contents. This is true whether or not you visually scan a list of records or do it with a computer program.

Relational Databases

Relational databases are designed to either eliminate or at least minimize the inherent deficiencies of flat-file tables. Like a flat-file database, a relational database may contain many different tables, but in this environment they are designed to be linked together in such a fashion as to significantly improve performance, flexibility and efficiency.

Again, consider the simple table shown in Figure 8-1 and the discussion regarding the addition of a new field for fax numbers. In a relational database, this problem is easily solved. Figure 8-2 shows the same table with one new field added. The number field (No.) stores a unique simple integer for each name in the address book. Figure 8-3 shows a new table with the same number field, an "AC" (Area Code) field and "Fax Number" field.

Name and Address Table						
No.	Name	Street Address	City	ST	Zip	AC Telephone
1	Jane Thomas	1121 E. Topeka Ave.	Kansas City	KS	66102	913 572-7495
2	John Smith	204 S. Main St., #5	Forest Grove	OR	97116	503 395-2938
3	Ellen Brown	1712 El Camino Drive	Los Angeles	CA	98682	360 594-9261

Figure 8-2. Relational Database Table 1

FAX Number Table		
No.	AC	Fax Number
1	913	573-4598
3	360	596-2895

Figure 8-3. Relational Database Table 2

Because the number field is unique for each person, a relational database can use it to link the two tables together. In our previous example, where it was assumed that only 10 people had fax numbers, the new table would only consist of 10 database records, one for each person with a fax number. The problem of wasted space in the previous example has gone away.

Similarly, the performance is significantly improved. In this case, only 10 records instead of 150 would have to be searched to find a specific fax number. The larger the database, the more important the issue of performance becomes. For example, large corporations have very large databases containing tens or hundreds of thousands and even millions of such records to keep track of their customers, suppliers, order numbers, and so forth. The performance factor in the design of such databases could easily be a crucial factor in the efficient operation of their business.

Using a Database

Figure 8-4 shows how the two tables shown in Figure 8-2 and Figure 8-3 are linked together with the unique No. field.

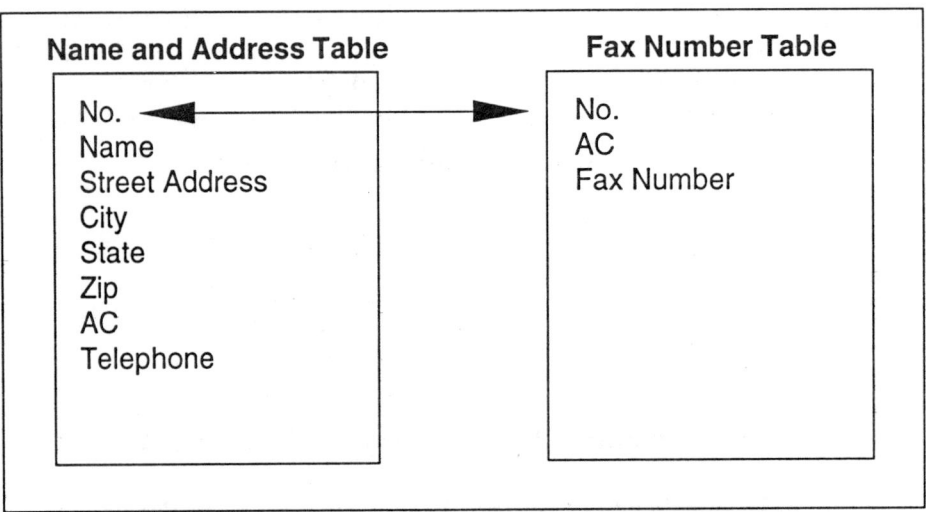

Figure 8-4. Linking Tables in a Relational Database

In addition to linking tables together, a relational database provides the capability for designing and running sophisticated queries. A database query enables you to search for information in the database that corresponds to virtually any specified criteria. The great advantage and capability of database queries will become more evident in the following sections.

SOURCE EXTRACTION INDEXING

In the Chapter 3 section, *Essential Elements for Genealogical Indexing*, you were introduced to the essentials of genealogical indexing. By now you should be able to see the advantages of using a database to implement your Source Extraction indexing.

I started experimenting with the indexing format introduced in Chapter 3, way back in the "old days," long before the age of personal computers, about 35 years ago. At first I used punched cards which had the distinct disadvantage of being restricted to only 80 characters per card.

The equipment of that day only permitted the development of very crude and inefficient flat-file tables, but they were, nevertheless, a beginning and much was learned. The tremendous advances in the development of personal computer hardware and software have enormously expanded the range of possibilities now available to us. Many former frustrating restrictions are now gone.

Again consider a record from the Source Extraction index first depicted in Figure 3-4, *Source Extraction Index Example,* from Chapter 3:

Given	Surname	Town	County	ST	Year	ECK	S R	Source
John	Chamberlain	Salem	Essex	MA	1790	/	M	1-001CS

You will notice that this format fits perfectly into a database table record. In an actual database, the various fields shown in this example would be designed to hold a sufficient number of characters to accommodate most, if not all actual information that you would want to store in these fields. In this and other examples, the fields have been compressed for purposes of illustration.

The database fields for Source Extraction indexing have been designed for maximum clarity and content, and it is hoped that no one will have difficulty in interpreting them and easily identifying the elements that were discussed in Chapter 3. Note that the heading "ECK" is used to designate the ERA Correlation Key character.

If you are using a database, it is a simple matter to include additional fields to provide further information, should you so desire. For example, early census records merely give the number of people in a household categorized by sexes and ages, and occasionally other miscellaneous information. The addition of only one or two fields would permit you to include the family structures in the index. This would be particularly useful if you are doing a descendancy genealogy where you are extracting everyone with a specific surname.

Using a Database

For example, consider the addition of a new field (Age Groups) to the previous record.

Given	Surname	Town	County	ST	Year	ECK	S	R	Age Groups	Source
John	Chamberlain	Salem	Essex	MA	1790	/		M	1-2-1-0-0	1-001CS

The "Age Groups" field contains the actual census data given by this source. Interpreting all the definitions and descriptions thus far described, this record tells us that a John Chamberlain was living in Salem, Essex County, Massachusetts, in 1790, heading a family of 1-2-1-0-0. This information was indexed from Page 1 of Source Extraction file No. 1, which is a census record as indicated by the suffix "CS." (Refer to the Glossary entry "1790 Census," to interpret the 1790 age groups shown in this example.)

As in other similar situations, however, be cautious about adding too many fields to your index. In this example, the one additional field adds a great deal of information to the record without requiring very much space. With this much information, you would rarely have to go back to your original Source Extractions to recheck your data. If you get carried away and add too many other fields, your index may quickly get bogged down. Too much data can detract from the efficiency of your index. As your index to Source Extractions increases, you could easily have thousands of such records, and so it is important to optimize all of the space the index requires.

It is important to note that the Source Extraction index model that has been described is a flat-file table. Not withstanding the general disadvantages of flat-file tables as previously noted, they are well-suited for this particular purpose. It is a flat-file table because there is no unique data within it that could serve as a natural link to another table or database object. Nevertheless, this table can still reside within a relational database.

One of the most important advantages of using a relational database is the tremendous flexibility you gain in arranging and displaying desired information without having to change anything. For example, you could show the surname before the given name and put it in all capital letters; display the jurisdictional hierarchy in reverse order; sort your index in any kind of order hierarchy, such as alphabetical by surname, then given name, followed by jurisdictions (in any order); and finally the year of the event, just to name a few possibilities.

DATABASE QUERIES

Perhaps the most powerful feature of a relational database is the use of queries. As the name implies, a query is a database tool or method whereby you can specify nearly any kind of search parameters and conditions. A query can search for information spanning one or more tables that meets your criteria, and display it in virtually any desired order or arrangement. Queries can also perform complex calculations on tables, update information, create new tables, and so forth.

For example, suppose you have been working on a descendancy genealogy and have a fairly large table containing several thousand database records that represent the index to your Source Extractions to date. Because each source is indexed separately, the original order in your index corresponds to the Source Number.

Let's say that you want to search the index to find anyone with the surname *Bowne* that was associated with the state of New York (NY). You could first sort the entire index by name and state (ST), and then find *Bowne* by going to the place where it should occur alphabetically. However, rather than having to sort the entire file and go through all of these steps, it would be much simpler to use a database query.

Using a Database

Essentially a query to perform this search would involve a statement similar to the following:

   Surname = Bowne AND ST = NY

The underscored words in this expression are the names of the fields. The term "AND" is a Boolean operator that requires both conditions (in this example) to be true; that is, the Surname must be *Bowne* and the ST must be *NY* for the query to find the specified information, if any.

Such a query could extract entries similar to the following:

Given	Surname	Town	County	ST	Year	ECK	S	R	Source
Jacob	Bowne		Ontario	NY	1790	/		M	1-001CS
Anne	Bowne		Niagara	NY	1800	/		F	21-003CS
Eben	Bowne		Oneida	NY	1830	/		M	37-006CS

You can see that these records meet the criteria as defined in the query. While this is a very simple example, it does illustrate the principle. Suppose that in this example, your query finds quite a few records that meet the criteria. In that case, you might want to specify that the query will display the records in alphabetical order by given name and date, or jurisdiction and date, or some other combination.

It is always an advantage to use standard spellings in the creation of your records because they will greatly facilitate the development and use of various queries to locate information. If your spellings are not standardized, it will generally be more difficult to find the names in question. Queries can deal with spelling variations, but at some cost in performance. In a large database, this can be a critical factor.

As a second example, consider the database tables shown in Figure 8-5. Note the similarity to the example discussed in the preceding section, *Relational Databases*. Let's say that the tables depicted in Figure 8-5 are part of a database which has been developed and maintained by a mail-order company selling sporting goods. The Customer Table contains the names and addresses of all the company's current and former customers while the Order Table lists all of the products purchased by their customers. As in the previous example, the *No.* field is a unique number assigned to each customer.

Let's assume that the company has learned that some of the gas lanterns they carry, Product Code # 12306, have been found to have a manufacturing defect that could cause personal injury. After some research, the company determined that the defective lanterns were all part of a batch that were manufactured and shipped to their customers in the state of Michigan during the period from March 14, 1996 to June 20, 1996. The company wishes to contact all customers who may have purchased this product during the aforementioned time period, warning them of the potential hazard and to return the lanterns for exchange or credit.

A database query to find this information could contain statements similar to the following:

```
Order Table:Prod. Code = 12306   AND
Order Table:Date > 14 Mar 1996 and < 20 June 1996   AND   Customer Table:ST = MI
Sorting Order: Zip Code, Ascending
Displayed Fields:
   Name And Address Table:     No., Name, Street Address, City, ST, Zip
   Order Table:                Date
```

In this query statement the name of the table and the specified field are separated by a colon.

145

Using a Database

Customer Table

No.	Name	Street Address	City	ST	Zip	AC	Telephone
1	Bill Anderson	910 S. 9th Ave.	Pasadena	CA	94952	818	272-4937
2	Guy Adams	483 Anaconda Road	Butte	MT	59701	406	493-2593
3	Joseph Allen	12476 Carlisle Way	Aurora	CO	80012	303	892-7535
4	Kenneth Jones	45 East 10th, #15	Wichita	KS	67208	316	425-9457
5	Ralph Williams	9340 Winder St.	Kalamazoo	MI	49004	616	794-0662
6	Edith Campbell	304 Goodman Ave,	Phoenix	AZ	85020	602	582-4910
7	Tom Bartlett	89 Fisher Road	Detroit	MI	48212	313	615-8392
8	Ted Papay	1029 Pomona Dr	Green Bay	WI	54301	414	275-8091
9	Richard Smith	3483 Macadam St.	Miami	FL	33189	305	390-0353
10	Carlene Sill	4003 Fleet St.	Raleigh	NC	27609	919	942-1565

Order Table

No.	Prod. Code	Description	Date of Purchase
1	13123	3# Sleeping Bag	15 Jan 1996
1	12306	Gas Lantern	15 Jan 1996
5	12306	Gas Lantern	23 Apr 1996
7	11716	½ oz. Lead sinkers	18 Nov 1996
7	34168	Two-man tent	19 Jun 1995

Figure 8-5. Relational Database Example

The following list could represent a sampling of the data obtained by this query.

No.	Name	Street Address	City	ST	Zip	Date
374	Sarah Miner	Route 1, Box 23	Pinckney	MI	48169	24 May 1996
113	Joe Thomas	931 10th Ave.	Utica	MI	48316	5 May 1996
5	Ralph Williams	9340 Winder St.	Kalamazoo	MI	49004	23 Apr 1996
278	Clifford Dane	340 Rural Ave.	Kalamazoo	MI	49008	14 Jun 1996
425	Myron Phillips	1910 Berry St.	Sodus	MI	49126	31 Mar 1996
62	Mary Underwood	282 Crawford Ave.	Hesperia	MI	49421	3 May 1996
34	Keith Smith	2310 Kinder Road	Houghton	MI	49931	10 Jun 1996

It is hoped that these examples have given you some idea of the advantages of a relational database, both in the convenient storage of information and in the great flexibility and power of queries. The following sections will elaborate upon the techniques thus far described.

INDEXING FAMILY GROUP RECORDS

The database model described in the preceding section, *Source Extraction Indexing,* is not designed to connect individuals or families together, but merely to provide a means for easily indexing your Source Extractions. Now that you have a little familiarity with relational databases and their general capabilities, we can expand our previous discussions to view a larger picture.

Just as your Source Extractions represent the first phase in the genealogical process, the compilation of Family Group Records (FGRs) represents the second phase. (See Chapter 1, Figure 1-1, *Process Comparisons, Sources and Compiled Records.*) Similarly, it is important to prepare and maintain a suitable genealogical index to your FGRs just as you did for your Source Extractions.

Because the FGR index only describes identified individuals and families, it will be more complete and inclusive than the Source Extraction index. Essentially, the FGR index is designed to contain the primary data shown for each person in your various FGRs. In the previous section, *Relational Databases*, the key element that connected the different tables was the *No.* field. Without this field the tables could not be connected to each other in a relational environment.

The key element in your FGR index is the unique LifeNumber™ (LN) which serves the same purpose as the *No.* field did in the previous examples. Not only is the LN a unique identifier from a genealogical perspective, but it also provides the means to link all the individuals in your genealogy together in a relational database.

As a minimum, the FGR index should include the primary data for each individual as follows:

1. LifeNumber™ (LN).
2. Name (given, surname).
3. Sex or gender.
4. Race.

5. Birth data (date of birth and place of birth (jurisdictional hierarchy).

6. Death data (date of death date and place of death (jurisdictional hierarchy).

7. Burial data (date of burial, cremation or interment, name of cemetery or mausoleum, location of burial or interment (jurisdictional hierarchy).

8. Father's Name (given, surname).

9. Father's LN.

10. Mother's Name (given, maiden).

11. Mother's LN.

12. Marriages (if any). Names of spouses, dates and places of each marriage.

Other fields could be included, such as an ancestry field to show the generations from a progenitor for descendancy genealogies, or a note field for general comments and remarks. Relational database tables can accommodate a great number of fields, many more than suggested here, each specifically designed and formatted to best fit the data to be stored therein.

If you use a relational database for your FGR index, it can not only serve as the master record for each individual in your genealogy. Moreover, it can also enable its data to be dynamically linked to corresponding fields within word processing files representing individual FGRs. (A more detailed discussion of the technical issues involved in this suggestion is beyond the scope of this book.) The intent here is to make you aware of some of the great capabilities in these extremely powerful and flexible software tools to assist you in your genealogical endeavors.

In the Chapter 1 section, *Evolution of a System*, the suggested ideal genealogical system would comprise two sets of records; Source Extractions and compiled or composite records (FGRs). Thus, it follows that if you have a database designed for each set of records, you could also have an interface between them to assist you in your work.

Compilers of descendancy genealogies especially could use such a system to great advantage. Queries could be designed to search for matching information between the two databases to enable comparisons between identified persons in the FGR index database with unidentified individuals in the Source Extraction index database or vice versa.

This could easily be implemented by the addition of an LN field to the Source Extraction index. As people in the Source Extraction index are identified, their LNs could also be entered in the LN field. Thus, when reviewing your Source Extraction index you will know which individuals have been identified.

JURISDICTIONAL TRACKING

The concept and techniques of jurisdictional tracking were introduced in Chapter 5, *Jurisdictional Tracking*. The accompanying exercises in Appendix C, *Jurisdictional Tracking Exercises*, were provided to give you a good understanding of the jurisdictional tracking process.

The preceding section, *Indexing Family Group Records*, described the process of indexing all individuals in your FGRs. The LN which serves as the link between all records in the FGR index database also functions in a similar manner for jurisdictional tracking. Thus, jurisdictional tracking which is a special index, is in reality a subset of the FGR index.

The addition of a jurisdictional tracking table in the FGR index database is relatively simple to implement. Its function would be to provide a place for recording general jurisdictional information distilled from various narrative records and other sources not found in the primary data that comprises the FGR index.

The judicious use of queries would enable you to view the jurisdictional tracking records for any person, and if desired, to include a few fields from the FGR index to provide a more complete picture.

Using a Database

Figure 8-6 depicts a partial view of a suggested FGR index database. You will note similarities to the database depicted in Figure 8-4 with respect to linking the tables. Using this model, let's say that you want a query to display the jurisdictional tracking records for your great, great grandfather, John Sylvester (LN 46), and his wife, Emma Bradford (LN 67). In addition, you want to see the year and place (state) of their birth displayed. (Assume that the query can extract the year from the complete birth date.)

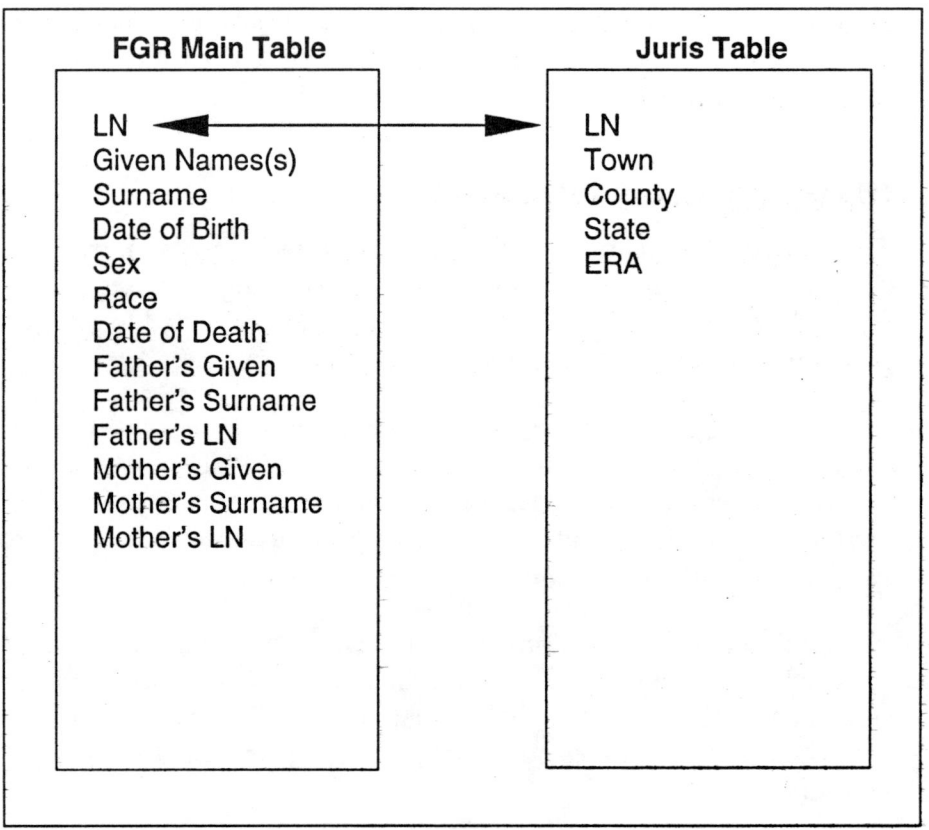

Figure 8-6. FGR Index Database

150

The query to find and display this information could contain statements similar to the following:

```
FGR Main Table:LifeNumber = 46 OR 67
Sorting Order (1): LifeNumber, Ascending; (2) ERA, Ascending
Displayed Fields:
   FGR Main Table:  LN, Given, Surname, Byr (birth year), BP (birth place), Sex
   Juris Table:     Town, County, ST, ERA
Display Order of Fields:
Given, Surname, Town, County, ST, Byr, BP, Sex, ERA, LN
```

The "OR" in the query statement is another Boolean Operator that in this case means either of the LNs meet the specified criteria.

The following listing could represent the results of such a query.

Given	Surname	Town	County	ST	Byr	BP	S	ERA	LN
John	Sylvester	Cleveland	Cuyahoga	OH	1827	OH	M	1827-1843	46
John	Sylvester		Erie	PA	1827	OH	M	1843/1847	46
John	Sylvester	Sacramento	Sacramento	CA	1827	OH	M	1855-1859	46
John	Sylvester	Forest Grove	Washington	OR	1827	OH	M	1859*1902	46
Emma	Bradford	St. Louis	St. Louis	MO	1833	MO	F	1833-1849	67
Emma	Bradford	San Francisco	San Francisco	CA	1833	MO	F	1849/1855	67
Emma	Sylvester	Sacramento	Sacramento	CA	1833	MO	F	1855-1859	67
Emma	Sylvester	Forest Grove	Washington	OR	1833	MO	F	1859>1902	67

This listing was designed to demonstrate different ERA Correlation Key (ECK) characters. (The ERA field in the above listing consists of three elements: beginning year, ECK, and ending year.) Note that Emma's surname changes to Sylvester in the year 1855 indicating she and John were married that year. A jurisdictional gap is shown for John Sylvester in that he was associated with Erie Co., PA, from about 1843 until 1847. Thereafter, his whereabouts remain unknown until he appeared in Sacramento, CA, in 1855. Emma survived her husband, and while the date of her death has not been found, she was believed to have remained in the same jurisdiction after her husband John's death in 1902.

Showing the year and place of birth is particularly useful if you were to sort your entire FGR index by jurisdictional hierarchy without regard for any particular individual, or to just sort alphabetically by names. In these instances, the year of birth and place of birth provide an important point of reference for each person when their tracking records are grouped together.

DATABASE SUMMARY

Only some of the most elementary characteristics of databases have been discussed in the preceding material. However, it is hoped that the information thus presented, will have given you some insights into the advantages of using a relational database in your genealogical work.

Summary 9

It is hoped that by now you have a good understanding of the concepts and techniques that have been presented and discussed in the previous chapters. To help put everything in perspective and serve as a quick recapitulation, let's summarize the most important elements:

- **The Planning Log**. This log or journal provides an easy way to chart your overall direction and scope of your genealogical research.

- **The Research Log**. This log is source-specific in that it provides a summary of all your research by each source.

- **Source Extraction Files**. These files contain the actual data you have extracted and numbered according to your Research Log.

- **Unique Identification**. The combination of a name, a time or date, and jurisdictional hierarchy (who, what, when, and where) is used to uniquely identify each person at the time of his or her birth. Assigning each person a number is an integral part of the unique identification process.

- **Jurisdictional Tracking**. A technique for building a jurisdictional history for each person from birth to death. A continuation of the unique identification process throughout a person's lifetime.

- **Compilation of Genealogical Records**. The Family Group Record (FGR) is a composite record built from merging various Source Extractions. The process of Data Analysis & Evaluation is a part of this process.

Summary

- **Chart Numbering**. The importance of using the correct numbering scheme for numbering pedigree charts and cross-referencing them with the applicable FGRs.

- **Genealogical Indexing**. A relational database provides an ideal solution for indexing individuals both in Source Extractions and in FGRs.

IMPORTANT CONCEPTS TO REMEMBER

While a number of different elements in genealogy have been presented and discussed, there are few principles that bear repeating because of their importance.

- **Precision**. The element of precision is vital to your work standing the test of time. Precision in your data extractions, proofreading everything you create, and never being quite satisfied that you've done everything possible will help you meet that goal.

- **Consistency**. Being consistent in the your usage of terms, special notation, and format, are of the utmost importance. If you're not consistent, when you do things one way here and another way somewhere else, your readers will never be quite sure of what you are doing. The best way to ensure consistency is to prepare a document, or a list of definitions of how you do things, and then adhere to your guidelines. Otherwise, after a passage of years, you yourself may not be sure of what you were thinking.

- **Analysis**. Being a really good genealogist requires that you train yourself to never overlook the slightest detail. Many times the answer or a very good clue to a knotty problem may be right in front of you, but you may never notice it. Train yourself to continuously analyze, sift, and evaluate your information, especially when you are grasping for straws in trying to penetrate the "stone wall."

- **Simplicity and Clarity**. No matter what system you select, always strive to keep it simple. If it isn't simple and clear, it won't survive. This is especially true when those who inherit your work have difficulty in deciphering your material. This not only applies to your verbiage and organization, but also just how you visually present it. An old rule that might apply here is: "Always write so that you cannot be misunderstood." A humorous way of expressing this rule might be the statement: "Keep it simple stupid!"

- **Rationale**. Every genealogist has to do a lot of guessing. It goes with the territory. It would be nice if we always had the whole story, but in the real world this rarely happens. There are areas in every family history of which you will probably never be quite sure. The important thing is to link every bit of information in your FGR to a specific source or sources, know what is a guess or estimate, and know what is solid and reliable.

  When you do guess or estimate, put down your rationale for conclusions drawn in the absence of definitive information. The better you can do this, the more your work will stand the test of time. This is because anyone else who might want to continue what you have begun will always know exactly where you were coming from, what you've done, and what you haven't done.

PREFERENCES IN NOTATION

A number of suggestions and recommendations have been made in the preceding chapters regarding the use of special characters, special notation, and selected words or phrases to convey additional precision and meaning in your records. The fact is you don't have to use what has been suggested. The underlying reason behind this discussion is to add a degree of precision to your work. You are always free to devise your notation, definitions and usages. The important point is to very clearly define whatever system you devise, and be very consistent in all areas. This way your readers will always clearly understand what you are doing.

Summary

CLARITY IN PRESENTATION

As a general rule, don't try to cram as much text as possible onto a page. An example to illustrate this point is in order.

Many years ago, a man who was unquestionably a very fine genealogist described (in a very capsulated style) his collection of material on a family surname he had researched for many years. Unfortunately, he seemed to be obsessed with saving paper, and put as much single-spaced text, along with many handwritten corrections as he possibly could onto each page. On top of this it appears that his typewriter ribbon was worn out before he even started. Though he does give a great deal of very valuable information in this compilation, it is so difficult to read and decipher that few people have had the patience to get through it.

There is a certain ratio of white space to text that if optimized will give your work a very strong and pleasing visual appeal. From a reader's point of view, it will almost surely guarantee that your work will be read and appreciated. Clear and uncluttered layout and design as well as concise, clear language will work wonders.

COMPUTER PROGRAMS FOR GENEALOGY

While not mandatory, the use of a computer provides such overwhelming advantages that it seems academic to enumerate them. Many of the concepts and techniques that have been described were depicted as being in a computer environment. It is true that you can research and generate a genealogy without using a computer. Genealogies were done for many years without them. But, it makes good sense to optimize your tools and take advantage of any technology that can save you time and money. This axiom applies to whatever kind of work in which you may be engaged. Some of the techniques, such as jurisdictional tracking and genealogical indexing would be very cumbersome and difficult to implement without the use of a computer.

Summary

But just having a computer is not enough. You need application software, especially designed for genealogy. Of course, if your computer expertise is sufficient, you could use more general purpose software which you could adapt to do any of the things discussed in this book. There have been well over 150 programs developed for genealogy at the time of this writing, and new ones are still appearing.

Sadly, none of the programs I have seen are capable of fully implementing the concepts and techniques laid down in this book. Every program has some merit, and a few do have a wide range of capabilities, but are also very complex to use and difficult to learn. This is quite discouraging for those who just want to do genealogy and not have to first become computer experts.

Naturally, anyone using a computer has to have some knowledge of it. Virtually everyone drives a car, and to successfully operate one does require some knowledge and training. Before you can start driving a car you first have to have a driver's license which requires you to pass a written test as well as a driving test. You also have to learn when to put in fuel, what kind, and when to have the tires checked, the oil changed, and so forth.

What is true of operating a car is also true for computers. You do have to learn something about them to effectively take advantage of the capabilities they confer. But it is at this point, where there are many divergences in computer application software. Some software is very difficult and unintuitive to use. Other programs may have inferior documentation and support, and some just plainly lack any real capability, flexibility and power.

A new program, GenStor™, currently under development, has been especially designed to implement the concepts and techniques of genealogical record-keeping which have been described in this book. A major design goal for this program is to make it intuitive and easy to use and yet represent state-of-the-art capabilities to be a powerful and sophisticated tool for a genealogist.

Summary

GenStor™ is expected to be available by late 1998. If you are interested in learning more about this program, please write to the author in care of the publisher.

Planning Log Examples

Appendix A supplements the material presented in Chapter 2, *Planning Your Genealogical Work,* by providing some examples of Planning Log entries. These examples have been designed to give you a better idea of how useful a Planning Log can be in your work.

EXAMPLE 1

Date: 22 June 1995. At home.

Objective   I have decided to do a genealogy of my family that I can give to my children. I've read some books and have a good idea of how to get started. I have already made out a Family Group Record for my own family, my husband, myself and our children.

My mother's older sister Helen is living in Florida. So one of the first things I want to do is to write to her and send copies of what I have compiled so far from my own personal knowledge and what I remember that my mother told me about her family.

My father is still alive and I have already called him and we are going to have him over for dinner this Sunday and will spend some time going over his family.

Date: 28 June 1995. At home.

Objective   I have sent away for some forms that I found listed in a catalog that will help me keep track of things better.

Planning Log Examples

Date: 14 July 1995. At the city library.

Objective Joined a small genealogical society located in Adams Grove which is not far away and they do have some books and films. I am planning to go next Tuesday and will make out a list of things I want to try and find.

EXAMPLE 2

Date: 17 Aug 1993. At the Family History Library, SLC, Utah

Objective I was re-reading this section in Tullidges' *History of Utah* for the tenth time and for the first time noticed the emphasis placed on the "Scotch Cap" worn by my great, great, great grandfather Nathaniel Brown while serving in the War of 1812. I am now thinking that this is probably a strong indication that he was a Scotchman. This might also explain the family tradition about his younger children not understanding the language used by their father's relatives when visiting. A thick Scotch accent might indeed be difficult for small children to understand. Heretofore, we had sort of assumed this family to be of English origin.

EXAMPLE 3

Date: 24 June 1994. At home.

Objective I just received a letter from my cousin Sally Johnson about my inquiry on information she may have on the Allen family that we both connect into. Because of her mother's ill health at the present, she is unable to try and find the family bible at this time as it is packed in one of the many boxes of her mother's things. She can probably get to it sometime this year.

Because it is inadvisable to try and do any library research on the Allen family until I can get a copy of the information in the Samuel Allen family bible I will stop work on mother's family and instead concentrate on my father's family.

Planning Log Examples

EXAMPLE 4

Date: 14 Feb 1990. The Rosedale cemetery, Los Angeles, CA.

Objective   I was visiting the Matthew's plots in the cemetery where my father's uncle Joe is buried along with some of his own family. I found the grave of a Sarah Ann Stone (1812-1879) who I can not identify but the inscription says she was a native of Arkansas. This may be an important clue as my father always said his great grandmother was supposed to have come from Arkansas but he never knew her name. When I get back home I will check this out further.

EXAMPLE 5

Date: 22 June 1980. At home.

Objective   I am preparing to go to the library tomorrow and will be concentrating on my ancestor Isaac Hill. I want to make sure that I check the following records for Isaac Hill or Hills:

Federal census records from 1820 through 1840 for Albany and Schoharie counties in New York for Isaac Hill.

Land records for Albany and Schoharie counties, N.Y.

Probate records for Albany and Schoharie counties, N.Y.

Check library catalog for other local records of this locality.

EXAMPLE 6

Date: 3 Jan 1985. At home.

Objective   I have been carefully reviewing all the material thus far acquired on my mother's family and have pretty well exhausted the knowledge of all my aunts, uncles and cousins or those who would possibly know anything about the family. With what I now have I think I will start preparing a list of objectives for my next visit to the library to see what resources might be available to extend these lines on back. Currently, I have identified the following surnames in my mother's family: Allen, Woolley, Woodward, and Adams.

Planning Log Examples

EXAMPLE 7

Date: 18 Nov 1992. State Library, Salem, Oregon

Objective Today, I found the journal of one William Gage, a former business partner of my grandfather's brother Sam Allen in the library's manuscript collections. It was just luck that I thought to look through this journal. The only reason I did was that this man was living in the same town as my great grandfather Joseph Allen which was cross-referenced in the library's catalog which is what caught my eye. Anyway, the interesting thing was that he mentioned my grandfather in connection with the statement that he had originally came from Camden county, N.J. Up until now we never did know where my great grandfather had come from.

Source Extraction Examples and Exercises

SOURCE EXTRACTION EXAMPLES

Chapter 3, *Source Extractions,* described the use of a Research Log and the process of Source Extraction. This appendix contains several examples to further illustrate how different types of sources can be identified in a Research Log, how the data could be extracted, and how the extracted names might be indexed. Following the examples are some indexing exercises which have been prepared to give you some hands-on practice in this process. You may find it useful to refer to Chapter 3, Table 3-1, *Era Correlation Key Characters and Interpretation,* to interpret the meaning of the character shown in the column heading "ECK," while reviewing the indexing examples and exercises.

Each of the following examples tries to depict a different type of source to give you a more rounded view of the Source Extraction process. Note that these examples are not intended to be complete. Their purpose is only to illustrate how these different types of sources might appear and how an index could look. Particularly, the illustrated indexes do not reflect an exact correspondence with what is shown in the facsimile of the applicable Source Extraction file.

Example 1

Let's say that you have a letter (consisting of one page) written by a brother of a great, great grandmother that has been preserved by the family. While most of it is just about the usual daily events in people's lives, there are a few little family clues contained in it. In any case, the letter is an original source and should be part of your source files. Of course, since it's an original family treasure, you wouldn't even think of three-hole punching it and just putting it in a binder along with everything else.

Source Extraction Examples and Exercises

First, carefully place it inside a high archival quality plastic sleeve to protect it from further wear and deterioration. You could put the sleeve in a binder, but it would be better to put a photocopy of the original in your Source Extraction file. The original could then be stored in another, and perhaps safer place. In this case, however, affix a label to the plastic sleeve that briefly describes what the contents are and state that a photocopy was made which is identified according to your Research Log entry. This would be especially useful to help someone else correctly identify your records.

Figure B-1 shows how this source might be described in your Research Log. Figure B-2 shows a portion of the photocopied letter (facsimile) identified by the unique Source Number assigned by your Research Log. According to the Research Log, this letter consists of one page (written on both sides) and is numbered from RC2-1 through RC2-2. The typed transcript of this letter (not shown) also consists of two pages numbered from RC2-3 through RC2-4. As you can see, additional information involving a source can simply be added without affecting the existing pagination of the Source Extraction file.

Figure B-3 shows a few of the names taken from this letter and how they might be genealogically indexed. In this example, the suffix "LT" has been used to indicate a letter. A paragraph preceding the index explains certain basic assumptions that were made when preparing the index. In this case, it was decided that the denoted year was to represent either a known or an estimated birth date.

You will observe from reading the first page of the letter that a few other details were given which are not reflected in the index. Later, we will address this issue in more detail. For now, remember that the purpose of this type of index is not to document every single bit of information that may be given by the source, but to only identify a person with a time and place.

Source Extraction Examples and Exercises

NO.		
2	**Title**	Letter written by Annaniah Gifford Wilbert, Forked River, N.J., to Mrs. Catherine (Chamberlin) Dickerson, American Fork, Utah, 20 Mar 1894. Annaniah Gifford Wilbert was the younger brother of Amy Wilbert, the mother of Mrs. Catherine (Chamberlin) Wilbert. This document consists of one handwritten page written on both sides.
	Call No.	Not applicable
	Location	Original in possession of David C. Chamberlin, 2682 S.E. Singing Woods Drive, Hillsboro, Oregon 97123.

Date: 14 June 1989

Objective Study the letter for possible genealogical data that may be contained therein.

Result Genealogical data was found relating to the Wilberts, the Giffords, and the Chamberlins. A photocopy was made of the original and numbered RC2-2 through RC2-3. Page RC2-1 provides a general description of the letter.

Date: 14 Oct 1991

Objective Transcribe handwritten letter to a typed copy.

Result A typed transcript of the original was made which consists of two pages numbered RC2-4 through RC2-5.

Date: 2 Sep 1991

Objective Identify and index all the names found in the letter.

Result Indexed all names and added the printout as an additional page, numbered RC 2-6. RefCode Suffix: LT (DCC).

Figure B-1. Research Log, Example 1

Source Extraction Examples and Exercises

> Forked River, New Jersey
> March 20th, 1894
>
> Mrs. Catherine Dickerson
> American Fork, Utah
>
> My Dear Niece,
>
> Your very welcome letter of the 10th ult., was an agreeable surprise and I appreciate the motives that impelled you to write, first Paternal obedience, second as a token that when you left here or rather in this section of this great country so many years ago has not been entirely forgotten. I have often thought about you and also the other members of the family, especially John, from whom in the sixties I had several letters.
>
> Yes, I remember you well as you were the oldest except for Hyrum who died in his infancy (perhaps a year old). I think Henry was the baby in '51 when I went away to sea. Sarah, my sister was born, I think in January 1839, but am not positive. Angeline has the bible containing the family record, but Sarah was about 7 years younger than me and I was born September 27th, 1831. Sarah died in July 1861, am not positive about the day of the month. My memory is not entirely reliable as to dates or names in all cases, of which this is one, but I think about the second in regard to our ancestry. Amy ought to be able to tell you more than me, she being the oldest child can remember of having seen, heard and learned things which I had not opportunity to do.
>
> To begin, my Grandfather Wilbur's given name was John. I could not tell what year he was born or died in. I remember him about the year 35-36 or 37, he was an old man then. He had brothers but don't know how many of their descendants or some of them are now living at or near Toms River, our County seat. My grandmother Wilbur's maiden name as I have been told was Lippincott, but don't know as I ever heard her given name. My father's name was John L. Wilbert. He always wrote his name with a "t," where he got it from or why he put it there I never knew. He was generally called Jack, I presume to distinguish his name from his father's. He was born at or near Toms River in the year 1785. My mother was Sarah Gifford, the daughter of Joshua Gifford and Amy Johnson of Old Monmouth County, New Jersey. My mother was born in the year 1794 being nine years younger than Father. She died in the year 1857. Father died in the year 1864 in his 79th year.
>
> ... [Etc.]
>
> RC2-2

Figure B-2. Source Extraction Example 1

Source Extraction Examples and Exercises

It was decided to have the index for this source show the birth dates for each person which were either specifically given or estimated. Annaniah's grandmother Lippincott's given name was unknown to him and so the index can only give her name as "Daughter Lippincott." Her birth date was estimated, as was the one for John Wilber, Joshua Gifford, Amy Johnson, Henry Chamberlin, and Hyrum Chamberlin. The jurisdictions shown were given in the second page of the letter which is not shown in the preceding facsimile.)

Given	Surname	Town	County	ST	Year	ECK	S	Source
Henry	Chamberlin	Forked River	Monmouth	NJ	1849	-	M	2-002LT
Hyrum	Chamberlin	Forked River	Monmouth	NJ	1837	-	M	2-002LT
Joshua	Gifford		Monmouth	NJ	1770	-	M	2-002LT
Sarah	Gifford		Monmouth	NJ	1794	-	F	2-002LT
Amy	Johnston		Monmouth	NJ	1772	-	F	2-002LT
Daughter	Lippincott		Monmouth	NJ	1760	-	F	2-002LT
John	Wilber		Monmouth	NJ	1759	-	M	2-002LT
Amy	Wilbert	Toms River	Monmouth	NJ	1816	-	F	2-002LT
Angeline	Wilbert	Toms River	Monmouth	NJ	1835	-	F	2-002LT
Annaniah	Wilbert	Toms River	Monmouth	NJ	1831	-	M	2-002LT
John L	Wilbert	Toms River	Monmouth	NJ	1785	-	M	2-002LT
Sarah	Wilbert	Toms River	Monmouth	NJ	1839	-	F	2-002LT

... [Etc.]

RC2-6

Figure B-3. Source Extraction Index, Example 1

Example 2

Now let us assume that your next source is a taped interview of your grandmother that contains some genealogical data and other information. Figure B-4 shows when the recording was done, where it was done, and who had the tapes at the time the entry was recorded in the log.

Source Extraction Examples and Exercises

NO.		
3	Title	Interview with Grandmother (Nancy Tilton) conducted by her daughter, Mary Anne (Brown) Jones. In Aug 1992, the original tapes were in possession of Mrs. Alice Ruth Belton, 3425 South Oak Lane, Hillsboro, Oregon 97123.
	Call No.	Not Applicable
	Location	The interview was conducted at grandmother's home on Beeson Road, Rural Route 17, Canby, Oregon.

Date: 18 July – 21 July 1966

Objective	To learn as much about our grandmother's life as we could and told in her own words.
Result	The interview was conducted in five sessions on three reel-to-reel tapes at 3¼ inches/sec speed.

Date: 8 Sep 1990

Objective	To make a typed transcript of these tape recordings.
Result	A typed transcript was made by Mrs. Alice Ruth Belton which consisted of 145 pages and numbered RC3-1 through RC3-145.

Date: 12 Nov 1990

Objective	To add some notes to clarify many of the place names and other details given in the interview.
Result	Twelve additional pages were added to clarify many place names and personal names and define conventions used in the transcript. These pages were numbered RC3-146 through RC3-157.

Date: 24 June 1992

Objective	Index all personal names.
Result	All names were indexed and added as pages RC3-158 through RC3-160.

Figure B-4. Research Log, Example 2

Source Extraction Examples and Exercises

You could put the audio tapes in some containers within a file folder though it would not be very convenient. However, in this example, it is the transcription of the tapes that is incorporated into your Source Extractions file. The Research Log describes the original tapes and notes that they were transcribed by a member of the family who still has them.

The typed copy of the transcript is paginated according to the Source Number assigned by the Research Log. A portion of the transcribed interview is illustrated in Figure B-5. From this interview all the names we could find were extracted. A partial listing of the index that was prepared is shown in Figure B-6.

And then my Grandma, my mother said and one of my younger aunts told me, Grandma Brigham was a hard working woman. I kind of resemble her in my energy. My Grandpa was a quiet man. He liked to read. He was the type that would just sit and read, for hours. He was almost 16 or was it 18 years older than my Grandma? He was a man 33 and she was only 16 or so when they got married. He had a store, I remember my mother telling me, a little store in the village. It was a grocery (general) store. Kerosene, soap, everything, boots maybe. He was quite a philosopher. He was noted for his wit. At a party he'd always say something witty to everybody and knew how to joke when he was young. He was quick-witted. He was the one who had a good education and my Grandma couldn't even read when he married her. My Grandma's father died and her mother was left with two little girls. Her sister's name was Miriam. And so great-grandma was left, but her father was living, so he came over, a widower himself, to help his daughter left alone on the prairie. So when grandma was sixteen her grandfather decided that he should find a husband for her.

... [Etc.]

RC3-73

Figure B-5.   Source Extraction Example 2

Source Extraction Examples and Exercises

> Abraham Roseberry's place of birth is not known with certainty. My mother merely stated (P. 35) of the interview that her great grandmother's father was thought to have come from Virginia. Mother rarely mentioned a specific year for an event. Usually, she spoke of the ages people were at the time something took place. Thus, the dates shown are estimated birth years derived from the ages of the person correlated with known years.
>
> | Given | Surname | Town | County | ST | Year | ECK | S | Source |
> |---|---|---|---|---|---|---|---|---|
> | Ralph | Brigham | St. Louis | St. Louis | MO | 1837 | - | M | 3-078IT |
> | Cecile | Greene | | Lee | IA | 1853 | - | F | 3-047IT |
> | Joseph | Greene | Boston | Suffolk | MA | 1820 | - | M | 3-132IT |
> | Emma | Roseberry | | Hamilton | OH | 1824 | - | F | 3-008IT |
> | Miriam | Greene | | Lee | IA | 1857 | - | F | 3-016IT |
> | Allen H | Lawrence | Doylestown | Bucks | PA | 1852 | - | M | 3-109IT |
> | Fannie | Lawrence | Des Moines | Des Moines | IA | 1890 | - | F | 3-068IT |
> | Abraham | Roseberry | | | VA | 1797 | - | M | 3-035IT |
>
> ... [Etc.]
>
> RC3-158

Figure B-6. Source Extraction Index, Example 2

Example 3

This example uses a Bible record as your next source. Your Research Log entry shown in Figure B-7 for this source describes the Bible in the space allotted for the title. This Bible has an inscription on the title page that identifies the person who originally owned it. At the time you made photocopies of the title page and the pages that contained the family information, the Bible was in the possession of a cousin whose name and address are given in the Research Log.

Figure B-8 shows a portion (facsimile) of the family information it contains. This example illustrates some interesting anomalies as noted in the Research Log. Figure B-9 shows a partial index to the names in this Bible record.

NO.		
4	**Title**	Family Bible record of Seth Knight. The title page of the bible is inscribed as belonging to Seth Knight. The bible was published by the J.B. Lippincott Co., Philadelphia, Pennsylvania, in 1832. It is a large book measuring approximately 16 inches high by 12 inches wide.
	Call No.	Not Applicable
	Location	On 15 July 1974, the bible was in the possession of Mrs. Sarah H. Young, 3645 North Lansing Drive, Peoria, Illinois.

Date: 15 July 1974

Objective   Extract all family information.

Result   A photocopy of the title page of the bible and the other pages (four in all) that contained family information were made and numbered RC4-2 through RC4-5.

Date: 18 Aug 1974

Objective   Make a transcript of the information found in the bible.

Result   A typed transcript of the photocopy was made which consists of two pages numbered RC4-6 through RC4-7.

Date: 22 June 1994

Objective   Prepare an index to all proper names found in this source.

Result   As I really studied this bible record, I saw for the first time that the publication date of the bible is 1832, some 15 years after the birth of their first recorded child. Perhaps there was an earlier family bible or some of the information contained in this bible was copied from some other record. This might explain why the birth of Esther Knight in 1821 (known to be their daughter) is not found recorded in this bible. This needs to be checked further.

A genealogical index was made of the family members listed in the bible which consists of one page numbered RC4-8.

Figure B-7.   Research Log, Example 3

Source Extraction Examples and Exercises

(Flyleaf of Bible)

Seth C. Knight, His Bible

Seth C. Knight was born April 8th 1790, in Coberskill, Schoharie County, State of New York. Annie Evans Knight was born July 5th, 1793, Albany County, State of New York

Seth C. Knight and Annie Evans were married June 22nd, 1815, by J.L. Noe, Justice of the Peace, Albany, New York

Births

Joseph Knight was born April 5th 1817.

Seth C. Knight Jr. was born May 24th 1818.

Isaac Evans Knight was born 28 July 1819.

James C. Knight was born June 22nd 1823.

Eliza Knight was born April 10th 1825.

George Washington Knight was born January 25th 1827, in Newberg, State of Ohio.

James Andrew Knight was born February 12th 1829 in Menter, Geauga County, Ohio.

Susan Mariah Knight was born April 9th 1831 in Erie, Erie County, State of Pennsylvania.

Seth C. Knight 3rd was born March 23rd 1833.

Hester Knight was born March 7th 1835.

Sidney William Knight was born September 9th 1836 in Fredonia, Shetauque County, State of New York.

... [Etc.]

RC4-2

Figure B-8. Source Extraction Example 3

From the section in the bible labeled "Deaths" was found the death records of a child that died young and whose birth was not recorded in the Births section.

Given	Surname	Town	County	ST	Year	ECK	S	R	Source
Seth C	Knight	Cobleskill	Albany	NY	1790	-	M		4-002BR
Annie	Evans		Albany	NY	1793	-	F		4-002BR
Nathaniel	Knight			NY	1815	*	M		4-004BR
Joseph	Knight			NY	1817	-	M		4-002BR
Seth C	Knight			NY	1818	-	M		4-002BR
Isaac Evans	Knight			MI	1819	-	M		4-002BR
James C	Knight			MI	1823	-	M		4-002BR
Eliza	Knight			OH	1825	-	F		4-002BR
George Washington	Knight	Newbury	Cuyahoga	OH	1827	-	M		4-002BR
James Andrew	Knight	Mentor	Geauga	OH	1829	-	F		4-002BR
Susan Mariah	Knight	Erie	Erie	PA	1831	-	F		4-002BR
Seth C	Knight			NY	1833	-	M		4-002BR
Hester	Knight			NY	1835	-	F		4-002BR
Sidney William	Knight	Fredonia	Chautauqua	NY	1836	-	M		4-002BR

... [Etc.]

RC4-8

Figure B-9. Source Extraction Index, Example 3

Example 4

Let us say that your next source to be recorded is a photocopy of the will of one of your ancestors. In this case you made the photocopies from a microfilm of the original document in the county surrogate's office for the county and state in which this person resided. In the Research Log (Figure B-10), you recorded the accession numbers for the microfilm that you examined at the library and also some information about the identification and location of the original document when it was microfilmed. The reason for this is that even though the microfilm is a copy of the original document, it is technically a secondary source. Moreover, in the event someone wanted to examine the original, it would be useful to know where it is located and its special accession number.

Source Extraction Examples and Exercises

Figure B-11 shows a portion of the photocopied will. Figure B-12 shows how the names found in this source could be indexed according to the genealogical guidelines that have been presented. In this example, the year the will was dated is used as a reference for each person named and shows the stated relationships in the variable field.

NO.		
5	**Title**	Will of Thomas Chamberlin; Case No. 9922M, Surrogate's Office, Monmouth Co., N.J. (The Surrogate's Office for Monmouth County, N.J. is located at Toms River, N.J.)
	Call No.	Film 548,091
	Location	Family History Library, 35 North West Temple, Salt Lake City, Utah
	Date: 26 June 1976	
	Objective	Transcribe the will from microfilm.
	Result	A photocopy of the will was made from the microfilm which consists of five pages numbered RC5-2 through RC5-6.
	Date: 14 Nov 1977	
	Objective	Prepare a typed transcript of the will.
	Result	A typed transcript of the will was made which consists of four pages numbered RC5-7 through RC5-10.
	Date: 19 Sep 1984	
	Objective	Index all names found in the will.
	Result	A genealogical index was made and a printout was made which was numbered RC5-11.

Figure B-10. Research Log, Example 4

Source Extraction Examples and Exercises

In the name of God Amen, I Thomas Chamberlin, of the Township of Stafford and County of Monmouth and State of East Jersey, this ninth day of January one thousand eight hundred and twenty-nine, do make this my last will and testament in the manner following:

First, all my honest debts and funeral charges are to be paid. I give to my son James W. Chamberlin the place whereon he now lives and the cedar swamp on the middle branch of Forked River, I give to him, his heirs and assigns forever. My son Joseph has had his share before and my daughter Asenath Brown has had her share and my daughter Lida Chamberlin has had her share, but I give her all that she owes me on the books.

I give to my son Thomas Chamberlin the place whereon he now lives that is to say, the south side of this place to certain marks that I have made, which land I give to my son Thomas Chamberlin on conditions that he is to pay one hundred and twenty-five dollars to my daughter Penelope Brown all. Also I give to my son Thomas one equal half of cedar swamp on Oyster Creek which I give to him, his heirs and assigns forever.

The residue of this place whereon I now live from Oyster Creek to the marks which I have made and the residue of swamp to be sold and one thousand dollars to be given to my grandchildren, Thomas B. Chamberlin, and Samuel B. Chamberlin, and Mary B. Chamberlin, to be put out for investing for their bringing up and when of age, to be equally divided among them all. Also, one hundred and twenty-five dollars to be given to my daughter Penelope Brown.

I give to my loving wife all my moveable estate on the place or elsewhere. I make and ordain my wife Mary Chamberlin and James W. Chamberlin my son, Executors of this my last will in trust for the intent and purposes in this my last will contained. In witness, I the said Thomas Chamberlin have hereunto set my hand and seal the day and year above written, January ninth 1829. Signed and sealed by the said Thomas Chamberlin for his last will and testament in the presence of:

    Amos Birdsall   Thomas Chamberlin
    John Parker
    Jeremiah Predmore

... [Etc.]

RC5-2

Figure B-11. Source Extraction Example 4

Source Extraction Examples and Exercises

> This index shows the presence of a variable field to indicate relationships in the will.
>
> | Given | Surname | Town | County | ST | Year | ECK | S | R | Rel. | Source |
> |---|---|---|---|---|---|---|---|---|---|---|
> | Thomas | Chamberlin | Stafford | Monmouth | NJ | 1829 | / | M | | Testator | 5-001WL |
> | James W | Chamberlin | | Monmouth | NJ | 1829 | / | M | | Son | 5-001WL |
> | Joseph | Chamberlin | | Monmouth | NJ | 1829 | / | M | | Son | 5-001WL |
> | Asenath | Brown | | Monmouth | NJ | 1829 | / | F | | Dau | 5-001WL |
> | Thomas | Chamberlin | | Monmouth | NJ | 1829 | / | M | | Son | 5-001WL |
> | Lida | Chamberlin | | Monmouth | NJ | 1829 | / | F | | Dau | 5-001WL |
> | Penelope | Brown | | Monmouth | NJ | 1829 | / | F | | Dau | 5-001WL |
> | Thomas B | Chamberlin | | Monmouth | NJ | 1829 | / | M | | Gndson | 5-001WL |
> | Samuel B | Chamberlin | | Monmouth | NJ | 1829 | / | M | | Gndson | 5-001WL |
> | Mary B | Chamberlin | | Monmouth | NJ | 1829 | / | F | | Gnddau | 5-001WL |
> | Mary | Chamberlin | Stafford | Monmouth | NJ | 1829 | / | F | | Wife | 5-001WL |
>
> ... [Etc.]
>
> RC5-11

Figure B-12. Source Extraction Index, Example 4

Example 5

This example concerns an actual case I encountered when I first became interested in genealogy. A book was consulted which had information on my family. As I gained some experience and started asking questions, I learned that the author of this book had obtained his information from the widow of my great grandfather's brother who had been dead for some 24 years, and whose knowledge of the family was second-hand, at best.

The author had made the unfortunate mistake of not consulting those in the family who really knew the facts. As a result of the erroneous information given, a considerable amount of work already done had to be discarded. This is a good example of what often happens when consulting a secondary source.

Figure B-13 shows the Research Log entries for this source. Figure B-14 shows a portion of the photocopied material from this book. Figure B-15 contains the names indexed from this source.

Source Extraction Examples and Exercises

NO.		
6	Title	Pioneers and Prominent Men of Utah, by Frank Esshom, Published by the Utah Pioneers Book Publishing Company, Salt Lake City, Utah, 1913. 1319 pages.
	Call No.	979.2 D3e 1913
	Location	Genealogical Section, Los Angeles City Library, 5th & Hope Streets, Los Angeles, CA

Date: 22 June 1958

	Objective	See if there is any information about my great, great grandfather Joseph Chamberlin in this source.
	Result	I found short biographical sketches of Joseph Chamberlin and his son James Thomas Chamberlin with some information on their connections to New Jersey. Noted their surname was spelled *Chamberlain* in this source. I made photocopies of this material and put it on two pages numbered RC6-1 and RC6-2.

Date: 26 July 1958

	Objective	Incorporate this material into Family Group Records
	Result	Prepared Family Group Records for Joseph Chamberlin and his son James Thomas Chamberlin based upon the information found in this book.

Date: 7 Dec 1963

	Objective	Other information now obtained indicate this source to be highly unreliable. My grand uncle told me that the man who compiled this book went to the widow of his uncle (James Thomas Chamberlin) for information on the Chamberlins instead of going to the people in the Chamberlin who knew the facts and as a result most of the information in this source is wrong.
	Result	Corrected the Family Group Record for Joseph Chamberlin and his son James Thomas Chamberlin.

Figure B-13. Research Log, Example 5

Source Extraction Examples and Exercises

Pioneers and Prominent Men of Utah, by Frank Esshom, Published by the Utah Pioneers Book Publishing Company, Salt Lake City, Utah, 1913. 1319 pages.

Genealogical Section, Los Angeles City Library, 5th & Hope Streets, Los Angeles, CA

Call No. 979.2 D3e 1913

22 June 1958

Found short biographies of Joseph Chamberlain (pp. 798-99); James T. Chamberlain (P. 799); Thomas Roscoe Chamberlain (P. 799); William Henry Chamberlin Jr. (P. 799). Noted variations in spelling of surname.

PP. 798-99:

"CHAMBERLAIN, JOSEPH (son of Thomas Chamberlain, of Toms River, Ocean county, New Jersey). Born May 12, 1812, in Ocean county, N.J. Came to Utah, Dec. 9, 1853, Preston Thomas company.

Married Amy Wilbert, Barnegat, Ocean county, N.J. (daughter of James Wilbert and Mary Gifford of Ocean county, N.J. Their children: Katherine, m. John Dickinson; John, m. Elizabeth Smart; Althea, m. James Brown; Rebecca, m. John Aldous; James Thomas, b. March 18, 1847, m. Susanna A. Alston July 23, 1882; Josephine, m. Harold P. Johnson; Henry, m. Frances Brown; Hyrum, died. Family home, Salt Lake City.

Owned first sawmill in Parley's canyon. Engaged in salt and lumber business. Died April, 1879."

P. 799:

CHAMBERLAIN, JAMES T. (son of Joseph Chamberlain and Amy Wilbert). Born ..."

...[Etc.]

RC6-1

Figure B-14. Source Extraction Example 5

Surname	Given	Town/City	County	ST	Year	ECK	S	R	Source
Chamberlain	Joseph		Ocean	NJ	1812	-	M		RC6-001HI
Chamberlain	Joseph	Salt Lake City	Salt Lake	UT	1879	*	M		RC6-001HI
Wilbert	Amy	Barnegat	Ocean	NJ	1835	/	F		RC6-001HI
Wilbert	James		Ocean	NJ	1792	-	M		RC6-001HI
Gifford	Mary		Ocean	NJ	1794	-	F		RC6-001HI
Chamberlain	James T		Ocean	NJ	1847	-	M		RC6-001HI
Alston	Susanna A	Salt Lake City	Salt Lake	UT	1882	/	F		RC6-001HI
... [Etc.]									

RC6-5

Figure B-15. Source Extraction Index, Example 5

In the preceding index, Joseph Chamberlin was listed twice to indicate different jurisdictions. The dates for Amy Wilbert, James Wilbert, and Mary Gifford are estimated. The information from this source eventually proved to be grossly inaccurate. It is included here to illustrate a typical situation when a particular source proves to be inaccurate.

Effectively estimating dates is a skill that generally comes with experience and usually involves working from the known to the unknown. It is expected that every genealogist has his or her own criteria for this process. From my own empirical experience, I have found that the average age of first marriages to be about 23 years for the man and a little younger for the woman. On the average the man is about two years older than the woman. I usually assume the active child-bearing age of a woman to range from about 17 to 44 years.

Besides these factors, there may other facts available to you which can modify the preceding assumptions, and of course, there are many exceptions to these suggested numbers. However, they are a good starting point, and as you gain experience and expertise, this process will come to you quite naturally.

Source Extraction Examples and Exercises

SOURCE EXTRACTION EXERCISES

The following few exercises have been developed to give you a little information and practice in implementing the principles of genealogical indexing using the principles described in the Chapter 3 section, *Essential Elements for Genealogical Indexing*. As in all things, "practice makes perfect," and this is no exception to that old saying. Even if you do not have a lot of names to index, it is recommended that you index them, just to gain practice in doing it this way.

The idea is for you to become really comfortable with this format and method of presentation. The expertise you develop will serve you very well in the future when indexing becomes a real necessity. Another benefit is that this type of indexing will train you to think more logically in correlating the essential elements required in the process of unique identification. Do not worry too much if your answers differ slightly from the ones given in the text. There will be some situations where there may be more than one way to do it.

Exercise 1

Let us say that you have been searching for a Joseph Anderson who may have lived in Crawford County, Indiana, perhaps as early as 1825. In reviewing a history of this county, you find mention of a Joseph Anderson, of Fredonia in said county, who appeared on a list of petitioners...dated 27 September 1830. You copy this information for inclusion in your Source Extraction file No. 78. Prepare an index record for this man, based on the information given. Compare your record with the following:

Given	Surname	Town	County	ST	Year	ECK	S	R	Source
Joseph	Anderson	Fredonia	Crawford	IN	1830	/	M		78-001HI

In this record, the suffice "HI" was used to indicate this source was a history. The forward slash is used because all we know is that he was in this jurisdiction for the given year, but could have been there for sometime before 1830 and afterwards.

Source Extraction Examples and Exercises

Exercise 2

In an interview with your great grandmother, she spoke of her grandfather, Elias Keyes. She didn't know where or when he was born, but did remember that he often used to speak of living in Niagara County, New York, close to Niagara Falls, after the close of the War of 1812, and just before her father was born in the year 1815. She added that the family lived there until her father was about 10 or 11 years old. From this information, prepare an index record for Elias Keyes. (Assume a Source Number of 36, and use a suffix of your own choice and arbitrary page number.) Compare your record with the following:

Given	Surname	Town	County	ST	Year	ECK	S	R	Source
Elias	Keyes		Niagara	NY	1814	-	M		46-003PR

There are several ways this index entry could be done. The one shown indicates he was in this jurisdiction a little before 1815, so you could show 1814 followed by the hyphen to indicate the earliest known date in the jurisdiction. You could show 1820 (a rough average of 1815 and 1826) followed by a forward slash to denote an approximate correlation. (The "PR" suffix and page number are arbitrary choices for illustration purposes.)

Exercise 3

From a family Bible you have extracted a number of names. One of them is an Elizabeth Dale who married a William Brown, 25 Nov 1861, at Nashville, Barton Co., MO. Prepare index records for Elizabeth Dale and William Brown. Assume an arbitrary Source Number, page number, and suffix of your own choice.) Compare your record with the following:

Given	Surname	Town	County	ST	Year	ECK	S	R	Source
Elizabeth	Dale	Nashville	Barton	MO	1861	/	F		123-001BI
William	Brown	Nashville	Barton	MO	1861	/	M		123-001BI

181

Source Extraction Examples and Exercises

The forward slash is used for both these entries to denote an approximation as either one or both could have been in this jurisdiction preceding 1861. A hyphen could also be used though it is not as good a fit. Note that these records do not show a connection between these two people except for the date, jurisdiction, and Source Extraction file number. Remember that the purpose of the index is not to make a genealogical connection, but just to index names associated with jurisdictions and dates. However, once a person has been identified in your Family Group Records (FGRs), his or her genealogical connections will be given in the FGR index.

Exercise 4

After going through some birth records, you have extracted the names of two people you want to track. The first one is an Ebenezer Sloan, born 17 Aug 1694, Boston, MA, to a Samuel and Betsey Sloan. The second one is only identified as "Child of Samuel & Betsey Sloan, b. 26 June 1692, also at Boston, MA. Prepare index records to reflect this information. (Assume an arbitrary Source Number, page number, and suffix of your own choice.) Compare your record with the following:

Given	Surname	Town	County	ST	Year	ECK	S	R	Source
Child	Sloan	Boston	Suffolk	MA	1692	-	C		12-002BR
Ebenezer	Sloan	Boston	Suffolk	MA	1694	-	M		12-002BR

In the first record, the given name is just given as "Child" because that is the way it appears in the records and the sex is indicated by a "C."

You may be wondering why the parents of these children have not been shown. Many of the names you may be indexing will not give this kind of information. The index format has been designed to accommodate any kind of record. If it is too specialized, this flexibility will be compromised.

However, the parents could be indexed in the following way:

Given	Surname	Town	County	ST	Year	ECK	S	R	Source
Samuel	Sloan	Boston	Suffolk	MA	1692	/	M		12-002BR
Betsey		Boston	Suffolk	MA	1692	/	F		12-002BR

Source Extraction Examples and Exercises

The year 1692 (an average of 1692 and 1694) followed by a forward slash approximately covers the years for the two births that you have already indexed. Betsey's surname could be shown as Sloan, though we know this is her married name. You could also leave this field blank because we don't know her maiden name. Another variation might be to show her married name, but in the Sex/Gender field, perhaps use "W" in lieu of "F" to indicate she is a married woman. In any case, as you compare information within your index, the Source Extraction file number will always provide the connecting link to group the indexed names from this source.

Exercise 5

You have just completed the extraction of several families in the 1850 Federal Census for Chicago, Cook Co., Illinois. One of these people is a John F. Martin, whose age is given as 52 years old and born in New York. Prepare an index record for this man based upon this information. (Assume an arbitrary Source Number, page number, and suffix of your own choice.) Compare your record with the following:

Given	Surname	Town	County	ST	Year	ECK	S	R	Source
John F	Martin	Chicago	Cook	IL	1850	/	M		41-001CS
John F	Martin			NY	1798	-	M		41-001CS

In this example, we show two records for this man because we want to pick up both jurisdictions. The first establishes his presence in Chicago in 1850 (denoted by the slash symbol). The ECK (hyphen) in the second record infers his estimated year of birth in the state of New York.

Exercise 6

You have included the will of an ancestor, Eli Brown, in your Source Extraction files. Eli Brown, was of Stafford, Monmouth County, New Jersey, when he made his will on 31 Oct 1815; proved 21 Apr 1816. A selected portion of this document reads as follows:

Source Extraction Examples and Exercises

> "Second, I give and bequeath to my granddaughter Mary Brown, daughter of my deceased son David, the sum of Fifty pounds, as in right of her father's share, to be paid out of the proceeds of my real estate..."

From this information, prepare index records for Eli Brown and the people who are given in the quoted portion of his will. (Assume an arbitrary Source Number, page number, and suffix of your own choice.) Compare your records with the following:

Given	Surname	Town	County	ST	Year	ECK	S	R	Source
Eli	Brown	Stafford	Monmouth	NJ	1816	*	M		13-001PR
David	Brown	Stafford	Monmouth	NJ	1815	<	M		13-002PR
Mary	Brown	Stafford	Monmouth	NJ	1815	/	F		13-002PR

For Eli Brown, the asterisk ECK indicates his death as having occurred in 1816, the date his will was proved (admitted to probate). In the record for his son David Brown, the less-than symbol following the year 1815, indicates that he was dead before this date (as stated in his father's will). All we know of Mary Brown (as given in the will), is that she was alive on the date that her grandfather made his will and thus the forward slash is appropriate. Of course, she may have not been living in this jurisdiction, but was associated with it. The Source Number suffix of "PR" was chosen to denote a probate record.

Exercise 7

Another section of the same will (as described in Exercise 6), reads as follows:

> "First, I give and bequeath to my dear wife Sarah Brown, the use of any two rooms in my present dwelling house which she may think proper to occupy...together with the sum of three hundred pounds to be paid to her out of the proceeds of my moveable estate...are made to my dear wife during the term of her natural life or widowhood...which I bequeath to her forever..."

Source Extraction Examples and Exercises

Though Eli's widow Sarah was given various bequests under the terms of the will, there appears to be no further mention of her in this document or in other sources consulted. From this information, prepare an index record for Sarah Brown. (Assume an arbitrary Source Number, page number, and suffix of your own choice.) Compare your records with the following:

Given	Surname	Town	County	ST	Year	ECK	S	R	Source
Sarah	Brown	Stafford	Monmouth	NJ	1816	>		F	13-003PR

The greater-than symbol following the year 1816 indicates that Sarah died sometime after this date as she was alive when her husband's will was proved. Suppose that in this exercise, it was known from the probate records that Sarah received bequests over a period of several years, say from 1816 through 1823, when her name is mentioned for the last time in this source. In this case, the index record for her could be stated:

Given	Surname	Town	County	ST	Year	ECK	S	R	Source
Sarah	Brown	Stafford	Monmouth	NJ	1823	>		F	13-003PR

Exercise 8

You have been trying to trace a certain man in your ancestry named Philemon Foster. You haven't been able to find a record of his death. However, you did come across a land record in which one Thomas Foster, known to be Philemon's son, conveyed several parcels of land in 1712. In this instrument, he mentioned that his father, Philemon Foster, of Billerica, MA, had purchased this same property in 1701.

Prepare index records for Philemon Foster and his son Thomas Foster, based upon this information. (Assume an arbitrary Source Number, page number, and suffix of your own choice.) Compare your record with the following:

Given	Surname	Town	County	ST	Year	ECK	S	R	Source
Philemon	Foster	Billerica	Middlesex	MA	1712	<		M	31-002LR'
Thomas	Foster	Billerica	Middlesex	MA	1712	/		M	31-002LR

Source Extraction Examples and Exercises

The less-than symbol serves quite well to show that Philemon was dead by 1712. Many genealogical sources frequently give information in this fashion when exact dates of death are not known. Another possibility for him would be to state the year as 1701 and the ECK as a forward slash. For Thomas Foster, all we know about him from this one source is that he sold land in 1712, thus the forward slash indicates his presence in the stated jurisdiction at this time. The Source Number suffix of "LR" was chosen to denote a land record.

Exercise 9

Let us say that you have been going through a history of Ontario county, New York, and have come across the following entry:

> "... Mr. John Andrews came to this community (Gorham) in the year 1817 where he owned and operated a livery stable. In 1823, he sold this business and moved to the town of Hopewell, a new community organized in 1822 from part of Gorham. He purchased a homestead there and also operated a hotel there for a number of years. In 1851, he conveyed his homestead and hotel in Hopewell and other property in Gorham, when it is presumed that he removed to the state of Iowa, to live with a daughter."

Prepare an index records for John Andrews, based upon this information. (Assume an arbitrary Source Number, page number, and suffix of your own choice.) Compare your records with the following:

Given	Surname	Town	County	ST	Year	ECK	S	R	Source
John	Andrews	Gorham	Ontario	NY	1817	-	M		97-007HI
John	Andrews	Hopewell	Ontario	NY	1822	-	M		97-007HI
John	Andrews			IA	1851	/	M		97-007HI

The first record uses the hyphen ECK as he was stated to have first been associated with the jurisdiction in that year. The second uses the same ECK for the second jurisdiction. The last record only shows the state of Iowa (IA) as that is all we know about him from the information at hand. The Source Extraction suffix of "HI" was chosen to denote the source as a history.

Exercise 10

You have been going through the death records for Gloucester, Essex Co., Massachusetts, in search of all persons with the surname Knight. Among the entries you extract is the following:

"Old Mr. Knight, dyed October ye 19th, 1697."

Prepare an index record for this man, based upon this information. (Assume an arbitrary Source Number, page number, and suffix of your own choice.) Compare your record with the following:

Given	Surname	Town	County	ST	Year	ECK	S	R	Source
Mr	Knight	Gloucester	Essex	MA	1697	*	M		114-003VR

This is a case in which we do not have this man's given name but can instead just use "Mr." The Source Extraction file number suffix of "VR" was chosen to denote the source as a vital record.

Jurisdictional Tracking Exercises   C

Appendix C supplements the material presented in Chapter 5, *Jurisdictional Tracking*, by providing additional examples to give you a little practice in creating jurisdictional tracking records. Do not worry if your answers differ somewhat from the ones given for each exercise. There will be some cases where there may be more than one way to do it.

EXERCISE 1

One of your ancestors is a man named Henry Stillwell. Though you know a lot about him, there are periods of time in his life for which you are unable to account. Let's say that you know he was born in Herkimer County, New York, in the year 1790. Of his early life you know nothing. He did have military service during the War of 1812, having enlisted in the year 1813 at Albany, New York, and was stationed at Ft. George in Niagara County for most of the same year (1813).

He next appears about the year 1818, where you believe him to be a petitioner along with a number of other men (all in the lumbering business) in Wayne County, Michigan. You know he was still in this area as late as 1821 when he sold a sawmill. By 1823, he was already married and living near Clymer, in Chautauqua County, New York. He lived in this place until his death in 1836. From this information, and assuming his LifeNumber to be 481, prepare a jurisdictional tracking record for this man and compare your results with the following:

Given	Surname	Town	County	ST	S	Era	LN
Henry	Stillwell		Herkimer	NY	M	1790-	481
Henry	Stillwell	Albany	Albany	NY	M	1813/	481
Henry	Stillwell	Fort George	Niagara	NY	M	1813/	481
Henry	Stillwell		Wayne	MI	M	1818-1821	481
Henry	Stillwell	Clymer	Chautauqua	NY	M	1823*1836	481

Jurisdictional Tracking Exercises

This exercise was designed to give you practice in using the forward slash (/) to designate indeterminate or approximate periods. In this exercise, he was associated with two different jurisdictions in 1813, not an uncommon occurrence.

EXERCISE 2

One of your ancestors had a child name Mary Adams (LifeNumber 93) who was born in the year 1745, Dracut, Middlesex County, MA. She was said to have died young but you can find no record of her death. Assuming a LifeNumber 93, prepare a jurisdictional tracking record for her and compare your results with the following:

Given	Surname	Town	County	ST	S	Era	LN
Mary	Adams	Dracut	Middlesex	MA	F	1745>	93

If you didn't know anything about this person and only found this one record for her, you would assume it to mean that she was born in 1745. The greater-than character indicates that she died soon after 1745. (The lowest year appearing in any tracking record for a given person is inferred to be either a known or estimated birth year.)

EXERCISE 3

Let's say you have an ancestor, Thomas Brown, who was born 19 Dec 1688, Boston, Suffolk County, MA. In 1702, he removed with his parents to Worcester, then a part of Hampshire county, MA. He lived in this area for the rest of his life and made his will there on 23 Nov 1753. While you have been unable to find a record of his death, you do know that his eldest son, John Brown, conveyed some of his father's property in the year 1761, Worcester, Worcester County, MA. (Note that in 1731, Worcester County was formed from part of Hampshire County.)

Assuming this man had a LifeNumber of 127, prepare a jurisdictional tracking record for him and compare your results with the following:

Given	Surname	Town	County	ST	S	Era	LN
Thomas	Brown	Boston	Suffolk	MA	M	1688-1702	127
Thomas	Brown	Worcester	Hampshire	MA	M	1702-1731	127
Thomas	Brown	Worcester	Worcester	MA	M	1731-1753	127
Thomas	Brown	Worcester	Worcester	MA	M	1753<1761	127

The less-than character is effective in the last record as it shows that Thomas Brown died sometime between 1692 and 1700. Also, the change of county jurisdiction when Worcester County was formed from Hampshire County in 1731. In this exercise, you could have also done it thusly:

Given	Surname	Town	County	ST	S	Era	LN
Thomas	Brown	Boston	Suffolk	MA	M	1688-1702	127
Thomas	Brown	Worcester	Hampshire	MA	M	1702-1731	127
Thomas	Brown	Worcester	Worcester	MA	M	1731<1761	127

While this tracking record is basically correct, it lacks precision. With an Era indicated as 1731<1761, we have a 30-year period of uncertainty for his death year. In the previous example, we incorporated the date that he made his will (1753) into the tracking record (Era: 1753<1761); which now results in an uncertainty of only eight years.

EXERCISE 4

One of your ancestors is a man named John H. Edmunds who was born in 1843, Berlin, Knox Co., Ohio. He lived in this area until 1862, when he enlisted in the Union Army during the Civil War. In 1865, after the close of the war, he returned to Ohio and lived for a brief period in the town of Xenia, in Greene County. Later that same year, he was married at Dayton, Montgomery Co., Ohio. In the following spring (1866), he and his bride moved to Pike County, Illinois, where he purchased land and started a farm on the outskirts of Detroit. About 1872, he left his family in Illinois to visit California.

Jurisdictional Tracking Exercises

His family received one letter from him in August of that year from San Francisco, saying that he had found work and expected to send for them in the near future. After this, he seems to have disappeared, and his family feared that he was dead. Then, three years later, in 1875, he suddenly appeared at the family home. It seems that he had been shanghaied on some nondescript vessel while in San Francisco and was in servitude for three years. He was finally able to escape to a small village on the coast of South America and from there, he slowly made his way home. Apparently this experience cured him of all desire to ever leave home again. He and his wife remained on the family homestead where he died in 1915.

From this information, prepare a jurisdictional tracking record for this man. Assume an arbitrary LifeNumber of your own choice for this exercise. For the period of time when he served in the Union Army, assume his residence to be Washington, D.C. Compare your results with the following:

Given	Surname	Town	County	ST	S	Era	LN
John H	Edmunds	Berlin	Knox	OH	M	1843-1862	133
John H	Edmunds		Washington	DC	M	1862-1865	133
John H	Edmunds	Xenia	Greene	OH	M	1865/	133
John H	Edmunds	Dayton	Montgomery	OH	M	1865-1866	133
John H	Edmunds		Pike	IL	M	1866-1872	133
John H	Edmunds	San Francisco	San Francisco	CA	M	1872/	133
John H	Edmunds	Detroit	Pike	IL	M	1875*1915	133

In this exercise, the period from 1872 to 1875 is basically unknown and does not appear in the tracking record. You will undoubtedly encounter similar situations in your own genealogy wherein there will be unaccounted-for periods of time.

EXERCISE 5

One of your ancestors is a woman named Mary Anne Thomas. She was born in 1837, New York City, N.Y. At the age of 16, she was employed in a garment factory in New York City. A year later, she met a young man named James Edwards, who she married in 1854, at Brooklyn, Kings Co., NY. They took up residence at Flatbush in the same county. The marriage did not last long, and they parted company the following year (1855). After this she returned home to live with her parents.

In 1858, she married again, this time to a man named Samuel F. Atkinson, at a resort in Flushing, Queens Co., NY. The couple returned to New York City where they remained for several months. In the spring of 1859, they moved to Syracuse, Onondaga Co., NY, where her husband took over the family business (a farm implements & hardware store) from his father. By this marriage, she had two children, a son born in 1859 and a daughter (your grandmother) born in 1863.

They resided at Syracuse until 1884, when she was widowed. Soon afterwards she sold the family business and went to live with her daughter in Erie, Erie Co., PA. After this, she seems to have disappeared. She is not buried beside her husband at the cemetery in Syracuse, nor in any cemetery in Erie, PA, her last known residence. Probably, she married again, and her name at this time has been forgotten by present-day descendants.

Jurisdictional Tracking Exercises

From this information, prepare a jurisdictional tracking record for this woman. Assume an arbitrary LifeNumber of your own choice for this exercise and compare your results with the following:

Given	Surname	Town	County	ST	S	Era	LN
Mary Anne	Thomas	New York City	New York	NY	F	1837-1854	67
Mary Anne	Edwards	Brooklyn	Kings	NY	F	1854/	67
Mary Anne	Edwards	Flatbush	Kings	NY	F	1854-1855	67
Mary Anne	Edwards	New York City	New York	NY	F	1855-1858	67
Mary Anne	Edwards	Flushing	Queens	NY	F	1858/	67
Mary Anne	Atkinson	New York City	New York	NY	F	1858-1859	67
Mary Anne	Atkinson	Syracuse	Onondaga	NY	F	1859-1884	67
Mary Anne	Atkinson	Erie	Erie	PA	F	1884/	67

This exercise was principally designed to focus on the change of surname. Because you have a unique number for identification, you can easily and immediately locate the Family Group Record (FGR) for this person and obtain all the details. This system of retrieval is entirely unaffected by any name changes.

EXERCISE 6

Let us assume that you have compiled a FGR for a family in your ancestry. The following is an abbreviated portion of this fictional FGR:

	LN
HUSBAND: William Allen Jameson	56
Father: William E. Jameson	29
Mother: Susanna Alice Carey	30

Born: 23 May 1825, Philadelphia, Philadelphia Co., PA
Died: 28 Feb 1902, Chicago, Cook Co., IL
Buried: 2 Mar 1902, Holy Evangelists Cemetery, Chicago, IL
Married: 22 June 1851, Springfield, Co., Greene, MO

	LN
WIFE: Mary Jane Adams	71
Father: Jonah D. Adams	82
Mother: Elizabeth Smith	83

Born: 19 Aug 1831, St. Louis, St. Louis Co., MO
Died: 14 Nov 1915, Seattle, King Co., WA
Buried: 17 Nov 1915, Evergreen Cemetery, Tacoma, Pierce, WA

CHILDREN

M   128   Jonah William Jameson, b. 12 July 1853, Springfield, MO. At the age of 16, he was sent to a military academy in Bowling Green, Caroline county, Virginia. While on a school outing, he drank contaminated water from which he contacted typhoid fever, and died shortly afterwards on 10 Sep 1871.

F   129   Betsey Anne Jameson, b. 17 Sep 1856, Mount Vernon, Lawrence Co. MO. When she was 17 years old, she attended a school for young ladies in Chicago, IL for a period of two years. In the summer of 1875, she returned to live at home until she married Elias F. Champney, 28 Nov 1876, at the home of her parents in Mount Vernon, MO. After her marriage, she and her husband lived in the same city for a number of years until 1892, when they moved to Seattle, WA. They were both still living there in 1924, according to a city directory.

Jurisdictional Tracking Exercises

From the biographical section of the FGR for this family is the following excerpt:

"William Jameson left home at the age of 21 and made his way to St. Louis, Missouri, where he found employment in a men's clothing store. While living here, he met his bride-to-be, Mary Adams. They were married at the home of her parents in Springfield, Missouri, June 22nd, 1851... Later that year, they journeyed to Mount Vernon, Missouri, where he operated a small department store in partnership with a cousin of his wife. In only a few years, he became sole owner and greatly expanded the business. In 1880, he sold out and moved to Chicago where he was a partner in a large department store..." After her husband's death in 1902, his widow Mary continued to live in Chicago until the summer of 1905, when she went to live with her daughter and son-in-law who were living in Seattle, WA..."

From this information, prepare jurisdictional tracking records for each member of this family (except for the parents of the husband & wife). The LifeNumbers for the parents are in the right margins; those for the children are in the left margins. Assume an arbitrary LifeNumber for Elias F. Champney. Compare your results with the following:

Given	Surname	Town	County	ST	S	Era	LN
William Allen	Jameson	Philadelphia	Philadelphia	PA	M	1825-1846	56
William Allen	Jameson	St. Louis	St. Louis	MO	M	1846-1851	56
William Allen	Jameson	Springfield	Greene	MO	M	1851/	56
William Allen	Jameson	Mount Vernon	Lawrence	MO	M	1851-1880	56
William Allen	Jameson	Chicago	Cook	IL	M	1880*1902	56
Mary Jane	Adams	St. Louis	St. Louis	MO	F	1831-	71
Mary Jane	Adams	Springfield	Greene	MO	F	1851/	71
Mary Jane	Jameson	Mount Vernon	Lawrence	MO	F	1851-1880	71
Mary Jane	Jameson	Chicago	Cook	IL	F	1880-1905	71
Mary Jane	Jameson	Seattle	King	WA	F	1905*1915	71
Jonah William	Jameson	Springfield	Greene	MO	M	1853-1853	128
Jonah William	Jameson	Mount Vernon	Lawrence	MO	M	1853-1869	128
Jonah William	Jameson	Bowling Green	Caroline	VA	M	1869*1871	128
Betsey Anne	Jameson	Mount Vernon	Lawrence	MO	F	1856-1873	129
Betsey Anne	Jameson	Chicago	Cook	IL	F	1873-1875	129
Betsey Anne	Jameson	Mount Vernon	Lawrence	MO	F	1875-1876	129
Betsey Anne	Champney	Mount Vernon	Lawrence	MO	F	1876-1892	129
Betsey Anne	Champney	Seattle	King	WA	F	1892/1924	129
Elias F	Champney	Mount Vernon	Lawrence	MO	F	1876-1892	301
Elias F	Champney	Seattle	King	WA	F	1892/1924	301

Note that Betsey Anne and her husband Elias were still living in 1924. Hence, the forward slash is used to indicate an approximation because we have no information past 1924.

EXERCISE 7

For this last exercise, develop a jurisdictional tracking record for yourself beginning with your birth up to the present time. Show every jurisdiction in which you have lived in, including residences, schools (if away from home), places you worked, and so forth. You may be surprised at all the different jurisdictions with which you have been associated.

Family Group Record Examples

This appendix contains additional examples of Family Group Record (FGR) sections as described and referenced in Chapter 6, *The Family Group Record*.

FGR PARENTS

Figures D-1 and D-2 illustrate additional examples of a Parent's Section.

```
                                                                    LN
HUSBAND:  Ebenezer⁴ Williams      "Eben/Eb"                         25
    Father:  John³ Williams                                         20
    Mother:  Anne Underwood                                         21
Born:  About 1694 (?), probably Shrewsbury, Monmouth Co., N.J.
Died:  10 July 1770, Good Luck, Monmouth Co., N.J.
Buried:  Good Luck Cemetery, Forked River, Monmouth Co., N.J.
Married:  About 1719, Monmouth Co., N.J.
Other Marriages:


                                                                    LN
WIFE:     Jane Lippincott                                          301
    Father:  Joel Lippincott                                       353
    Mother:  Rebecca                                               354
Born:  28 Aug 1696, Shrewsbury, Monmouth Co., N.J.
Died:  After 14 Aug 1770, probably Monmouth Co., N.J.
Buried:  Good Luck Cemetery, Forked River, Monmouth Co., N.J.
Other Marriages:  (1) George Wardell, 17 Sep 1718, Shrewsbury, N.J.
```

Figure D-1. Parent's Section Example 1

Family Group Record Examples

	LN
HUSBAND: Henry^6 Harrington "Colonel"	49
Father: Samuel^5 Harrington	153
Mother: Elizabeth Thomas	154

Born: About 1843, Pike Co., IL
Died: 23 Dec 1897, Chicago, Cook Co., IL
Buried: Masonic Cemetery, Chicago, IL
Married: (1) Abigail E. Stevens, 14 Oct 1866, Pike Co., IL
Other Marriages: (2) Samantha Alicia Brown, 17 Sep 1879, Chicago, IL

	LN
WIFE (1): Abigail E Stevens "Nabby"	209
Father: Thomas Stevens	164
Mother: Mary Adams	165

Born: About 1845, Pike Co., IL
Died: 17 Nov 1878, Chicago, Cook Co., IL. "aged 33 years"
Buried: Masonic Cemetery, Chicago, IL
Other Marriages:

	LN
WIFE (2): Samantha Alicia Brown	61
Father: William Brown	52
Mother: Mary Overholzer	53

Born: 23 Oct 1854, New York, New York Co., NY
Died: 19 May 1922, Pasadena, Los Angeles Co., CA
Buried: Ramona Cemetery, Pasadena, CA
Other Marriages:

Figure D-2.   Parent's Section Example 2

Family Group Record Examples

FGR CHILDREN

Figure D-3 illustrates another example of a Children's section which also shows the use of Event Modifiers. The LN is the number preceding each name.

		CHILDREN (Order uncertain - probably others)
M	28	James^5 Chamberlin, b. About 1720, probably Shrewsbury Twp., Monmouth Co., N.J. Married —?—, about 1748 (?), probably Monmouth Co., N.J. Died about Feb-Mar 1802, Stafford Twp., Monmouth Co., N.J. +
M	29	William^5 Chamberlin, b. About 1723, probably Shrewsbury Twp., Monmouth Co., N.J. Married Catherine Longstreet, by License dated 22 Dec 1746, Monmouth Co., N.J. Died 18 Dec 1759, probably Dover Twp., Monmouth Co., N.J. +
M	30	Thomas^5 Chamberlin, b. About 1726 (?), probably Shrewsbury Twp., Monmouth Co., N.J. Married Catherine Gant, by License dated 4 May 1747, Shrewsbury, N.J. Died after July 1770, perhaps Monmouth Co., N.J. +
M	31	John^5 Chamberlin, b. About 1728 (?), probably Shrewsbury Twp., Monmouth Co., N.J. Married Mary Gant, by License dated 1 Dec 1749, Shrewsbury, N.J. Died after July 1770, perhaps Monmouth Co., N.J. +
M	27	Samuel^5 Chamberlin, b. About 1730 (?), probably Shrewsbury Twp., Monmouth Co., N.J. Probably married Betsey —?—, about 1755 (?), probably Monmouth Co., N.J. In 1808, he was living at or near Forked River, N.J. +
F	32	Valeria^5 Chamberlin, b. About 1732, probably Shrewsbury Twp., Monmouth Co., N.J. Married Uriah Lippincott, by License dated 17 Aug 1752, Monmouth Co., N.J. +
F	33	Zilphia^5 Chamberlin, b. About 1733 (?), probably Shrewsbury Twp., Monmouth Co., N.J. Married Ephraim Bates, by License dated 30 May 1755, Monmouth Co., N.J. +

Figure D-3. Children's Section Example

Family Group Record Examples

FGR BIOGRAPHICAL

Figures D-4 and D-5 show various items (set off by quotation marks) that could be included in an FGR Biographical section. (Note most of the individual paragraphs are unrelated to each other.)

BIOGRAPHICAL

"Richard Goddard was of Upham and Swindon, Wiltshire, England. He was the eldest son of his parents and resided in handsome mansion at Upham, built "on and with the ruins of a still larger house, the hunting lodge of John of Gaunt...." The initials R.G. and E.G., with the date 1599 are carved on the porch, for Richard Goddard and his wife Elizabeth; also the initials T.G. & A.G. for Thomas Goddard and Anne Goddard, the father and mother of Richard..."

"The following illustration is a partial copy of an ancient document bearing William Chamberlain's signature as Constable:"

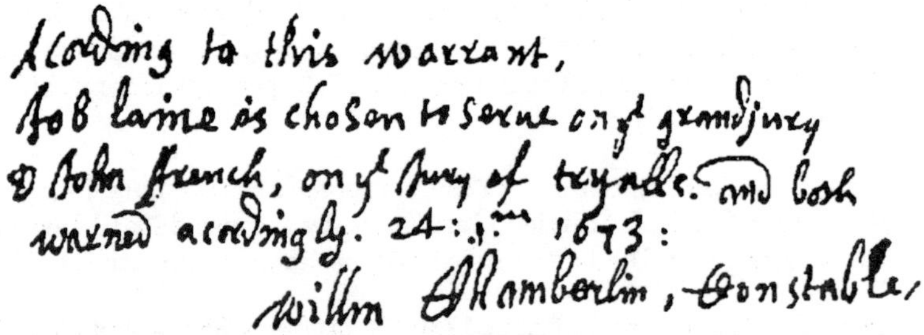

[handwritten document image]

William Chamberlin was a grantee in East Jersey, 1762-63. He and his son William, Jr., were taxed in Shrewsbury in 1764. William Chamberlin of Shrewsbury (now Barnegat), sold land to his son Thomas of the same place, ½ acre of a tract in Barnegat, on the south side of Oyster Creek, 20 Jan 1747.

"Mrs. Mary Chamberlin, along with Elizabeth Spragg and David Woodmansee of Turkey Foot Township, conveyed land on 28 May 1805 to Samuel Woodmansee of Dover Township for $50. This land consisted of three lots on the highway leading over Cedar Creek bridge. All parties in this transactions were heirs of David Woodmansee, deceased. The same people also sold land in Dover to David and Francis Woodmansee."

Figure D-4. Biographical Section Example 1

BIOGRAPHICAL

George Washington Brown, son of Nathaniel Brown, had his father's biographical sketch published in Tullidge's *History of Utah*, (Vol. 2, pp. 211-214; 1889). In this sketch, he related many incidents of his father's life. While the year of Nathaniel Brown's birth and the place of his death as ascribed by George W. Brown are questionable in light of other evidence, the narrative is most interesting and valuable. He began his narrative by telling of his father's bravery and patriotism during the War of 1812...

In May 1838, Avis, Nathaniel's widow, became a convert to the Mormon church, established only a few years before by Joseph Smith. Within the next two years, she took her children and removed to the Mormon settlement then established at Nauvoo, Illinois. By September 1840, Avis and her children had settled in Lee county, Iowa, near the town of Montrose, living in a Mormon settlement known as the "Ambrosia Branch." (Lee county, Iowa, was just across the Mississippi river from Nauvoo.) The records of the Ambrosia branch states that George W., James A., and Susan M. were baptized in Lee County, Iowa, in September 1840. The Ambrosia branch was not formally organized until 14 Sep 1844, and has provided us with a most valuable record of the Brown family, without which we would be much less informed. A restored copy of this record reads:

> *Avis Brown, widow of Nathaniel Brown and daughter of Isaac and Avis Hills, was born April 8th 1800, in Coberskill, Schoharie County, State of New York. Baptised in May A.D. 1838 by Matthias Bovee in Shetauque County, New York.*
>
> *George W. Brown was born January 25th 1827, in Newberg [Newbury], — [Cuyahoga] County, State of Ohio. Baptised September AD 1840 in Lee County, Iowa.*
>
> *James Andrew Brown was born February 12th 1829 in Menter, Geauga County, Ohio.*
> *Baptised September 1840.*
>
> *Susan Mariah Brown was born April 9th 1831 in Erie, Erie County, State of Pennsylvania. Baptised September A.D. 1840 in Lee County, Iowa.*
>
> *Sidney William Brown was born September 9th 1836 in Fredonia, Shetauque County, State of New York. Baptised May 11th 1845 by George W. Voorhees. [Etc.]*

Figure D-5.   Biographical Section Example 2

Family Group Record Examples

DATA ANALYSIS & EVALUATION

Example 1

"William Chamberlin, a resident of Shrewsbury township, Monmouth Co., N.J., made his will in 1765 (proved 1770). It was believed that he was a son of an earlier William Chamberlin, who had come to Monmouth County, New Jersey, in the early 1680s with his brother Henry, who died in 1689, leaving only one son, John. In 1717, this same John was named as guardian to a Henry Chamberlin. This record indicates that Henry was a minor, assumed to be between the age of 14 and 21 years (hence born between 1697 and 1703).

The William who made his will in 1770, named a number of sons including one James Chamberlin. This son James had land surveyed in Monmouth County as early as 1741. Assuming James to be at least of legal age to engage in land transactions yield a birth date for him at least as early as 1720. In addition, other evidence indicates that James was the eldest son of his father. Thus, his father William was probably born before 1700.

An exhaustive search of all available records for New Jersey, and in particular, Monmouth County and the East and West Jersey Proprietor's records has revealed that Henry, William, John, and Henry Chamberlin were the only men of this surname mentioned from 1668 (the date that Monmouth county was organized) until the guardianship record of 1717.

It is known conclusively that John (born about 1688) was the only son of Henry and his wife Anne (West) Chamberlin. Thus, it appears logical from the preponderance of evidence, that the William who made his will in 1765 and the Henry whose guardianship was recorded in 1717, could only be sons of the earlier William Chamberlin. Both the names of William and Henry persisted for many generations in the descendants of both Henry and William the younger.

Thus, until further information comes to light, it will be tentatively assumed that the William of this record, born about 1694 (?), in Shrewsbury Twp., Monmouth Co., N.J., was a son of William[3] (John[2], Henry[1]) Chamberlin, a third generation descendant of Henry Chamberlin, Blacksmith, of Hingham, MA, 1638/39."

Family Group Record Examples

Example 2

"Thomas Blake Smith usually went by the name Howard or T.H. Smith in later life. In the 1850 and 1860 censuses, his name is given as Thomas B. No proof that his middle name was "Blake," but the continuing use of the initial "B" in his name, and his mothers maiden name being Blake points to it. However, Aunt Sally's records list a child "Biddle" in his father's family, that cannot otherwise be identified. Her list of children for this man's father matches the known list with the child Biddle in the same family position as this man. Hence, it is believed that "Biddle" was perhaps this man's nickname when a child. Another possibility is that his middle name was Biddle and not Blake."

Example 3

The following example was chosen to illustrate the kind of problems that often arise when comparing sources.

"Tullidge's *History of Utah*, (Vol. 2, pp. 211-214; 1889), contains a biographical sketch of Nathaniel Brown as given by his son George Washington Brown (1827-1906). In this sketch, George Brown related many incidents of his father's life, including the statement:

> 'After the war [War of 1812] my father betook himself to the woods. He went to the headwaters of the river St. Clair, and began the manufacture of shingles...'

The headwaters of the St. Clair are located near the present-day city of Port Huron, Michigan. The St. Clair river issues forth from the southern end of Lake Huron and flows southward about 42 miles where it empties into Lake St. Clair. As such, it forms the boundary between St. Clair County, Michigan, and the Canadian (then British) Province of Ontario. Isaac Brown, eldest surviving son of Nathaniel Brown, was born in this region according to several other sources, including information given by himself. A final passage about Nathaniel Brown from the sketch in the *History of Utah* reads:

> 'He died in 1837, in the fiftieth year of his age, at his home near the head waters of the river St. Clair, in Michigan.'

Family Group Record Examples

This statement conflicts with information given in the records of the Ambrosia Branch of the Mormon church. In May 1838, Nathaniel's widow became a convert to the Mormon church. By September 1840, she and her children were in Lee county, Iowa, near the town of Montrose, living in a Mormon settlement known as the "Ambrosia Branch" (not formally organized until 14 Sep 1844).

The Ambrosia record of the Brown family gives the following (abbreviated) birth information for the four youngest (surviving) children: George A., 1827, Newbury, Cuyahoga Co., OH; James A., 1829, Mentor, Geauga Co., OH; Susan M., 1831, Erie, Erie Co., PA; Sidney W., 1836, Fredonia, Chautauqua Co., NY. (This information has also been corroborated by several other sources.) We also know that Avis and her children were living in Chautauqua county in May 1838.

These facts indicate that beginning in the early 1820s, Nathaniel Brown and his family began a slow migration from the St. Clair region in Michigan, southerly to the northwestern part of Ohio, and thence eastward along the southern shores of Lake Erie through Ohio, Erie county, Pennsylvania, and into Chautauqua county, N.Y.

From other information given by George W. Brown, we know that Nathaniel had sustained a number of serious injuries in his last years which all but incapacitated him. In light of these facts, it does not seem possible nor logical, that Nathaniel could have left Chautauqua county after September 1836, to travel some 300 miles across the frontier back to the headwaters of the St. Clair river; a region he had left some 15 or 16 years previously, and then die almost immediately afterwards.

No death record of Nathaniel Brown has ever been found. It is difficult to understand why Nathaniel's son George could be mistaken about where his father died, but in light of the other evidence, there can really be no doubt that the *History of Utah* is in error on this point. Possibly the error is due to the manner in which the information from George Brown was communicated to the author of the *History of Utah*, who probably wrote the article from notes made during an interview with George Brown. Thus, the discrepancy could be attributed to faulty notes, etc.

Based upon the foregoing analysis, the place of Nathaniel's death will be given as Chautauqua Co., N.Y., until such time as other information either confirms or refutes this assumption."

Example 4

This example, which is a true story, uses an indirect approach in the analysis of available information to trace a person's place of origin in the absence of definite information. The following analysis could be considered as a basis for future research on this particular family.

"Henry Chamberlin, Blacksmith, first appears in America at Hingham, MA, on 17 Feb 1638/39, when he was received as a townsman. He was accompanied by his wife and at least six children. A record of Henry's emigration to the New World has not been found in any of the extant ship's passenger lists nor in any of the emigration records in England. None of the records of this man and his family in New England give the slightest clue as to his place of origin (assumed to be England). The task at hand is to develop some approach or line of research that may yield some clue to solve this problem.

Henry was a Blacksmith, a skilled craftsman that was very much in demand in those days. He was given a generous allotment of land grants in Hingham by the Proprietors. He was made a Freeman of the Massachusetts Bay Colony on 13 Mar 1639, by the General Court. These facts indicated that while probably not wealthy, he was definitely a man of obvious means and high standing in the community. Virtually all of the property he received from the town in 1638/39 was not conveyed until after his death in 1674.

This information suggests that Henry did not just "wander into the town of Hingham." He probably arrived in America during the late summer or fall of 1638. In August 1638, a large group of people did come to Hingham, MA, from Hingham, England. (Among this group was another Henry Chamberlin, a shoemaker, who does not appear to be related to the man of this discussion, Henry Chamberlin, Blacksmith.)

Examination and analysis of the extant records in Hingham, England, make no specific mention of him, which suggests that he did not come from this place. After arriving in Massachusetts, Henry Chamberlin and his family may have lived temporarily in another town near Hingham or perhaps with another family in Hingham until he was officially received by the town (during the winter of 1638/39). Logic says that he undoubtedly came to Hingham because he probably knew some people already living there, or perhaps was even related to them. In many, many instances, people that were involved in migrations, either from Europe to America or just westward across America, usually did so in groups or with people they knew in their former residence.

The Hingham Proprietor's records contain a very good list of the town's inhabitants at this time. Other sources provide the names of the people who emigrated from Hingham, England, in 1638. By comparing these two lists, it should be a relatively simple matter to derive a list of the town's inhabitants who did not come from Hingham, England.

These remaining families could be checked against other records in New England, especially passenger lists and records of emigration from England, for possible clues as to their English origins. Of course, there are no guarantees this approach will work, and it is definitely a "long shot," but it just might work. All English jurisdictions thus identified, could then be examined in detail for possible clues or references to Henry Chamberlin, etc.

Family Group Record Examples

FGR REFERENCES

Figure D-6 shows a format with the Source Extraction file numbers in the left-hand column followed by a description of the source.

PREPARATION OF THIS RECORD

This record was prepared by James H. Jones, 134 S.W. Adams Street, Peoria, IL 61602, using data obtained from various sources as listed. Comments and additional information are welcome. This FGR last updated on 10 Jan 1996.

References

SE	Description
5	Family Bible of William F. Thomson, in possession of Mr. Robert S. Evans, 2495 East Bates Avenue, Denver, CO 80210 (1978).
13	Personal Knowledge of Mrs. Lucille S. Young, 492 North 13th Street, Red Bluff, CA 96080 (1990).
17	Gravestone Inscriptions, Old Waretown Cemetery, Waretown, N.J., copied by Donald F. Gray, 401 Dowd Avenue, Elizabeth, N.J. 07206, 21 May 1984.
28	Letter to Samuel D. Tompkins from Andrew C. Moore, Jersey City, N.J., 18 July 1872, in possession of Mrs. Laura L. Anderson, Route 3, Box 139, Talent, OR 97540 (1989).
31	History of the Town of Hingham, MA. Published by the town, 1893; three volumes in four; Library Call No. 974.482/H1. Vol. 3, pp. 178-182.
42	Essex County, Massachusetts, Records of the Probate Court, 1638-1881; Essex County Court House, Register of Probate, Salem, MA; Index to the Probate Docket, Vols. 9-12, K-Ri, 1638-1840. Family History Library (35 North West Temple, Salt Lake City) Film No. 0860478, pp. 138-39.
69	U.S. Federal Census, Licking County, Ohio, Hartford Twp., National Archives Microcopy, M-19, Roll. No. 134; Family History Library (35 North West Temple, Salt Lake City) Film No. 337,945, P. 486.
104	Monmouth County, New Jersey, Deeds, Vol. M, 1800-1802. Maintained and housed at the Monmouth County Clerk's Office, Freehold, N.J.; Family History Library (35 North West Temple, Salt Lake City) Film No. 0592651, pp. 387-93.

[DISK ID LN25]

Figure D-6. FGR References Section Example

Family Group Record Examples

This format is more suitable when you wish to use the Source Numbers as footnote references throughout the FGR. The order or grouping of references depends somewhat upon their bulk. If you have very few references, say less than ten, the order is not going to be critical. If on the other hand, you have quite a number of references it would be advisable to list them in order by the Source Extraction file as shown here.

Figure D-7 shows an example of using Source Numbers as footnote subscripts in an FGR Parent's section to identify the specific source(s) for this information. A partial and abbreviated listing of the sources cited is also shown:

	LN
HUSBAND: Levi^6 Anderson $_{1,3}$	45
Father: Samuel^5 Anderson $_{1,3}$	66
Mother: Abigail $_{1,3}$	67
Born: 18 Apr 1808, Amwell Twp., Hunterdon Co., N.J. $_{1,3,8}$	
Died: 10 July 1878, Hightstown, Mercer Co., N.J. $_3$	
Buried: Methodist Church Burying Ground, Mercer Co., N.J. $_8$	
Married: (1) 11 Apr 1832, Sparta, Sussex Co., N.J. $_3$	
Other Marriages: (2) Mrs. Alice Duckworth, 17 May 1845, Mercer Co., N.J. $_{3,5}$	
	LN
WIFE: Joanna Conover $_{3,19}$	123
Father: Thomas Conover $_{3,19}$	124
Mother: Samantha Roberts $_{3,19}$	125
Born: 9 Aug 1811, Probably Sussex Co., N.J. $_3$	
Died: 16 Dec 1844, West Windsor Twp., Mercer Co., N.J. $_{3,8}$	
Buried: Methodist Church Burying Ground, Mercer Co., N.J. $_8$	
Other Marriages:	

SE	Description
1	Some of the Descendants of Nicholas Anderson, [Etc.]
3	Family bible of Levi Anderson, [Etc.]
5	Marriage Records, Mercer County, N.J., Book A, pp. 45-46, [Etc.]
8	Sexton's Records, Methodist Church Burying Ground, [Etc.]
19	Will of Thomas Conover, [Etc.]

Figure D-7. Linking FGR References to Key Events

Family Group Record Examples

By using the Source Numbers as subscripts they cannot be confused with the superscripted generation numbers which you may be using. This method allows you to place these subscripts wherever applicable to reference the source or sources that apply to a particular bit of information. With your references listed in numerical order by Source Number it is an easy matter to quickly identify and immediately retrieve your pertinent Source Extraction file(s).

Pedigree Chart Numbering — E

This appendix supplements the material in Chapter 7, *Genealogical Charts and Numbering,* by providing tables to help you find the correct numbers for extending pedigree charts and provides an introduction to numbering systems. Table E-1 gives the equivalents for powers of two for a selected range of values.

Table E-1. Powers of 2[1]

$2^0 = 1$	$2^8 = 256$	$2^{15} = 35,768$
$2^1 = 2$	$2^9 = 512$	$2^{16} = 65,536$
$2^2 = 4$	$2^{10} = 1,024$	$2^{17} = 130,072$
$2^3 = 8$	$2^{11} = 2,048$	$2^{18} = 262,144$
$2^4 = 16$	$2^{12} = 4,096$	$2^{19} = 524,288$
$2^5 = 32$	$2^{13} = 8,192$	$2^{20} = 1,048,576$
$2^6 = 64$	$2^{14} = 16,284$	$2^{21} = 2,097,152$

NUMBERING FROM THE FIRST CHART

Table E-2 shows the extended chart numbers from the first chart in the pedigree which has been identified as Chart No. 0 (zero). The numbers in the Chart 0 column are the 16 Ancestors, Nos. 15-30, with the corresponding extension chart number in the adjacent column. Thus, if you are extending ancestor 18 (fourth line), the correct extension chart number is 4.

---

[1] A number raised to the zero power is always equal to one. A number raised to the first power is always equal to the number itself; i.e., $2^1 = 2$, $8^1 = 8$, $16^1 = 16$, and so forth.

Pedigree Chart Numbering

Use Table E-3 if you have identified your first chart as No. 1. The calculated numbers in the following tables are based upon the standard four-generation pedigree chart.

Table E-2.   Extended Pedigree Chart Numbers (First Chart No. 0)

Chart 0	Ext. Chart
15 (1st)	1
16 (2nd)	2
17 (3rd)	3
18 (4th)	4
19 (5th)	5
20 (6th)	6
21 (7th)	7
22 (8th)	8

Chart 0	Ext. Chart
23 (9th)	9
24 (10th)	10
25 (11th)	11
26 (12th)	12
27 (13th)	13
28 (14th)	14
29 (15th)	15
30 (16th)	16

Table E-3.   Extended Pedigree Chart Numbers (First Chart No. 1)

Chart 1	Ext. Chart
16 (1st)	2
17 (2nd)	3
18 (3rd)	4
19 (4th)	5
20 (5th)	6
21 (6th)	7
22 (7th)	8
23 (8th)	9

Chart 1	Ext. Chart
24 (9th)	10
25 (10th)	11
26 (11th)	12
27 (12th)	13
28 (13th)	14
29 (14th)	15
30 (15th)	16
31 (16th)	17

As shown in Tables E-2 and E-3, the numbering for the first 16 extension charts is very straight-forward. Remember that your first chart shows the first four ancestral generations; the next 16 charts show generations five through eight, the next 256 charts show generations nine through 12, and so forth.

Pedigree Chart Numbering

As you proceed to succeeding generations, the numbering becomes more involved because the extension numbers increase exponentially according to the power of 16 for each set of four generations.

EXTENDED CHART NUMBERING

To clarify the foregoing discussion, let's call generations one through four, *Range A*, generations five through eight, *Range B*, generations nine through 12, *Range C*, and generations 13 through 16, *Range D*, and so forth. Consider the ranges as the sequence of charts for a four-generation grouping. Table E-4 defines the mathematical relationships between the first six ranges which are also illustrated in Figure E-1.

Table E-4. Chart Grouping by Ranges

Range	Generations	Number of Charts in Range	Cumulative Number of Charts	Number of Ancestral Extensions[‡]
A	1-4	1 (16^0)	1	16
B	5-8	16 (16^1)	17	256
C	9-12	256 (16^2)	273	4,096
D	13-16	4,096 (16^3)	4,369	65,536
E	17-20	65,536 (16^4)	69,905	1,048,576
F	21-24	1,048,576 (16^5)	1,118,481	16,777,216

[‡] The number of ancestral extensions refers to the total within the entire range.

Chart Numbers From Tables

Table E-5, arranged by ranges as previously described, will enable you to directly find the correct chart extension numbers for the first 16 generations. The numbers in Table E-5 were computed on the basis of the first pedigree chart being identified as No. 0 (zero). If you identified your first chart as No. 1, you must add a one (1) to the numbers in Table E-5.

Pedigree Chart Numbering

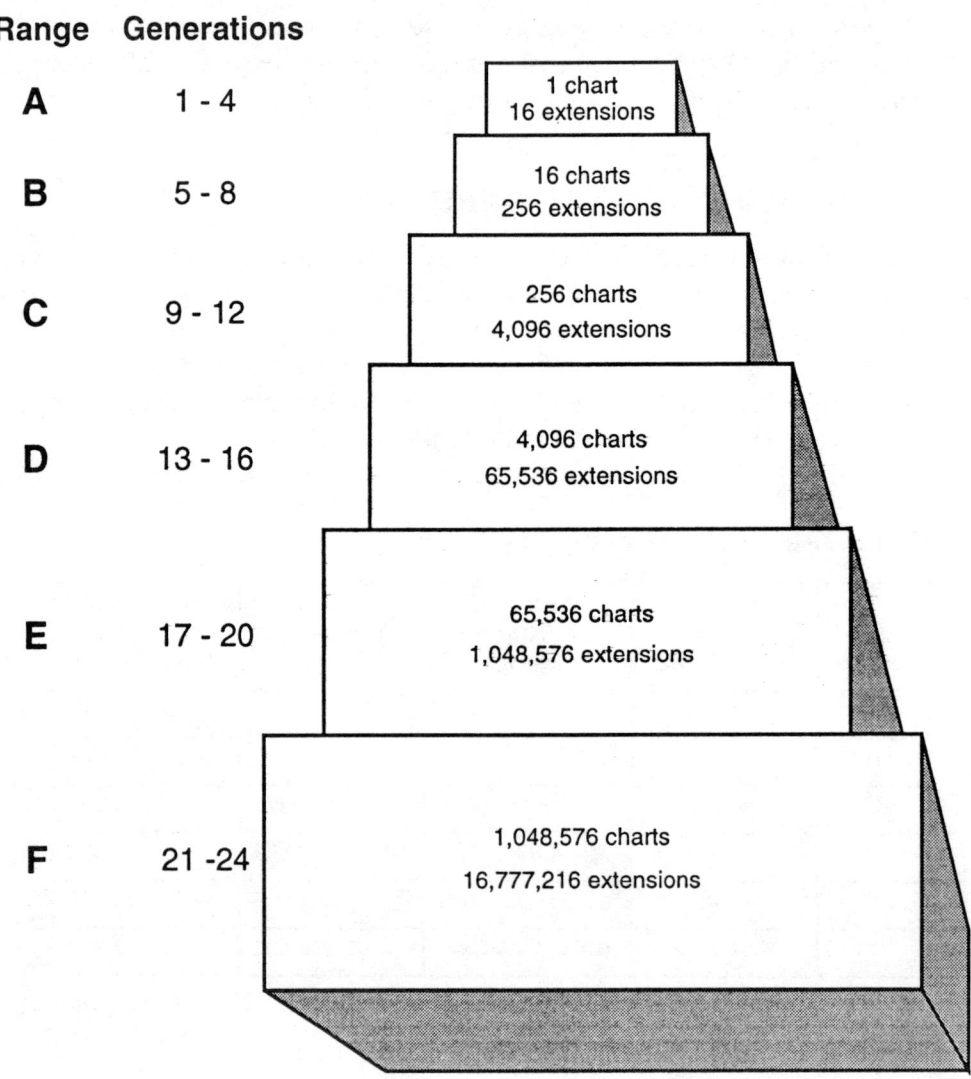

Figure E-1. Chart and Range Relationships

Table E-5. Pedigree Chart Numbers for Ranges C and D

B	Anc. Ext. Line	C	D	B	Anc. Ext. Line	C	D
1	1st	17	273	3	1st	49	785
	2nd	18	289		2nd	50	801
	3rd	19	305		3rd	51	817
	4th	20	321		4th	52	833
	5th	21	337		5th	53	849
	6th	22	353		6th	54	865
	7th	23	369		7th	55	881
	8th	24	385		8th	56	897
	9th	25	401		9th	57	913
	10th	26	417		10th	58	929
	11th	27	433		11th	59	945
	12th	28	449		12th	60	961
	13th	29	465		13th	61	977
	14th	30	481		14th	62	993
	15th	31	497		15th	63	1,009
	16th	32	513		16th	64	1,025
2	1st	33	529	4	1st	65	1,041
	2nd	34	545		2nd	66	1,057
	3rd	35	561		3rd	67	1,073
	4th	36	577		4th	68	1,089
	5th	37	593		5th	69	1,105
	6th	38	609		6th	70	1,121
	7th	39	625		7th	71	1,137
	8th	40	641		8th	72	1,153
	9th	41	657		9th	73	1,169
	10th	42	673		10th	74	1,185
	11th	43	689		11th	75	1,201
	12th	44	705		12th	76	1,217
	13th	45	721		13th	77	1,233
	14th	46	737		14th	78	1,249
	15th	47	753		15th	79	1,265
	16th	48	769		16th	80	1,281

Table E-5. Pedigree Chart Numbers for Ranges C and D (Continued)

B	Anc. Ext. Line	C	D	B	Anc. Ext. Line	C	D
5	1st	81	1,297	7	1st	113	1,809
	2nd	82	1,313		2nd	114	1,825
	3rd	83	1,329		3rd	115	1,841
	4th	84	1,345		4th	116	1,857
	5th	85	1,361		5th	117	1,873
	6th	86	1,377		6th	118	1,889
	7th	87	1,393		7th	119	1,905
	8th	88	1,409		8th	120	1,921
	9th	89	1,425		9th	121	1,937
	10th	90	1,441		10th	122	1,953
	11th	91	1,457		11th	123	1,969
	12th	92	1,473		12th	124	1,985
	13th	93	1,489		13th	125	2,001
	14th	94	1,505		14th	126	2,017
	15th	95	1,521		15th	127	2,033
	16th	96	1,537		16th	128	2,049
6	1st	97	1,553	8	1st	129	2,065
	2nd	98	1,569		2nd	130	2,081
	3rd	99	1,585		3rd	131	2,097
	4th	100	1,601		4th	132	2,113
	5th	101	1,617		5th	133	2,129
	6th	102	1,633		6th	134	2,145
	7th	103	1,649		7th	135	2,161
	8th	104	1,665		8th	136	2,177
	9th	105	1,681		9th	137	2,193
	10th	106	1,697		10th	138	2,209
	11th	107	1,713		11th	139	2,225
	12th	108	1,729		12th	140	2,241
	13th	109	1,745		13th	141	2,257
	14th	110	1,761		14th	142	2,273
	15th	111	1,777		15th	143	2,289
	16th	112	1,793		16th	144	2,305

Table E-5. Pedigree Chart Numbers for Ranges C and D (Continued)

B	Anc. Ext. Line	C	D	B	Anc. Ext. Line	C	D
9	1st	145	2,321	11	1st	177	2,833
	2nd	146	2,337		2nd	178	2,849
	3rd	147	2,353		3rd	179	2,865
	4th	148	2,369		4th	180	2,881
	5th	149	2,385		5th	181	2,897
	6th	150	2,401		6th	182	2,913
	7th	151	2,417		7th	183	2,929
	8th	152	2,433		8th	184	2,945
	9th	153	2,449		9th	185	2,961
	10th	154	2,465		10th	186	2,977
	11th	155	2,481		11th	187	2,993
	12th	156	2,497		12th	188	3,009
	13th	157	2,513		13th	189	3,025
	14th	158	2,529		14th	190	3,041
	15th	159	2,545		15th	191	3,057
	16th	160	2,561		16th	192	3,073
10	1st	161	2,577	12	1st	193	3,089
	2nd	162	2,593		2nd	194	3,105
	3rd	163	2,609		3rd	195	3,121
	4th	164	2,625		4th	196	3,137
	5th	165	2,641		5th	197	3,153
	6th	166	2,657		6th	198	3,169
	7th	167	2,673		7th	199	3,185
	8th	168	2,689		8th	200	3,201
	9th	169	2,705		9th	201	3,217
	10th	170	2,721		10th	202	3,233
	11th	171	2,737		11th	203	3,249
	12th	172	2,753		12th	204	3,265
	13th	173	2,769		13th	205	3,281
	14th	174	2,785		14th	206	3,297
	15th	175	2,801		15th	207	3,313
	16th	176	2,817		16th	208	3,329

Table E-5. Pedigree Chart Numbers for Ranges C and D (Continued)

B	Anc. Ext. Line	C	D	B	Anc. Ext. Line	C	D
13	1st	209	3,345	15	1st	241	3,857
	2nd	210	3,361		2nd	242	3,873
	3rd	211	3,377		3rd	243	3,889
	4th	212	3,393		4th	244	3,905
	5th	213	3,409		5th	245	3,921
	6th	214	3,425		6th	246	3,937
	7th	215	3,441		7th	247	3,953
	8th	216	3,457		8th	248	3,969
	9th	217	3,473		9th	249	3,985
	10th	218	3,489		10th	250	4,001
	11th	219	3,505		11th	251	4,017
	12th	220	3,521		12th	252	4,033
	13th	221	3,537		13th	253	4,049
	14th	222	3,553		14th	254	4,065
	15th	223	3,569		15th	255	4,081
	16th	224	3,585		16th	256	4,097
14	1st	225	3,601	16	1st	257	4,113
	2nd	226	3,617		2nd	258	4,129
	3rd	227	3,633		3rd	259	4,145
	4th	228	3,649		4th	260	4,161
	5th	229	3,665		5th	261	4,177
	6th	230	3,681		6th	262	4,193
	7th	231	3,697		7th	263	4,209
	8th	232	3,713		8th	264	4,225
	9th	233	3,729		9th	265	4,241
	10th	234	3,745		10th	266	4,257
	11th	235	3,761		11th	267	4,273
	12th	236	3,777		12th	268	4,289
	13th	237	3,793		13th	269	4,305
	14th	238	3,809		14th	270	4,321
	15th	239	3,825		15th	271	4,337
	16th	240	3,841		16th	272	4,353

The numbers in Ranges B and C are consecutive; the numbers in Range D are in increments of 16. (The difference between any two consecutive numbers in Range D is 16. See *Argument* in the Glossary.) The first number in Range D is the number of the *first ancestral extension line* for the corresponding chart number in Range C. Once you have the first ancestral extension number in Range D, it is a simple matter of counting down to obtain the correct number for the desired ancestral extension from Range C.

If Range E were shown, its increments would be 256; Range F increments would be 4,096, and so forth. Because of the rapid increase in the size of the table increments, the calculations required to interpolate these values are more cumbersome and prone to error than if you just used one of the formulas derived in Chapter 7, *Computing Pedigree Chart Numbers*. For this reason, the higher ranges of numbers are not shown.

Chart Numbering Examples

As an example, assume that you want to begin your chart numbering with No. 0, and further suppose you have been working on your pedigree and have an ancestral line as described thusly:

Range A	Range B	Range C	Range D
First Chart	2nd Chart	3rd Chart	4th Chart
11th Extension	7th Extension	5th Extension	14th Extension

In Range A, the 11th ancestral extension connects to Chart No. 11 (Table E-2) in Range B. The 7th ancestral extension from Chart No. 11 connects to Chart No. 183 (Range C, Table E-5), adjacent to Chart No. 2,929 in Range D. As previously defined, the number in Range D, adjacent to the number in Range C, is for the 1st ancestral extension. Because we are interested in the 5th ancestral extension, we must add five to the value in Range D (2,929 + 5) obtain the correct value. Thus, the 5th ancestral extension from Chart No. 183 connects to Chart No. 2,934.

Using Formula 3, derived in Chapter 7, we would proceed as follows:

(3) $16C + 1 = N$
   $16 \times 2{,}934 + 1 = N$
   $46{,}944 + 1 = 46{,}944$ (the number of the first ancestral extension).
   $46{,}944 + 14 = 46{,}958$, the correct chart number for the 14th ancestral extension.

If you had identified your first chart as No. 1, then you would have to use Table E-3 and add a one to the values in E-5 to obtain the correct number. You also have to use Formula 2 (See Chapter 7, *Computing Pedigree Chart Numbers*.)

NUMBERING SYSTEMS

As briefly mentioned in Chapter 7, binary or hexadecimal numbers have been proposed for use in numbering pedigree charts. I do not endorse their use for the simple reason that so few people will be familiar with or comfortable using them.

However, the following discussion may be useful for those who wish to know something about numbering systems in general, but with a focus on binary and hexadecimal numbers. It is not the intent here to present an in-depth description of this subject, which is quite beyond the scope of this book. Those who wish to pursue the subject further can find many excellent books available to study.

The following material should provide sufficient information to enable you to use and understand binary and hexadecimal numbers, while still keeping the mathematics simple. An elementary knowledge of algebra should enable you to understand the following discussion with little or no difficulty.

Positional Notation

Positional notation is a form of notation in which the value of a particular numeral depends not only on the numeral which is written, but also on the position of the numeral within the number. For example, the decimal whole number 3,333 may be expressed as a series of powers of 10 as follows:

$$3 \times 10^3 + 3 \times 10^2 + 3 \times 10^1 + 3 \times 10^0 = 3,000 + 300 + 30 + 3 = 3,333$$

Because the digit at the right represents the smallest quantity of the number, it is called the least significant digit (LSD). The digit at the left, which represents the greatest quantity of the number, is called the most significant digit (MSD).

Fractional numbers may also be expanded in a similar power series. For example, the fraction 0.1713 can be expressed as:

$$1 \times 10^{-1} + 7 \times 10^{-2} + 1 \times 10^{-3} + 3 \times 10^{-4}$$

Radix

Each system of positional notation has a radix, which is defined as the base of the power series which represents the number. A power series can be expressed in the following general form:

$$\ldots + aN^4 + bN^3 + cN^2 + dN^1 + eN^0 + fN^{-1} + gN^{-2} \ldots$$

In this series, N is the radix and the coefficients *a* through *g* are the characters of the number. When N is equal to 2, the series is a binary number; when N is equal to 8, the series is an octal number; when N is equal to 10, the series is a decimal number, and when N is equal to 16, the series is a hexadecimal number, and so forth.

Pedigree Chart Numbering

The characteristics of a radix are as follows:

1. The radix of an enumeration system is equal to the total number of different characters which are used in the system. The binary system, with a radix of 2, has only two characters which are the numerals 0 and 1.

2. The value of the radix is always one unit greater than the largest basic character that is used. This is because the radix is equal to the total number of the characters which are used wherein the numbering always starts from zero. For example, the octal system which has a radix of 8, uses the numerals 0, 1, 2, 3, 4, 5, 6, and 7.

3. Positional notation does not, in itself, indicate the radix. The quantity 312 could represent a number expressed in octal (base 8), decimal (base 10), or in any system that has a radix of 4 or greater. Binary numbers are usually recognizable by the repetitive appearance of only the numerals 0 and 1.

4. To prevent confusion, numbers that are not written in the decimal system sometimes have the radix appear as a decimal number subscript, similar to the following octal number:

    3157_8

Counting

The rules for the counting of numbers that are written in a system of positional notation are the same for every radix. The octal system which follows, is used as an example.

> Starting from 0, add 1 to the least significant digit until all of the basic characters have been used:
>
> ... 0, 1, 2, 3, 4, 5, 6, 7, ...

Because 7 is the largest character in the octal system, the next consecutive number that is larger than 7 requires two digits. The series of two-digit numbers starts with 0 as the least significant and 1 as the most significant digit:

... 6, 7, 10, 11, 12, 13, 14, 15, 16, 17, ...

When a digit reaches its maximum value (7, in this case), replace the digit with 0 and add 1 to the next most significant digit:

... 16, 17, 20, 21, ... 26, 27, 30, 31, ... 36, 37, 40, 41, ...

When two or more consecutive digits reach the maximum value, replace each digit with 0 and add 1 to the next most significant digit:

... 76, 77, 100, 101, ... 176, 177, ... 200, ... 776, 777, ... 1000, ...

The radix in any system of enumeration is always represented by the two-digit number 10. This is true because the radix of a system is always one unit larger than the largest character used in the system, and by the rules of counting, its value is written as 10.

For example:

Binary 10	=	2	The radix of the binary system.
Octal 10	=	8	The radix of the octal system.
Decimal 10	=	10	The radix of the decimal system.
Hexadecimal 10	=	16	The radix of the hexadecimal system.

Multiplication and Division by Radix

Any number of a system may easily be multiplied or divided by the radix of the system. When a number is multiplied by 10 in the decimal system, the decimal point is moved one place to the right:

3456.0 × 10 = 345.60

When the same decimal number is divided by 10, the decimal point is moved one place to the left:

$$3456.0 \div 10 = 345.6$$

In a like fashion, a binary number is multiplied by 2 when the binary point is moved one place to the right:

$$10101.0 \times 2 = 101010$$

And when the same binary number is divided by 2, the binary point is moved one place to the left:

$$0101.0 \div 2 = 1010.10$$

These equations can be verified by computing the decimal equivalents of the binary numbers.

NUMBER STRUCTURE

A number may consist of two parts: the integer, or whole number (the part of the number equal to or greater than 1); and the fraction (the part of the number that is less than 1). This section deals only with integers because fractional numbers are of no consequence in genealogical numbering.

Equivalent Numbers

If two numbers that are written in different number systems represent the same magnitude, the numbers are said to be equivalent. That is, the two numbers are actually equal, even though they are not composed of the same digits. For example, the octal number 11 is equal to the decimal number 9.

There are two characteristics of equivalent numbers that may be of interest:

1. Consider a pair of equivalent numbers, such as octal 11 and decimal 9. Both of these numbers may be multiplied by 2, and the products of the multiplication will still be equivalent. Both of the original numbers may be divided by 5 and, again, the quotients of the division will be equivalent. Any arithmetic operation which is performed equally on both of the equivalent numbers will yield two equivalent numbers.

2. When two numbers are equivalent, two separate equations can be stated concerning the numbers. The integral part of one number is equal to the integral part of the other number; and the fractional part of one number is equal to the fractional part of the other number. Any change which retains the equivalence of the original numbers will result in a new pair of equivalent integers and a new pair of equivalent fractions. By the use of the equality of the parts of numbers, it is possible to convert numbers that are expressed in any number system to any other number system; that is, to change the radixes of the numbers.

Binary Numbers

Binary numbers are the foundation of all computer architecture because they have only two basic characters or numerals, (0 and 1), in contrast to the decimal system which has 10 basic numerals (0, 1, 2, 3, 4, 5, 6, 7, 8, and 9). In the binary system, all numbers are represented by combinations or groups of the numerals 0 and 1.

These characteristics are easily represented in an electronic digital system or computer by the two stable states of a bistable electronics element. Because there are many simple electronic devices which possess two stable states, information represented by binary numbers can easily be electronically generated, transferred, transformed, and stored. Moreover, such binary electronic devices are very economical and easily manufactured.

Pedigree Chart Numbering

Conversely, the 10 numerals of the decimal system would require the use of electronic elements having 10 stable states. Devices which would possess 10 stable states have not been economically feasible to design and manufacture because of their inherent complexity. For these reasons, computers and other digital systems use the binary number system.

Although the binary system has the advantage of only requiring two characters, it generally requires the use of more digits than its decimal equivalents. In general, a binary number requires between three and three and one-half times as many digits as the equivalent decimal number. For example, the decimal number 32 (2 digits) is the equivalent of the binary number 100000 (6 digits).

DECIMAL-BINARY EQUIVALENTS

In the binary system, which has a radix of 2, the position of a digit in a number shows the power of 2 by which that digit must be multiplied to indicate its magnitude. For example, the binary whole number 10101 may be written in the power series form as:

$$1 \times 2^4 + 0 \times 2^3 + 1 \times 2^2 + 0 \times 2^1 + 1 \times 2^0 = 10101$$

Evaluating this expression gives:

$$16 + 0 + 4 + 0 + 1 = 21$$

This example shows that the binary number 10101 is equal to the decimal number 21. Table E-6 lists binary and decimal equivalent pairs up to decimal 15. Note that the binary numbers, which use the two characters 0 and 1, follow the rules for counting as previously discussed.

Table E-6. Decimal-binary Equivalents

Decimal Count	Binary Count
0	0000
1	0001
2	0010
3	0011
4	0100
5	0101
6	0110
7	0111

Decimal Count	Binary Count
8	1000
9	1001
10	1010
11	1011
12	1100
13	1101
14	1110
15	1111

Table E-7 shows powers of the base 2 up to the sixth power, and their decimal and binary equivalents. All binary numbers can be formed by grouping together the binary equivalents of the appropriate powers of the base 2.

Table E-7. Powers of 2 and Equivalents

Power of 2	Decimal Equivalent	Binary Equivalent
2^0	1	1
2^1	2	10
2^2	4	100
2^3	8	1000
2^4	16	10000
2^5	32	100000
2^6	64	1000000

BINARY TO DECIMAL CONVERSION

Binary integers can be converted to the equivalent decimal integers as follows:

1. Select the powers of the base 2 which are represented by a coefficient of 1 in the binary number.

2. Express each of these powers of the base 2 in the decimal equivalent. These are the partial decimal equivalents.

Consider the binary number 10111001 which is expressed in the following binary power series:

$$1 \times 2^7 + 0 \times 2^6 + 1 \times 2^5 + 1 \times 2^4 + 1 \times 2^3 + 0 \times 2^2 + 0 \times 2^1 + 1 \times 2^0$$

Evaluating this expression gives:

$$128 + 0 + 32 + 16 + 8 + 0 + 0 + 1 = 185$$

In this expression, 185 is the decimal equivalent of the original binary number, 10111001.

DECIMAL TO BINARY CONVERSION

Decimal integers can be converted to equivalent binary integers by performing a series of divisions, the rules of which, are as follows:

1. Divide the decimal number by 2 to obtain a quotient and a remainder.

2. Tabulate the remainder. The remainder is the LSD of the binary number. (When a number is divided by 2, the remainder can only be 0 or 1.)

3. The quotient in Step 1 now becomes a new dividend. Divide the new dividend by 2 to obtain a new quotient and remainder. (The remainder obtained in Step 1 is not included in the division.)

4. The remainder obtained in Step 3 is the next most significant digit.

5. Repeat the procedures given in Steps 3 and 4 above until the quotient is 0 and the remainder is 1. This final remainder is the MSD of the binary number.

To illustrate the preceding steps, the decimal number 117 will be converted to the equivalent binary number as shown in Table E-8.

Table E-8. Decimal to Binary Conversion

Decimal Number	Quotient	Remainder	Binary Equivalent
117 ÷ 2	58	1	1
58 ÷ 2	29	0	01
29 ÷ 2	14	1	101
14 ÷ 2	7	0	0101
7 ÷ 2	3	1	10101
3 ÷ 2	1	1	110101
1 ÷ 2	0	1	1110101

Thus, the binary number 1110101 is equivalent to the decimal number 117.

Hexadecimal Numbers

Hexadecimal numbers are common in the computer industry, because it is so much easier to use them in place of their binary equivalents which require so many more numerals. Because the hexadecimal base of 16 itself, is equal to the fourth power of 2, it is very easy to convert numbers back and forth between binary and hexadecimal. In this sense, hexadecimal is like a shorthand version of binary, which is the actual numbering system used in a digital computer.

DECIMAL-HEXADECIMAL EQUIVALENTS

In the hexadecimal system, which has a radix of 16, the position of a digit in a number shows the power of 16 by which that digit must be multiplied to indicate its magnitude. For example, the hexadecimal whole number 1028 may be written in the power series form as:

$$1 \times 16^3 + 0 \times 16^2 + 2 \times 16^1 + 8 \times 16^0$$

Evaluating this expression gives:

$$1 \times 4096 + 0 + 2 \times 16 + 8 \times 1 = 4,096 + 32 + 8 = 4136$$

This expression shows that the hexadecimal number 1028 is equal to the decimal number 4136. Table E-9 lists the hexadecimal and decimal equivalent pairs up to decimal 31.

Table E-9. Decimal-hexadecimal Equivalents

Decimal Count	Hexadecimal Count
0	0
1	1
2	2
3	3
4	4
5	5
6	6
7	7
8	8
9	9
10	A
11	B
12	C
13	D
14	E
15	F

Decimal Count	Hexadecimal Count
16	10
17	11
18	12
19	13
20	14
21	15
22	16
23	17
24	18
25	19
26	1A
27	1B
28	1C
29	1D
30	1E
31	1F

Table E-10 shows powers of the base 16 up to the eighth power, and their decimal and hexadecimal equivalents. All hexadecimal numbers can be formed by grouping together the hexadecimal equivalents of the appropriate powers of the base 16.

Table E-10. Powers of 16 With Decimal and Hexadecimal Equivalents

Powers of 16	Decimal Equivalent	Hexadecimal Equivalent
16^0	1	1
16^1	16	10
16^2	256	100
16^3	4,096	1,000
16^4	65,536	10,000
16^5	1,048,576	100,000
16^6	16,777,216	1,000,000
16^7	268,435,456	10,000,000
16^8	4,294,967,296	100,000,000

HEXADECIMAL TO DECIMAL CONVERSION

Hexadecimal integers can be converted to the equivalent decimal integers as follows:

1. Select the powers of the base 16 which are represented by a coefficient of 1 in the hexadecimal number.

2. Express each of these powers of the base 16 in the decimal equivalent. These are the partial decimal equivalents.

Consider the hexadecimal number 390A2, which is expressed in the following hexadecimal power series:

$$3 \times 16^4 + 9 \times 16^3 + 0 \times 16^2 + 10 \times 16^1 + 2 \times 16^0$$

Note that you must use the decimal equivalent of the *A* character (10) to evaluate the preceding expression which gives:

$$196,608 + 36,864 + 160 + 2 = 233,634$$

Thus, 233,634 is the decimal equivalent of the original hexadecimal number, 390A2.

DECIMAL TO HEXADECIMAL CONVERSION

Decimal integers can be converted to equivalent hexadecimal integers by performing a series of divisions, in the same manner as was described for decimal to binary conversion, except that the divisor is 16. The rules for decimal to hexadecimal conversion are as follows:

1. Divide the decimal number by 16 to obtain a quotient and a remainder.

2. Tabulate the remainder. The remainder is the LSD of the hexadecimal number.

3. The quotient in Step 1 now becomes a new dividend. Divide the new dividend by 16 to obtain a new quotient and remainder. (The remainder obtained in Step 1 is not included in the division.)

4. The remainder obtained in Step 3 is the next most significant digit.

5. Repeat the procedures given in Steps 3 and 4 above until the quotient is 0 and the remainder is less than 16. This final remainder is the MSD of the hexadecimal number.

Pedigree Chart Numbering

To summarize the preceding steps, the decimal number 32,768 will be converted to the equivalent hexadecimal number as shown in Table E-11.

Table E-11. Decimal to Hexadecimal Conversion

Decimal Number	Quotient	Remainder	Hexadecimal Equivalent
32,768 ÷ 16	2,048	0	0
2,048 ÷ 16	128	0	0
128 ÷ 16	8	0	0
8 ÷ 16	0	8	8

Thus, the hexadecimal number 8,000 is equivalent to the decimal number 32,768.

Conversions Between Binary and Hexadecimal Numbers

Converting numbers back and forth between binary and hexadecimal numbers is very easy because the base 16 is equal to the fourth power of 2 which eliminates the need for any involved multiplication or division procedures. Table E-12 lists the binary, decimal, and hexadecimal equivalents up to decimal 15 to facilitate the following procedures.

Table E-12. Decimal-binary-hexadecimal Equivalents

Decimal Count	Binary Count	Hex Count	Decimal Count	Binary Count	Hex Count
0	0000	0	8	1000	8
1	0001	1	9	1001	9
2	0010	2	10	1010	A
3	0011	3	11	1011	B
4	0100	4	12	1100	C
5	0101	5	13	1101	D
6	0110	6	14	1110	E
7	0111	7	15	1111	F

Pedigree Chart Numbering

BINARY TO HEXADECIMAL

For example, let us assume you have the binary number 11101010011. Separate these characters into groups of four digits, moving from right to left, as in the following:

0111 0101 0011

Note that we have added a 0 to complement the first group which does not change its value because it is the MSD of the expression. Table E-12, shows the decimal equivalent of the first group of binary numbers, 0111, to be 7. Similarly, the second group of binary numbers, 0101, equals 5; the third group, 0011, equals 3. Now write these decimal equivalents in same order as the groups of original binary numbers thusly:

0111 0101 0011 ⇒ 7 5 3 ⇒ 753

Thus, 753, is the hexadecimal equivalent of the original binary number 11101010011.

For another example, assume you have the binary number, 10101. Separating it into two groups of four digits and evaluating them gives:

0001 0101 ⇒ 1 5 ⇒ 15

Thus, 15, is the hexadecimal equivalent of the original binary number, 10101.

HEXADECIMAL TO BINARY

Assume you have the hexadecimal number 13F83. Separate these five characters into groups by inserting some space in between them as follows:

1 3 F 8 6

Pedigree Chart Numbering

Now write down the binary equivalents of these individual digits as found in Table E-12. (Remember that the character *F* is equal to decimal 15.) Arrange the binary equivalents in the same order as in the original hexadecimal number as follows:

0001 0011 1111 1000 0110

Thus, the binary number 10011111110000110, is the equivalent of the original hexadecimal number 13F86.

For a second example, assume you have the hexadecimal number 8DE. Separate these three digits into three groups and evaluate each group for its binary equivalent as in the following:

8 D E ⇒ 1000 1101 1110 ⇒ 100011011110

Thus, the binary number 100011011110, is the equivalent of the original hexadecimal number 8DE.

Glossary

The following definitions are provided to give you a better understanding of the special terms used in this book. Additional selected terms are listed that may be of use or interest. Each entry is generally categorized as follows:

- *Abbreviation; Genealogical.* General abbreviations commonly used in genealogical literature.

- *Abbreviation; Latin.* Selected Latin abbreviations that often appear in genealogical literature.

- *Computer Science.* Selected terms or words specifically related to the field of computer science.

- *Genealogy.* Words or terms commonly used in genealogical literature.

- *General.* Terms not specific to any one field of endeavor.

- *Latin.* Latin words or phrases commonly used in genealogical literature.

- *Mathematics.* Selected terms or words specifically related to the field of mathematics.

- *Special.* Special terms or words introduced in this book with their special meanings.

All of the glossary entries are also cross-referenced in the index under the foregoing categories.

Glossary

1790 Age Groups. *Genealogy*. In the 1790 federal census, each person in an enumerated family was placed in one of five categories according to age and other criteria according to the form: 1-1-1-0-0. An abbreviated definition of the five categories is:

Column 1	Free white males of 16 years and upwards, including Heads of Families.
Column 2	Free white males under 16 years.
Column 3	Free white females, including Heads of Families.
Column 4	All other free persons.
Column 5	Slaves

Acronym. *General* A word formed from the initial letters of a name, or by combining initial letters or parts of a series of words.

Address. *Computer Science*. A location in computer mass storage or memory.

Adm. *Abbreviation, Genealogical*. Administrator/Administration. A common term used in genealogy to indicate that an estate was administered upon, the administrator of an estate.

Ahnentafel. *Genealogy*. A German word that means *ancestor table*. The Ahnentafel number is used to denote an ancestor on a pedigree chart. The Ahnentafel number for a person's father is simply twice the value of the preceding number. The Ahnentafel number for the mother is twice the value of the preceding number plus one. See Sosa-Stradonitz system.

Aliq. *Abbreviation* [perhaps for *aliquant*.] Defined to mean: as in—assumed.

ante. *Latin*. Appearing before, having prior aspect. Before, in front, in front of, prior, precedent, earlier, etc.

Ancestral Chart. *Genealogy*. A chart that shows an individual's ancestors. See pedigree.

Ancestral Extension. *Special*. A pedigree chart that is being extended from another chart of preceding generations.

Glossary

Ancestral Genealogy. *Genealogy.* A genealogy that traces all the known ancestors of a given individual.

Architecture. *Computer Science.* In computer terminology, architecture most commonly refers to the design parameters of a computer system.

Argument. *Mathematics.* The independent variable of a function. The most common example is probably found in mathematical tables, wherein the value of any two numbers appearing in consecutive rows represent a constant value which is calculated from a mathematical function.

Aristotelian. *General* A person whose thinking and methods tend to be empirical or scientific.

b. *Abbreviation; Genealogical.* Born.

Bp. *Abbreviation; Genealogical.* Baptized. A Christian religious ceremony. This term is usually associated with a date and jurisdiction.

Base. *Mathematics.* The base of a power series which represents a number. Synonym for Radix.

Binary. *Mathematics.* Binary is a system of numbering with the base of 2 as its radix. All numbers in binary are represented by combinations or groups of the numerals 0 and 1.

Birth-order Numbering. *Genealogy.* A system using lower case Roman numerals to indicate the birth order of each child in a family.

Bit. *Computer Science.* A bit is a unit of information used by digital computers and represents the smallest piece of addressable memory within a computer. A bit expresses the choice between two possibilities. (binary 0 and 1 numerals). See Byte.

Boolean Logic. *Mathematics.* Named after George Boole who defined an algebra of logical operations such as AND and OR, on the two values of true and false statements. An AND operator will only allow the resulting condition to be True when all of its elements are True. An OR operator will allow the resulting condition to be True if any of its elements are True.

Glossary

Byte. *Computer Science.* A byte is the minimum amount of storage a computer requires to store one alphanumeric character. Each byte is comprised of a unique combination of eight bits (binary 0 and 1 numerals). See Bit.

Ca. *Abbreviation; Latin.* About. See Circa.

Chr. *Abbreviation; Genealogical.* Christened. A Christian religious ceremony. This term is usually associated with a date and jurisdiction.

Calendar. *General* Various systems of reckoning time in which the beginning, length, and divisions of a year are defined. The following is only the briefest summary of the calendar as it applies to recorded genealogical events that may be encountered in various European and American jurisdictions. Much more complete information and all technical details can be obtained from virtually any good encyclopedia.

The Julian calendar was imposed in the year 46 A.D., by the Roman emperor Julius Caesar. Because of its inherent inaccuracy, cumulative errors soon became noticeable within a few hundred years. The Venerable Bede, (673?-735) an Anglo-Saxon theologian and historian introduced the method of dating events from the birth of Christ using the notation "A.D." or Anno Domini which means: *In the Year of Our Lord.* In the year 730 A.D., Bede announced that the Julian calendar was already in error by more than five days, but nothing was done about it for the next 800 years.

In the year 1582, Pope Gregory, by Papal decree, ordered that the day following October 5th (St. Francis Day) was to be October 15th. The new calendar which became known as the Gregorian calendar was immediately instituted in Rome and the Italian states of Portugal and Spain. After this edict, Gregorian dates were often followed by the notation "N.S." or New Style. Other European countries slowly adopted the new calendar during the next 336 years.

In 1918, Russia was the last major country to make the change from the Julian calendar when the cumulative error amounted to 13 days. Many dates recorded after 1582 in countries still using the Julian Calendar were followed by the notation "O.S." or old style. Great Britain did not adopt the new calendar until 1752 when it was decreed that the day following September 2nd, 1752, would be September 15, 1752, a cumulative error of 12 days. See Double-dating.

Circa. *Latin.* About. Abbreviation: Ca.

Glossary

Computerize. *Computer Science.* A term that is used to mean organizing data into a specific format that is compatible in a computer environment usually a within computer applications such as word processing or relational database management.

d. *Abbreviation; Genealogical.* Died.

d.s.p. *Abbreviation; Latin.* See decessit sine prole.

d.s.p.m. *Abbreviation; Latin.* See decessit sine prole mascula.

Data Analysis & Evaluation. *Special.* A name that is given to the process of resolving discrepancies or differences between sources. A Data Analysis & Evaluation section within the Family Group Record provides a convenient forum for this process, as well as a good place to record remaining questions, leads to be followed, notes to yourself, comments, hunches, and ideas for future research, and so forth.

Data Compilation. *Special.* A phrase that refers to the process of combining data from various sources into a composite record. See Family Group Record (FGR).

Data Extraction. *Special.* A phrase that refers to the process of extracting desired data from a specific source or reference. See Source Extraction.

Data Storage & Retrieval. *Computer Science.* A phrase used to denote a computer process that stores information in a manner that can be easily retrieved. Synonymous with Information Storage & Retrieval.

Database. *Computer Science.* An organized collection of interrelated data that is stored according to a definite plan or design. In a generic sense, a database can be any collection of data, but without an organized structure it can never operate properly to permit sophisticated database functions.

Database Field. *Computer Science.* A field is represented as a column in a database table. A category of information, such as name or address. On a database form, a field is an area where data can be entered.

Database Management. *Computer Science.* A collection of software subsystems required for using a database; facilities for defining, maintaining, retrieving from, and updating a database.

Glossary

Database Query. *Computer Science.* A sophisticated technique that allows requested information from a relational database to be displayed in virtually any form or organization according to user-specified criteria.

Database Record. *Computer Science.* A set of information that belongs together, such as all the information on one person. A record is generally a single line or row of data with a varying number of fields or columns within a database table.

Database Record Format. *Computer Science.* The organization of fields or columns within a database record.

Database Table. *Computer Science.* A collection of data with the same subject or topic. A table stores data in records (rows) and fields (columns).

Date Modifier. *Special.* A term given to the use of the words *about, before, after,* and *between,* in connection with citing specific dates or years. The word *about* is also used in conjunction with special notation; (?) and (??) for additional precision.

Decessit sine prole. *Latin.* Died without offspring or issue. Abbreviation: d.s.p.

Decessit sine prole mascula. *Latin.* Died without male issue). Abbreviation: d.s.p.m.

Decimal. *Mathematics.* Decimal is a system of numbering with the base of 10 as its radix. All numbers in decimal are represented by combinations or groups of the numerals 0, 1, 2, 3, 4, 5, 6, 7, 8, and 9.

De facto. *Latin.* In reality or fact; actually. An unofficial standard.

Descendancy Chart. *Genealogy.* A chart that graphically depicts lines of descent from an ancestor or progenitor.

Descendancy Genealogy. *Genealogy.* A genealogy that attempts to trace all the descendants of a given pair of ancestors or progenitor to the present day.

Dewey Decimal Classification System. *General* A system of classifying books, maps, and other materials in a library. Originated by Melvil Dewey (1851-1931), an American librarian, in 1876.

Glossary

Double-dating. *Genealogy.* A system of expressing dates prior to 1752 in America and the British Colonies that occurred within the period of January through March 24th. Thus, a date occurring within this period was often expressed in the following form: 22 Feb 1732/33, 19 Jan 1697/98, 15 Mar 1743/44, and so forth. This situation came about because March 25th was the old New Year's Day in England from 1155 until the year 1752.

When the Julian calendar was imposed in 46 A.D., January 1st was the first day of the year. However during the succeeding centuries and certainly by the Middle Ages, most European countries had adopted March 25th as New Years Day. This day was the Christian Feast of the Annunciation Day, also known as Lady Day.

In England, before 1066 (the date of the Norman Conquest), the legal first day had been either March 25th or December 25th (Christmas Day). From 1087 to 1155, January 1st again became the legal first day of the year. From 1155 to 1752, Lady Day (March 25th) was again the first legal day of the new year. By 1564, France had restored January 1st as the first day of the year. Before 1582, the Papal States and most of the rest of Italy had observed Christmas Day as the first day of the year.

When the Gregorian Calendar was finally adopted by Great Britain in 1752, January 1st again became the first legal day of the year. Note however, that Scotland had already decreed January 1st as New Year's Day in 1600. Every genealogist must be made aware that possible dating errors may be made because of the constantly changing of New Year's Day and the imposition of the Gregorian calendar in 1582, occurring at different times in different countries. See calendar.

Equivalent Numbers. *Mathematics.* If two numbers that are written in different number systems represent the same magnitude, the numbers are said to be equivalent. That is, the two numbers are actually equal, even though they are not composed of the same digits.

ECK. *Special.* An acronym for ERA Correlation key.

Era. *Special.* The name given to either a single year or a range of years in a database record. See Era Correlation key.

Era Correlation Key. *Special.* The name given to a special character that is associated with a Era or date in a database record. Acronym: ECK.

Glossary

Event. *Genealogy.* An occurrence or incident in a person's life that can be keyed to a time and place that has been recorded. Events include birth, marriage(s), death, graduation from a school, a period of military service, etc. There is virtually no limit to the number of events in a person's life.

Event Modifiers. *Special.* The name given to the use of predefined words or notation that are used in connection with citing key events. See Date Modifier and Jurisdictional Modifier.

Family Group Record. *Special.* A document of specific format and design to present all known information about a given family. Acronym: FGR.

FGR. *Special.* Acronym for Family Group Record.

Flat-file Database. *Computer Science.* A flat-file database comprises one or more tables, consisting of rows and columns. In each table, much of the data in the various rows and columns is repetitive and redundant, generally wasting storage space. Because the tables are not linked to each other, queries are very limited in scope. Because of these and other limitations, a flat-file database is generally considered to be inferior to a relational database.

Four-generation Chart. *Genealogy.* A pedigree chart that contains four generations of ancestors. The de facto standard for genealogists. This size chart is erroneously called a five-generation chart in most genealogical literature.

Fraction. *Mathematics.* An expression that indicates the quotient of two quantities.

GCS. *Special.* Acronym for *Genealogical Coordinate System*™.

Genealogical Coordinate System™. *Special.* A phrase for identifying the correlation of an *event* with a *name*, *time*, and *place*. Acronym: GCS.

Generation Numbering. *Genealogy.* A system using superscripts to indicate number of generations removed from an immigrant ancestor.

GenStor™. *Special.* A computer program under development designed to implement the concepts in this book.

Global Positioning Technology. *General* Devices using this technology communicate with satellites circling the globe to obtain latitude and longitude information within a few feet of the absolute. Originally developed for military purposes by the Department of Defense. Small hand-held commercial versions of these devices, about the size of a TV remote, are available to the general public. Acronym: GPS.

GPS. *General* Acronym for Global Positioning Technology.

Greater-than. *Mathematics.* The symbol > is used to denote that a quantity is greater than a preceding number or mathematical expression.

Henry System. *Genealogy.* A numbering system for descendancy genealogies very similar to the Index System. In this system, every person's number is based upon the birth order of his or her ancestor in the direct line. Numbers ten and beyond are used as parenthetical expressions; i.e., a tenth child is (10), the eleventh, is (11), the twelfth is (12), and so forth.

Hexadecimal. *Mathematics.* Hexadecimal or Hex, is a system of numbering with the base of 16 as its radix. All numbers in hexadecimal are represented by combinations or groups of the numerals 0, 1, 2, 3, 4, 5, 6, 7, 8, 9, A, B, C, D, E, and F.

Ibidem. *Latin.* In the same place. Used in footnotes and bibliographies to refer to the book, chapter, article, or page cited just before. Abbreviations: ib., ibid.

Ibid. *Abbreviation; Latin.* See Ibidem.

Index System. *Genealogy.* A numbering system for descendancy genealogies. Adapted from Dewey Decimal Classification System in 1900. In this system, every person's number is based upon the birth order of his or her ancestor in the direct line. A tenth child is assigned the letter "x;" an "a" for the eleventh, a "b" for the twelfth, etc.

Integer. *Mathematics.* A whole number which can be positive (1, 2, 3, . . .), negative (–1, –2, –3, . . .), or zero (0). In genealogical numbering an integer will usually be a positive whole number, but can be negative when used in generation numbering.

Glossary

Int. *Abbreviation; Genealogical.* Intention. In past times, marriage ceremonies were often preceded by the filing of an Intention of Marriage document by the parties in question, usually several months before the planned wedding date. The date of the Intention is often used in lieu of a missing marriage date. However, not all Intentions were consummated by marriage.

Inv. *Abbreviation; Genealogical.* Inventory. A term for associating the Inventory of a person's estate usually in connection with a date and jurisdiction.

Jurisdiction. *Special.* Any entity that creates records. A jurisdiction can be a civil entity, or organizations such as churches, fraternal groups, insurance companies, institutions, schools, universities, and corporations. The primary focus in this book deals with civil entities, such as a country, state, territory, province, county, district, township or town, and so forth. See also, Jurisdictional Hierarchy, Jurisdictional History, and Jurisdictional Tracking.

Jurisdictional Hierarchy. *Special.* A term specific to civil entities that describes their relationship to each other; i.e., state, county, town, and township are civil entities in the United States (country) in descending order of jurisdiction. When citing an event, the complete Jurisdictional Hierarchy should be given, insofar as information permits.

Jurisdictional History. *Special.* A chronological record of various jurisdictions with whom a person has been identified during their lifetime.

Jurisdictional Modifier. *Special.* The name given to the words *probably*, *perhaps*, *of* and *or* to indicate a degree of uncertainty in connection with a cited jurisdiction. See Event Modifiers.

Jurisdictional Tracking. *Special.* A process best implemented in a computer database to develop and maintain a chronological record of various jurisdictions associated with a person in a genealogy. See Jurisdictional History.

Key Event. *Special.* The name given to events of primary importance in a genealogical record; i.e., birth, marriage(s), death, burial, or cremation.

Landscape. *General* A publishing term that refers to page orientation wherein the shortest dimension of the page is vertical. See Portrait.

Laptop. *Computer Science.* A small portable computer.

Latitude. *General* The angular distance north or south of the earth's equator, measured in degrees along a meridian, as on a map or globe.

Least Significant Digit. *Mathematics.* The digit in the rightmost position of a numerical expression represents the least quantity of the number. It's acronym LSD.

Less-than. *Mathematics.* The symbol < is used to denote that a quantity is less than a number or mathematical expression which follows it.

Lic. *Genealogy.* License. A term often used in genealogical records that indicates a license (usually marriage) is associated with some stated event.

LifeNumber™. *Special.* A system for numbering an individual in either an ancestral or descendancy genealogy. The LifeNumber is a simple, arbitrary, and unique number, usually an integer. Acronym: LN.

LN. *Special.* Acronym for LifeNumber™.

Longitude. *General* Angular distance on the earth's surface, measured east or west from the prime meridian at Greenwich, England, to the meridian passing through a position, expressed in degrees (or hours), minutes, and seconds.

LSD. *Mathematics.* Acronym for least significant digit.

m. *Abbreviation; Genealogical.* Marriage.

Mass Storage. *Computer Science.* Special media for permanently storing computer information such as disk or tape drives. Not to be confused with computer memory.

Memory. *Computer Science.* Computer memory refers to electronic devices which retains memory electrically or magnetically. Magnetic memory devices are now quite rare but have the advantage of retaining their data when power is removed. Electronic memory devices are volatile which means they lose their data in the event of a power failure. See mass storage.

Modified Register System. *Genealogy.* A numbering system for descendancy genealogies adapted from the Register system, often called NGSQ. This system starts with a family male progenitor and assigns that person the number 1. From then all the descendants are numbered including those either that died young or who left no descendants. As in the Register System, spouses are not numbered. Each child of the progenitor is numbered in chronological order beginning with the next number.

Thus, the first child is 2, the second child is 3. In the third generation, the children of the first child in the second generation to be carried forward are numbered first, then the children of the second child in the second generation to be carried forward are numbered, and so on. In all cases, the numbers are sequential from the progenitor. See Register System.

Most Significant Digit. *Mathematics.* The digit in the leftmost position of a numerical expression represents the greatest quantity of the number. It's acronym MSD.

MSD. *Mathematics.* Acronym for most significant digit.

née (also **nee**). *General.* Usually used to indicate the maiden name of a married woman. Formerly known as the French feminine past participle of *naitre*, to be born, from old French *naistre;* from Latin *nasci*.

New England System. *Genealogy.* A numbering system for descendancy genealogies. See Register System.

NGSQ System. *Genealogy.* NGSQ is the acronym for the National Genealogical Society Quarterly. See Modified Register System.

Notebook. *Computer Science.* A portable computer smaller than a laptop.

Octal. *Mathematics.* Octal is a system of numbering with the base of 8 as its radix. All numbers in octal are represented by combinations or groups of the numerals 0, 1, 2, 3, 4, 5, 6, and 7.

op. cit. *Abbreviation; Latin.* See opere citato.

Opere citato. *Latin.* In the work cited). *Abbreviation*: op. cit.

Glossary

Pedigree. *Genealogy.* A person's ancestry; usually an ancestral chart which begins with a specific individual, and graphically depicts that person's direct ancestors on all lines back as far possible.

Performance. *Computer Science.* A term often used in the computer industry to denote the overall efficiency and speed of a hardware configuration or software application.

Planning Log. *Special.* A document whose format and design provides a convenient way to record notes, thoughts, ideas, and general plans, to plan genealogical goals.

Portrait. *General* A publishing term that refers to page orientation wherein the longest dimension of the page is vertical. The most common form of page layout. See Landscape.

Positional Notation. *Mathematics.* Positional notation is a form of notation in which the value of a particular numeral depends not only on the numeral which is written, but also on the position of the numeral within the number.

Power Series. *Mathematics.* A power series can be expressed in the following general form:

$$... + aN^4 + bN^3 + cN^2 + dN^1 + eN^0 + fN^{-1} + gN^{-2} ...$$

Where N is the radix and the coefficients *a* through *g* are the characters of the number. When N is equal to 2, the series is a binary number; when N is equal to 8, the series is an octal number; when N is equal to 10, the series is a decimal number, and when N is equal to 16, the series is a hexadecimal number, and so forth.

Powers of a Number. *Mathematics.* A number or symbol denoted as a superscript placed to the right of and above another number, symbol, or expression, denoting the power to which that number, symbol, or expression is to be raised.

Primary Source. *Genealogy.* An original record such as a birth certificate, marriage certificate, a deed, a family bible, a court record, a baptismal record, and so forth.

q.v. *Abbreviation; Latin.* See quod vide.

Quod vide. *Latin.* Which see. *Abbreviation*: q.v.

Glossary

Radix. *Mathematics*. The base of the power series which represents the number. See Power Series.

Range. *Special*. A range is a term to describe a sequence of pedigree charts within a group of generations. As defined, *Range A* comprises the first four generations in the first chart of a pedigree. *Range B* comprises generations five through eight. *Range C* comprises generations nine through 12. *Range D* comprises generations 13 through 16, and so forth. Ranges refer to the sequence of charts for a four-generation grouping.

Register System. *Genealogy*. A numbering system for descendancy genealogies. This system starts with a male progenitor and assigns that person the number 1. From then on only the descendants who are carried forward are numbered. Children that died young or who left no descendants are not numbered. Each child of the progenitor is numbered in chronological order beginning with the next number. Thus, the first child is 2, the second child is 3, so long as the child will be carried forward.

In the third generation, the children of the first child in the second generation who is carried forward are numbered first, then the children of the second child in the second generation who is to be carried forward are numbered, and so on. Most often, the children of female lines are not numbered, even though some females may be numbered. In all cases, the numbers are sequential from the progenitor. See Modified Register System.

Relational Database. *Computer Science*. A database in which information can be stored in more than one table, linked together in such a way as to allow efficient and nonredundant data storage and retrieval, as well as very sophisticated queries and reports, and great flexibility and power.

Research Log. *Special*. A Research Log is a document whose format and design enable the recording of details and results of each specific source that has been consulted for genealogical information. A Research Log is *Source-Specific*.

s.p. *Abbreviation; Latin*. See Sine prole.

s.p.m. *Abbreviation; Latin*. See Sine prole mascula.

Scientific Method. *General* Often referred to as the scientific approach which is based upon the Aristotelian philosophy.

Glossary

Secondary Source. *Genealogy.* A source that is generally compilation of primary sources. A published family history, a book listing all the marriages in a region, an index to vital records, and census indexes, etc., are examples of secondary sources.

sic. *Latin.* Thus; so. A Latin term frequently used in written texts to indicate that a surprising or paradoxical word, phrase, or fact is not a mistake and is to be read as it stands.

Sine prole. *Latin.* Without offspring or issue. [New Latin *sine prōlē*: Latin *sine*, without + Latin *prōlē*, ablative of *prōlēs*, offspring.] Abbreviation: s.p.

Sine prole mascula. *Latin.* Without male issue). Abbreviation: s.p.m.

Sosa-Stradonitz system. *Genealogy.* A system for numbering pedigrees invented in 1676 by Jerome de Sosa, a Spanish genealogist. It was subsequently revised in 1898 by Stephane Kekule von Stadonitz. This system appears be identical to the Ahnentafel system wherein the number for a person's father is simply twice the value of the preceding number. The number for the mother is twice the value of the preceding number plus one. See Ahnentafel.

Soundex. *Genealogy.* A special form of phonetic indexing first developed for use by the Census Bureau that categorizes names according to a specific methodology.

Source. *Special.* Any distinct entity which contains or provides information.

Source Extraction. *Special.* The extraction of desired data from a single, specific source.

Source Extraction File. *Special.* A file containing data extracted from a single, specific source. The numbering of multiple Source Extraction files is determined by the Source Number. See Source Number.

Source Number. *Special.* A unique integer that is arbitrarily assigned to each specific source that has been researched for possible genealogical data. The key or index to these numbers is maintained in the Research Log. See Research Log.

Spreadsheet. *Computer Science.* A computer application especially designed for creating and editing documents with the capability to perform various mathematical computations of all kinds.

Glossary

Standard Chart. *Special.* See four-generation chart.

Standard Numbering System. *Genealogy.* A system, so-called, that numbers pedigree charts according to a consecutive sequence of numbering that numbers all charts in a generation grouping. In this system, all possible or theoretical charts must be allocated a number even if they don't exist. Chart numbering based on the powers of two and the number of ancestral generations per chart. See pedigree and range.

Subnotebook. *Computer Science.* The smallest portable computer.

Unique Identification. *Special.* A phrase used to denote identification of a person, separate and distinct from anyone else in the world.

Word Processor. *Computer Science.* A computer application especially designed for creating and editing documents of all kinds; word processing.

Bibliography

The following selected references are provided for those who wish to learn more about some of the concepts and methods described in this book.

Baxter, Angus. *Do's and Don'ts for Ancestor Hunters*. 1988.

Friedman, Lawrence M. 2d ed. *A History of American Law*. New York: Simon & Schuster, 1985.

Harland, Derek. *Genealogical Research Standards*. Vol. 2. Bookcraft, 1958. Evidence evaluation and discrepancies; research procedures and pedigree analysis; source materials and their place in the genealogical structure. Volume 1 is *A Basic Course in Genealogy*.

Harland, Derek, and Frank Smith. *A Basic Course in Genealogy*. Vol. 1. Bookcraft, 1958. An introduction to record-keeping and research. Volume 2 is *Genealogical Research Standards*.

Jones, Vincent L. *Stamp Out Chaos! Eliminate Confusion!* Salt Lake City, UT: Progenitor Genealogical Society.

Jones, Vincent L, Arlene H. Eakle, and Mildred Christensen. *Family History For Fun and Profit*. Publisher's Press, Salt Lake City, UT: Publisher's Press, 1972. Originally published as: *Genealogical Research: A Jurisdictional Approach*.

Lackey, Richard. *Cite Your Sources: A Manual for Documenting Family Histories and Genealogical Records*. Jackson, MS: University Press of Mississippi, 1980.

Rubincam, Milton. Pitfalls in Genealogical Research. Salt Lake City, UT: Ancestry Publishing, 1987.

Shammas, et al. *Inheritance in America: From Colonial Times to the Present*. New Brunswick, NJ: Rutgers University Press, 1987.

Stevenson, Noel C. J.D. *Genealogical Evidence*. Rev. ed. Laguna Hills, CA: Argean Press, 1989. A guide to the standard of proof relating to pedigrees, ancestry, heirship and family history.

Index

A

Abbreviations
  Aliq., 238
  Genealogical, 87
    Adm., 238
    b., 239
    Bp., 239
    Chr., 240
    d., 241
    Int., 246
    Inv., 246
    Lic., 247
    m., 247
  Latin, 87
    Ca., 240
    d.s.p., 241
    d.s.p.m., 241
    ibid, 245
    op. cit., 248
    q.v., 249
    s.p., 250
    s.p.m., 250
Absolute Numbers. *See* LifeNumber™ System
Ahnentafel, 238
  Limitations, 117
  System, 116
Ancestral Charts. *See* Pedigree Charts
Aristotle, 3
Audience
  Targeting, 16
  Who is your, 16

B

Baptism
  Comparison with birthdate, 86
Base. *See* Radix
Binary. *See* Numbering Systems
Binary Electronic Devices, 225
Biographical. *See* Family Group Record
Biographical Section. *See* Family Group Record
Birth
  Unique identification, 47
Birth Date
  Estimating, 51
  Importance, 51
  Mandatory element, 51
Boolean Operator
  AND, 144
  OR, 151

C

Calendar
  Errors, 240
  Gregorian, 240
  Julian, 240
  New Year's Day, 243
Charts. *See* Pedigree or Descendancy Charts
Children's Section. *See* Family Group Record
Christening
  Comparison with birth date, 86
Compiled Records
  Indexing, 12

Index

C

Computer Programs
    Genealogical, 156
Computer Science
    Address, 238
    Architecture, 239
    Bit, 239
    Byte, 240
    Computerize, 241
    Data Storage & Retrieval, 241
    Database, 241
    Database Field, 241
    Database fields, 136
    Database Management, 241
    Database Query, 242
    Database Record, 242
    Database Record Format, 242
    Database records, 136
    Database Table, 242
    Flat-file Database, 244
    Laptop Computer, 246
    Mass Storage, 247
    Memory, 247
    Notebook Computer, 248
    Performance, 249
    Relational Database, 250
    Spreadsheet, 251
    Subnotebook Computer, 252
    Word Processing, 252
Computers
    A tool, 20
    Advantages, 19
    Can't think for you, 19
    Genealogical applications, 4
    What they do best, 19

D

Data Analysis & Evaluation, 11, 101
    Getting started, 102
    Rationale, 11
    Resolution of discrepancies, 102

Data Analysis & Evaluation Section. *See* Family Group Record
Database
    Definition, 135
    FGR Index, 150
    Flat-file, 137
        Limitations, 137
        Redundant data, 138
    Queries, 140
        General structure, 145
        Sophisticated searching, 143
    Relational, 138
        Example, 146
        Example Table 1, 139
        Example Table 2, 139
        FGR Indexing, 147
        FGR Primary data, 147
        Flexibility, 143
        Jurisdictional tracking, 149
        Linking Indexes, 149
        Linking tables, 139
        Linking Tables, 140
        Links to FGRs, 148
        Optimizing Jurisdictional tracking, 152
        Power and flexibility, 148
        Unique identification, 149
    Simple Flat-file table, 136
    Source Extraction Indexing, 140
    Source extraction record, 141
    Types of, 136
    Useful tool, 135
Date Modifiers
    Birth, Marriage, Death, 88
    Suggested notation, 88
Dates
    Correct notation, 85
Decimal. *See* Numbering Systems

Index

D

Descendancy Charts, 118
    Limitations, 118
    Typical Example Detail, 121
    Typical Example Outline, 120
Descendancy Numbering Systems, 121
    Comparisons, 125
    Henry, 122
    Index, 122
    Modified Register (NGSQ), 124
    Register, 123

E

ECK. *See* ERA Correlation Key
Era
    A range of years, 72
    Correlation Key, 73
Era Correlation Key
    Asterisk character, 40, 75
    Characters and Interpretation, 40, 74
    Forward slash character, 40, 74
    Greater-than character, 40, 75
    Hyphen character, 40, 74
    Less-than character, 40, 75
Event Modifiers
    Adding precision, 88
    Date and Jurisdiction, 87
    Predefined notation, 87
Events
    Chronological framework, 68
    Correlation elements, 47, 68
    Importance of location, 52
    Jurisdictions, 68
    Recorded, 68
    Types of, 68

F

Family
    Definition, 82
Family Group Record
    A composite, 11, 13, 81
    Biographical information, types of, 100
    Biographical section, 99
    Children's section, 98
    Compiling, 47
    Complete information, 13
    Data Analysis & Evaluation, 101
    Definition, 81
    Focal point, 82
    Focal point for merging information, 101
    Foundation, 81
    Indexing, 12
    Major elements, 91
    Merging of sources, 81
    Multiple marriages, 85
    Parents section, 93
    Preparation, 82
    References section, 103
    Structure, 91
Family Group Record (FGR) Outline, 92
FGR. *See* Family Group Record
    Biographical Section Example 1, 202
    Biographical Section Example 2, 203
    Children's Section Example, 201
    Data Analysis & Evaluation Section
        Example 1, 204
        Example 2, 205
        Example 3, 205
        Example 4, 206
    Database Index, 150
    Numbering Example 1, 131
    Numbering Example 2, 132
    Numbering Example 3, 133
    Parent's Section Example 1, 199
    Parent's Section Example 2, 200
    References Linking to Key Events, 209
    References Section Example, 208
    Typical Biographical Section, 101

Index

F

FGR
    Typical Children's Section, 97
    Typical Data Analysis & Evaluation Section, 103
    Typical Parent's Section, 96
    Typical References Section, 106
Formulas
    (1), 114
    (2), 114
    (3), 114
Four-generation chart, 108
Four-generation Chart. *See* Pedigree Charts

G

GCS. *See* Genealogical Coordinate System™
Genealogical Abbreviations. *See* Abbreviations
Genealogical Aids, 15
Genealogical Chart Numbering
    Descendancy systems comparison, 127
    Pedigree charts, 110
    Pedigree systems comparison, 118
Genealogical Charts, 107. *See* Pedigree or Descendancy Charts
    Ancestral and descendancy, 107
    Supplement to the FGR, 13
Genealogical Concepts, 154
    Analysis, 154
    Consistency, 154
    Precision, 154
    Rationale, 155
    Simplicity and Clarity, 155
Genealogical Coordinate System™, 12
    Adds Precision, 47
    Correlation of Elements, 47
Genealogical Indexing
    Correct principles, 35
    Database Optimization of fields, 142
    Database record, 142
    Essential criteria, 36
    Optimizing, 36
    Race, 39
    Sex or Gender, 37
    Source Extraction Exercise 1, 180
    Source Extraction Exercise 10, 187
    Source Extraction Exercise 2, 181
    Source Extraction Exercise 3, 181
    Source Extraction Exercise 4, 182
    Source Extraction Exercise 5, 183
    Source Extraction Exercise 6, 183
    Source Extraction Exercise 7, 184
    Source Extraction Exercise 8, 185
    Source Extraction Exercise 9, 186
Genealogical Notation
    Preferences, 155
Genealogical Numbering, 61
    Analogous to addresses, 63
    Assigning to identify, 64
    FGRs and charts, 107
    Generation, 90
    LifeNumbers, 62
    Simplicity a virtue, 60
Genealogical Overview, 153
    Compiling genealogical records, 153
    Concepts to remember, 154
    Genealogical indexing, 154
    Genealogical numbering, 154
    Jurisdictional tracking, 153
    Planning Log, 153
    Research Log, 153
    Source extraction files, 153
    Unique identification, 153
Genealogical Process
    Advantages of using a computer, 4
    Clarity in presentation, 156
    Compiling records, 11
    Data Analysis & Evaluation, 2
    Evolution of a System, 5
    Ideal, 7
    Internal elements, 12

Index

G

Genealogical Process
  Precision essential, 3
  Six basic steps, 7
  Source Extractions and Compiled
    Records, 13
  Summary, 12
  Underlying Concepts, 2
Genealogy
  1790 Age Groups, 238
  A giant picture puzzle, 2
  A living record, 2
  A science of life, 2
  Ahnentafel, 238
  An iterative process, 8
  Ancestral, 4, 239
    Characteristics of, 16
    Charts, 238
    Pedigree, 16
  Ancestral a subset of Descendancy, 16
  Ancestral and Descendancy, 15
  Basic elements, 1
  Birth-order numbering, 239
  Both art and science, 3
  Clarity a must, 17
  Computer programs, 156
  Correlating little bits of data, 2
  Definition, 1
  Descendancy, 4, 242
    Characteristics of, 17
    Charts, 242
  Double-dating, 243
  Events, 244
  Four-generation chart, 244
  Generation numbering, 244
  Henry System, 245
  Index System, 245
  Initial questions, 4
  Linking individuals, 82
  Modified Register System, 248
  Never done, 2
  Never-ending process, 82
  New England System, 248
  NGSQ System, 248
  Organization and compilation, 1
  Pedigree, 249
  Planning, 19
  Planning and goals, 4
  Planning your project, 8
  Primary Source, 249
  Reasons for doing, 8, 17
  Register System, 250
  Secondary Sources, 251
  Simple to understand, 18
  Sosa-Stradonitz system, 251
  Soundex, 251
  Standard Numbering System, 252
  Two sets of records, 5
Genealogy and Science
  Similarities, 3
General
  Calendar, 240
General Definitions
  Acronym, 238
  Aristotelian, 239
  Calendar, 240
  Dewey Decimal Classification System, 242
  Global Positioning Technology (GPS), 245
  Landscape, 246
  Latitude, 247
  Longitude, 247
  née, 248
  Portrait, 249
  Scientific Method, 250
GenStor™
  Computer program, 157
Geography
  Physical features, 53
  Political divisions, 54
Global Positioning Technology (GPS), 53
GPS. *See* Global Positioning Technology

259

Index

H

Henry System. *See* Descendancy Numbering Systems
Hexadecimal. *See* Numbering Systems

I

Index System. *See* Descendancy Numbering Systems

J

Jurisdictional Hierarchies, 77
    Correctly citing, 56
    Correlation with time, 55
Jurisdictional Modifiers
    Suggested notation, 89
Jurisdictional Tracking
    A special index, 76
    Correlation with time, 67
    Data record format, 70, 76
    Derivation from FGR, 71
    During lifetime, 67
    Era Correlation Key, 73
    Era Correlation Key interpretation, 77
    Exercise, 80
    Exercise 1, 189
    Exercise 2, 190
    Exercise 3, 191
    Exercise 4, 191
    Exercise 5, 193
    Exercise 6, 195
    Exercise 7, 197
    Incomplete time periods, 78
    Individual-specific, 73
    Key elements, 69
    Name changes, 78
    Relation to Unique Identification, 12
    Technique, 69
Jurisdictions
    Civil most important, 26
    Definition, 25
    Evolution, 54
    Knowing where to look, 55
    Political divisions, 54

L

Land and Property
    Descriptions, 53
    Physical measurements, 52
Latin Abbreviations. *See* Abbreviations
Latin Terms
    ante, 238
    circa, 240
    de facto, 242
    decessit sine prole, 242
    decessit sine prole mascula, 242
    ibidem, 245
    quod vide, 249
    sic, 251
    sine prole, 251
    sine prole mascula, 251
Law of Gender, 112
LifeNumber™ System, 62
    Absolute numbering, 129
    Advantages, 130
LN. *See* LifeNumber™

M

Marriage Anomalies, 84
Marriages
    Multiple, 85
Mathematical Terms
    Argument, 239
    Base, 239
    binary, 239
    boolean, 239
    Decimal, 242
    Equivalent numbers, 243
    Fraction, 244
    Greater-than, 245
    Hexadecimal, 245

Index

M

Mathematical Terms
    Integer, 245
    Least Significant Digit, 247
    Less-than, 247
    LSD, 247
    Most Signifcant Digit, 248
    MSD, 248
    Octal, 248
    Positional Notation, 249
    Power Series, 249
    Powers of a Number, 249
    Radix, 250
Modified Register System. *See* Descendancy Numbering Systems

N

Names
    Compression in writing, 50
    Identification when incomplete, 83
    Incomplete, missing or ambiguous, 83
    Literacy in spelling, 49
    Notation for females, 84
    Reproduction of sounds, 50
    Spelling, 49
    Spelling Derivations, 49
    Spelling factors, 50
    Susceptibility of vowels to change, 50
New England System. *See* Descendancy Numbering Systems
NGSQ. *See* Descendancy Numbering Systems
Numbering. *See* Genealogical Numbering
Numbering Systems, 220
    Binary, 111, 225
    Binary number characteristics, 226
    Binary to hexadecimal Conversion, 235
    Birth-order, 91
    Converting Binary to Decimal, 228
    Converting Decimal to Binary, 228
    Decimal to binary conversion example, 229
    Decimal to hexadecimal conversion, 233
    Decimal to Hexadecimal Conversion Example, 234
    Decimal-Binary Equivalents, 226
    Decimal-Hexadecimal equivalents, 230
    Equivalent numbers, 225
    Hexadecimal, 111, 230
        Relation to binary, 230
    Hexadecimal equivalents for powers of 16, 231
    Hexadecimal to binary conversion, 234
    Hexadecimal to binary Conversion, 235
    Hexadecimal to Decimal Conversion, 232
    Least significant digit (LSD), 221
    Mathematical basics, 220
    Most significant digit (MSD), 221
    Multiplication and division, 223
    Number of characters required, 223
    Power Series, 221
    Radix, 221
    Rules of counting, 222
    Structure, 224

O

Organization
    Advantages of, 18
    Flexibility, 20
    Genealogical process foundation, 2

P

Parent's Section. *See* Family Group Record
Pedigree Charts, 107
    A Relative picture, 115
    Ahnentafel numbering system, 116
    Calculating numbers, 211
    Cross-referencing, 112

Index

P

Pedigree Charts
  Design, 108
  Four-generation, 109
  Four-generation the standard, 108
  Grouping by Ranges, 213
  Linking, 108, 110
  Numbering, 110
  Numbering a function of the powers of 2, 110
  Numbering by generation groups, 213
  Numbering calculations, 113
  Numbering considerations, 110
  Numbering example using tables, 219
  Numbering formulas, 114
  Numbering from tables, 213
  Numbering males and females, 112
  Numbering paradox, 111
  Numbering ranges, 213
  Numbering systems, 115
  Numbering Systems Comparison, 118
  Numbering the first 16 extensions, 212
  Numbers for Ranges C and D, 215
  Range Grouping, 214
  Size limitations, 108
  Standard numbering system, 116
Pedigree Numbering. *See* Pedigree Charts
Pedigrees
  Proving, 56
Planning
  Advantages of, 18
  Essential to research, 15
  Guidelines, 20
  Keeps you on track, 20
  Setting goals, 20
Planning Log
  A genealogical tool, 21
  Differences with Research Log, 4
  Essential elements, 22
  Example 1, 159
  Example 2, 160
  Example 3, 160
  Example 4, 161
  Example 5, 161
  Example 6, 161
  Example 7, 162
  Overall goals, 4
  Overall objectives, 21
Political Divisions
  Relation to Jurisdictions, 54
Positional Notation, 221
Powers of 2, 211
  Binary and decimal equivalents, 227

R

Radix, 221
Range
  Grouping by generations, 250
References
  Essential elements, 104
References Section. *See* Family Group Record
Register System. *See* Descendancy Numbering Systems
Research Log
  An index, 10
  Comments/Notes, 32
  Current status, 10
  Date, 30
  Essential Elements, 30
  Evolution of, 6
  Example, 40, 42
  Example 1, 165
  Example 2, 168
  Example 3, 171
  Example 4, 174
  Example 5, 177
  Library Call Number, 31
  Respository or Location, 31
  Search Objectives, 32
  Source Description, 30
  Source Number, 30
  Source number prefixes, 33

Index

R

Research Log
    Source number suffixes, 35
    Source-specific, 4
    Source-specific tool, 29

S

Science
    Observations and measurements, 3
    Precision, importance of, 3
Scientific Method, 3
Sosa-Stradonitz System. *See* Ahnentafel
Source Extraction
    Example, 43
    Files, 6, 33
    Indexing Example, 44
    Number components, 34
    Process, 29
Source Extraction Indexing
    Example 1, 167
    Example 2, 170
    Example 3, 173
    Example 4, 176
    Example 5, 179
Source Extractions, 25, 29
    Comparison with compiled records, 13
    Example 1, 166
    Example 2, 169
    Example 3, 172
    Example 4, 175
    Example 5, 178
    Indexing, 10, 35
    Indexing Exercise 1, 180
    Indexing Exercise 10, 187
    Indexing Exercise 2, 181
    Indexing Exercise 3, 181
    Indexing Exercise 4, 182
    Indexing Exercise 5, 183
    Indexing Exercise 6, 183
    Indexing Exercise 7, 184
    Indexing Exercise 8, 185
    Indexing Exercise 9, 186
    Indexing Exercises, 180
    Logging and Indexing, 9
    Number, 33
    Organizing and Filing, 9
    Organizing with a computer, 9
    Precision a must, 7
    Precision, its importance, 8
    Resolving differences, 11
Sources
    Comparing, 5
    Definition, 25
    Importance of validating, 5
    Merging, 7
    Primary, 26
    Secondary, 27
Special
    Ancestral Extension, 238
    Data Analysis & Evaluation, 241
    Data Compilation, 241
    Data Extraction, 241
    Date Modifier, 242
    ECK, 243
    Era, 243
    Era Correlation Key, 243
    Event Modifers, 244
    Family Group Record, 244
    FGR, 244
    GCS, 244
    Genealogical Coordinate System™, 244
    GenStor™, 244
    Jurisdiction, 246
    Jurisdictional Hierarchy, 246
    Jurisdictional History, 246
    Jurisdictional Modifier, 246
    Jurisdictional Tracking, 246
    Key Event, 246
    LifeNumber™, 247
    LN, 247
    Planning Log, 249
    Range, 250
    Research Log, 250
    Source, 251

Index

S

Special
    Source Extraction, 251
    Source Extraction File, 251
    Source Number, 251
    Standard Chart, 252
    Unique Identification, 252
Spelling, 49
    Consistency, 51
    Standardizing, 37
Standard Chart. *See* Pedigree Charts
Standard Numbering System. *See* Pedigree Numbering Systems

U

Unique Identification
    An example, 64, 130
    And Jurisdictional Tracking, 12
    Begins with birth, 47
    Correlation of elements, 52
    Genealogical Numbering, 12
    Linking families, 59
    Name, 48
    Precision, 47
    Who, what, when and where, 12
    Within a family, 59

V

Vital Records
    Errors in, 57
    Fraudulent creation, 57